MULTILATERALISM VERSUS REGIONALISM:
TRADE ISSUES AFTER THE URUGUAY ROUND

EADI BOOK SERIES 19

Multilateralism versus Regionalism: Trade Issues After the Uruguay Round

edited by
MEINE PIETER VAN DIJK
and
SANDRO SIDERI

FRANK CASS
LONDON • PORTLAND, OR

in association with
EADI   The European Association of Development Research
and Training Institutes (EADI), Geneva

First published in 1996 in Great Britain by
FRANK CASS & CO. LTD.
Newbury House, 900 Eastern Avenue,
London IG2 7HH

and in the United States of America by
FRANK CASS
c/o ISBS
5804 N.E. Hassalo Street
Portland, Oregon 97213-3644

British Library Cataloguing in Publication Data
A catalogue record for this book
is available from the British Library

ISBN 0 7146 4270 3 (paperback)

Library of Congress Cataloging-in-Publication Data
Multilateralism versus regionalism; trade issues after the Uruguay
Round / edited by Meine Pieter van Dijk and Sandro Sideri.
   p.   cm. — (EADI book series; 19)
Includes bibliographical references (p.).
ISBN 0-7146-4270-3
  1. International Trade.   2. Regionalism.   3. Uruguay Round
(1987–1994)   4. World Trade Organization.   I. Dijk, Meine Pieter
van.   II. Sideri, S., 1934– .   III. Series: EADI-book series; 19.
HF1379.M848   1996
382—dc20   96-10878
                                             CIP

Typeset by Regent Typesetting, London
Printed in Great Britain by
Antony Rowe Ltd, Chippenham

Contents

Notes on Contributors

Alberto Brugnoli is at the Department of Economics, Università Commerciale L. Bocconi in Milan, Italy.

Meine Pieter van Dijk is an economist at the Economic Faculty of the Erasmus University in Rotterdam, and Research Associate, CERES, Research School, Utrecht, The Netherlands.

Mariarosa Lunati is at the Education, Employment, Labour and Social Affairs Department (EELSA) of the OECD in Paris, France.

Antonella Mori is at the Institute of Latin American Studies, Università Commerciale L. Bocconi in Milan, Italy.

Giorgio Barba Navaretti is at the State University in Milan and the Centro Studi Luca d'Agliano in Turin, Italy.

Sheila Page is at the Overseas Development Institute (ODI) in London, UK.

Francesco Passarelli is at the Department of Systems and Organisation Theory, University di Teramo, in Teramo, Italy.

Laura Resmini is at the Department of Economics, Università Commerciale L. Bocconi in Milan, Italy.

Bruno van Rompuy is at the Catholic University in Louvain, Belgium.

Sandro Sideri is at the Institute of Social Studies (ISS) in The Hague, The Netherlands.

Christopher Stevens is at the Institute of Development Studies (IDS) in Brighton, UK.

Siegfried Schultz is at the German Institute for Economic Research (DIW) in Berlin, Germany.

Jürgen Wiemann is affiliated to the German Development Institute (GDI) in Berlin, Germany.

Abbreviations

ACP	African, Caribbean and Pacific countries
AFTA	ASEAN Free Trade Area
ANZCERTA	Australian–New Zealand Closer Economic Relations Trade Agreement
AP	Andean Pact
APEC	Asia Pacific Economic Cooperation
ASEAN	Association of South-East Asian Nations
CACM	Central American Common Market
CAP	Common Agricultural Policy
CARICOM	Central American Common Market
CBI	Caribbean Basin Initiative
CE4	Czech Republic, Hungary, Poland and Slovak Republic
CEC	Commission of the European Community
CEEC	Central and Eastern European Countries
CET	Common External Tariff
CFA	Currency for Francophone Africa
CFC	Chlorofluorocarbons
CGE	Computable General Equilibrium
CIS	Commonwealth of Independent States
CMEA	Council for Mutual Economic Assistance
COM	Cadre d'Obligations Mutuelles
COMESA	Common Market for East and Southern Africa
CPI	Consumer Price Index
DAC	Development Assistance Committee
DC	Developed Countries
DIW	Deutsches Institut für Wirtschaftsforschung
DM	Deutsch Mark
EAI	Enterprise for the Americas Initiative
EBRD	European Bank for Reconstruction and Development
EC	European Community
ECU	European Currency Unit
ECOWAS	Economic Community of West African States
EDF	European Development Fund
EE5	five countries in association agreement with the EU
EEA	European Economic Area
EEC	European Economic Community

Abbreviations

EFTA	European Free Trade Association
EID	European Information Department
EIU	Economist Intelligence Unit
ELTAC	European Largest Textiles and Apparel Companies
EU	European Union
FDI	Foreign Direct Investment
FMO	Framework of Mutual Obligations
FOC	First Order Conditions
FTA	Free Trade Association
FT	Financial Times
GATS	General Agreement on Trade in Services
GATT	General Agreement on Tariffs and Trade
GCC	Gulf Cooperation Council
GDI	German Development Institute
GDP	Gross Domestic Product
GSP	Generalised System of Preferences
ICAs	International Commodity Agreements
ICoA	International Coffee Agreement
ICO	International Cocoa Organisation
IEO	Industry and Environmental Office
IHT	International Herald Tribune
IMF	International Monetary Fund
INRO	International Natural Rubber Organisation
IP	Intellectual Property
IPC	International Programme for Commodities
IPRs	Intellectual Property Rights
ISO	International Standards Organisation
LAFTA	Latin American Free Trade Association
LAIA	Latin American Integration Association
LDCs	Least Developed Countries
MERCOSUR	Mercado del Cono Sur
MFA	Multi-Fibre Arrangement
MFN	Most Favoured Nation
MNC	Multi-National Corporation
NAFTA	North American Free Trade Agreement
NGO	Non Governmental Organisation
NICs	Newly Industrialising Countries
NIEO	New International Economic Order
NIP	National Indicative Programme
NTB	Non Tariff Barriers
OCT	Overseas Countries and Territories
ODI	Overseas Development Institute

OECD	Organisation for Economic Co–operation and Development
OPEC	Organisation of Petrol Exporting Countries
OPT	Outward Processing Trade
PCP	Pentachlorophenol
PHARE	Poland and Hungary: Assistance for Economic Restructuring
PPMs	Process and Production Methods
ppm	parts per million
PTA	Preferential Trade Area for Eastern and Southern Africa
QR	Quantitative Restrictions
RAL	German Institute for Quality Assurance and Certification
R&D	Research and Development
SAARC	South Asian Association for Regional Cooperation
SACU	South African Custom Union
SADCC	Southern African Development Coordination Conference
SAPTA	South Asian Preferential Trade Arrangement (treaty signed by SAARC)
SEM	Single European Market
STABEX	Stabilisation of Export Revenues
SYSMIN	System of Stabilising Mining Revenues
TACIS	European Union Initiative for New Independent States and Mongolia
TBT	Technical Barriers to Trade
TDB	Trade Development Board
TNC	Transnational Corporation
TREPs	Trade Related Aspects of Environmental Policies
TRIMs	Trade-Related Investment Measures
TRIPs	Trade-Related Intellectual Property Rights
UK	United Kingdom
UNCED	United Nations Conference on Environment and Development
UNCTAD	United Nations Conference on Trade and Development
UNCTC	United Nations Center on Transnational Corporations
USA	United States of America
VERs	Voluntary Export Restraints
WTO	World Trade Organisation

The completion of the Uruguay Round in April 1994 did not solve all the issues. This book takes up where the newly created World Trade Organisation will have to start. The issue of regionalism versus multilateral agreements such as the Uruguay Round will be discussed in the first five chapters. Subsequently specific issues such as green protectionism, technical standards, intellectual property rights protection, the effects of disarmament on international trade, the effects of abolishing the Multi-Fibre Agreement and the external impact of the EU's Common agricultural policy will be discussed.

The Editors

1

Introduction: The Results of the Uruguay Round and the Agenda for the World Trade Organisation

MEINE PIETER VAN DIJK

I. INTRODUCTION

In April 1994 the seven-year long Uruguay Round of trade talks was closed formally in Marrakesh. Tariffs would be reduced substantially and a number of non-tariff barriers would be removed.[1] The agreement was signed there, together with the agreement to create the World Trade Organisation (WTO). Since then the major trading nations have ratified the GATT Accord. It became effective in 1995. During the middle of the 1980s the internationalisation of the economy accelerated. Since the fall of the Berlin Wall in 1989, the rise of East Asia and the prospect of further economic integration (Europe 1992 and the Uruguay Round of GATT), international relations have changed rapidly. Economic growth is high in East Asia and jobs are moving from Western to Eastern Europe and Asia. The internationalisation of the economy has led to increased trade and globalisation of capital flows. Technological development, improved communications, a more liberal investment climate in many developing countries and lower costs of transportation have all contributed to these developments. In particular the East Asian developing countries have benefited enormously from the gradual liberalisation of world trade since 1947. Development takes place where there are structures. Trade negotiations result in international structures which reduce risks and facilitate trade; of crucial importance is the role of the private sector in the development process. Rapid economic growth is largely the result of the market or private initiative, backed up by investments in infrastructure and education, liberalisation of trade and financial services and sound macro-economic policies.[2]

At the same time that multilateral negotiations have dragged on, regional agreements were reached with more ease and frequency than ever before.[3] In this book multilateralism will be confronted with regionalism (regional economic integration), with the tendency to agree on more liberal trade policies within a regional co-operation framework.[4] While the European Union (EU) and North-American Free Trade Agreement (NAFTA) are examples of the latter, the conclusion of the Uruguay Round is an example of successful multilateralism.

As a background to the articles in Part I dealing with multilateralism versus regionalism, we describe in this introduction the role of GATT, the achievements and possible effects of the Uruguay Round and the bones of contention that still exist. These have been put on the plate of WTO, the successor of GATT, which has come into existence as of 1 January 1995.

A list of issues in the field of trade that still exist after the Uruguay Round will be drawn up. Although we cannot deal with all these issues, in Part II eight important issues will be discussed. In the second part of the introduction we will discuss these issues while giving an overview of the whole volume. Preceding that, a special section will be devoted to the countries of Central and Eastern Europe. Their situation since the fall of the Wall may be described as being 'caught between multilateralism and regionalism'. These countries would favour multilateral trade agreements which would facilitate the redirection of their exports. However, being so close to the important West European market, they are forced to attach more importance to regional trade agreements with the EU.

II. THE ROLE OF GATT

The General Agreement on Trade and Tariffs (GATT) was signed in 1947. It meant the beginning of a period of increasing multilateralism in international trade. The agreement is the basis for a global rule-based trading system. Tariff concessions are linked to non-discrimination through the principle of Most-Favoured Nation (MFN) treatment. Through a series of Rounds GATT has contributed significantly to the liberalisation of world trade.[5] However, over time three trends can be detected. In the first place the number of countries participating in the negotiations increased, contributing to a lengthening of the time necessary to reach an agreement. Secondly, the issues became ever more complicated, when more sectors were discussed (for example also agriculture and the services sector) and when exports had become more important for many countries. Finally, the effects of just lowering tarifs gradually diminished, since tariffs had been reduced already in subsequent Rounds. Also, many countries became used to lower tariffs in the framework of regional associations or through the Generalised System of Preferences (GSP).

The Uruguay Round was the most ambitious Round of all multilateral trade negotiations ever undertaken under GATT.[6] It was the eighth Round and has been described as a victory for a rule-based multilateral trading system and a milestone in the evolution of international economic relations.[7] The new institutional economics points to the importance of rules and regulations to guide economic development. The opposite of rules is a series of *ad hoc* protective measures. The GATT Uruguay Round can be seen as the basis for emerging international institutions. The opposite of a rule-based system would be a system of arbitrary import restrictions, so-called anti-dumping policies and so-called Voluntary Export Restraints (VERs). Multilateral trading rules erode when countries resort to protectionist and anti-dumping actions, VERs and other discriminatory measures.

During the seven years of negotiations the economic position of the OECD countries deteriorated and, hence, their willingness to make concessions. The fall of the Wall in 1989 implied a change from power policies to economic motives to give Eastern Europe and the former Soviet republics a better chance. In December 1994 trade negotiators cleared last-minute hurdles to a formal agreement to inaugurate the WTO on 1 January 1995. The WTO will have to deal with dumping and monitoring the results of the Uruguay Round. The advantage of the WTO is that all participants share similar rights and obligations. Despite their economic power WTO's verdict is binding for all member states.

III. ACHIEVEMENTS OF THE URUGUAY ROUND

Because of the Uruguay Round, tariffs on manufactures will on average be 40 per cent lower compared with the previous GATT Round. The objective is to be achieved by the industrial countries over a period of five years, as the scope of GATT's multilateral trade negotiations was extended in the Uruguay Round. The achievements in market liberalisation, strengthening of rules and institutions and extension of discipline to new areas will be far-reaching, according to the International Monetary Fund [*IMF, 1994*]. Negotiations went beyond the question of tariffs which had preoccupied previous ones. We saw an extension of the trade negotiations to areas as government procurement, Trade Related Intellectual Property rights (TRIPs) and Trade Related Investment Measures (TRIMs). This time non-tariff barriers (such as standards, procurement procedures on state aid) and trade-related intellectual property rights issues were high on the agenda, while sectors other than manufacturing (for example, agriculture and services) also received attention.

The Uruguay Round will strengthen multilateral discipline and extend this to other areas than manufacturing. More than ever, the role of the private sector was central in the negotiations. Most developed countries admitted that they wanted to reinforce the position of their private sector internationally.[8] In second place came the improvement of the economic situation of developing and Eastern European countries.

3

Besides the lowering of import duties for industrial products, the major achievements of the Uruguay Round are:

(1) the reduction of non-tariff barriers to trade;
(2) the phasing out of the Multi-Fibre Arrangement (MFA);
(3) agreement concerning Trade Related Intellectual Property rights and Trade Related Investment Measures;
(4) an agreement on tropical and temperate agriculture;
(5) new ideas about the role of GATT (and its successor) in the settlement of trade disputes;
(6) agreement on technical standards;
(7) an agreement reached on services (such as financial services, telecommunications, transportation and movement of natural persons);
(8) the changing of safeguard provisions in GATT;
(9) the decision of contracting parties to create the WTO and suggestions made concerning the agenda of the WTO;
(10) the commitment of the Uruguay Round to the multilateral trade system.

Ad 1.

Grey area measures (non-tariff barriers) such as VERs and orderly marketing agreements will be phased out within four years. However, in the case of manufactures, protection remains possible because of the (altered) safeguard clause. However, developing countries benefit from the reduction of high tariff peaks on items in which they compete strongly with developed countries. Escalation (increasing tariffs when a product is processed further) will be eliminated. Growing misuse of anti-dumping will be reduced because the rules have been made clearer and more extensive, making it more difficult to resort to anti-dumping policies.

Ad 2.

The phasing out of the Multi-Fibre Arrangement (MFA) means that under the Uruguay Round most of the tariffs and quotas on textiles and clothing will gradually be eliminated after 1995 and completely abandoned in 2005. The dismantling of barriers to textile imports by such major markets as the United States (US) and the EU over a ten-year period is considered one of the major achievements of the trade pact [*IHT 8–12–1994*]. The MFA was a convenient device for developed countries, as they officially argued it would give them some time to restructure their industries to the competition from low income countries. The effects of the MFA will be discussed in more detail in Chapters 10 and 11.

Ad 3.

The section of the agreement on Trade Related Intellectual Property provides a good basis for the protection of intellectual property. Agreements on TRIPs and TRIMs oblige member countries to adjust their domestic legislation and policies with respect to the protection of Intellectual Property Rights (IPR) and Foreign Direct Investment (FDI) in order to avoid trade conflicts. Although developing countries may have to pay more for knowledge-intensive goods they received concessions on goods of export of interest to them and enjoy the advantages of a multilateral agreement over possibly tougher bilateral agreements. Trade-related investment measures that violate the GATT principles of national treatment and prohibition of quantitative restrictions (such as local content and foreign exchange balancing requirements) are to be eliminated within two years by industrial countries, within five years by developing countries and within seven years by Least Developed Countries or LDCs [*IMF 1994: 83*].

Ad 4.

An agreement on tropical and temperate agriculture has been reached. Trade in agricultural products will be brought within the ambit of the WTO and will be progressively liberalised. Temperate agriculture was the most conflicting issue in the negotiations. An agreement between the US and the EU in the field of agriculture was necessary before the Uruguay Round could be concluded. Such an agreement between the US and the EU delayed the closing of the Uruguay Round by one year. Tariffs on tropical products have been cut and an agreement has been reached to introduce market mechanisms in production and trade. Issues related to agriculture and trade will also be discussed in Chapters 12 and 13.

Ad 5.

The settlement of trade disputes has been agreed upon. A new dispute-settlement system permits limited sanctions against countries breaking world trade rules. The increased predictability and discipline provided by the integrated dispute settlement mechanism should stimulate export-oriented investment and the expansion of world trade.

Ad 6.

Product standards may be imposed, provided these standards are applied without discrimination against imported goods, and provided they are justified by technological needs (technical standards), or scientific evidence (environmental and health standards) and applied indiscriminately (the GATT principle of non-discrimination). Agreement has been reached on further harmonisation of technical standards in different countries (see also Chapter 7).

Ad 7.

An agreement has been reached on services: the General Agreement on Trade in Services (GATS). They have been brought for the first time within the multilateral framework of rules. Further, some degree of agreement on improved market access has also been reached. LDCs would like more liberalisation of migration while developed countries push for financial services liberalisation.

Ad 8.

The safeguard provisions in GATT have been changed. The objective was to discourage countries from using unilateral, selective restraints on imports outside the GATT as a substitute for existing GATT procedures which require consultation, non-selectivity and compensation without, however, bringing selectivity into the GATT [*Page et al., 1992*]. The safeguards clause has been altered in ways that may increase its use against LDCs although, in the past, developed countries have been reluctant to use it as a justification for import controls because these have to be applied against all suppliers. Some selectivity is admitted in the new agreement, if it can be established that imports from certain countries have increased disproportionately. Safeguards can be imposed for a maximum of eight years but, if selective, for four years at the maximum.

Ad 9.

The WTO is a single institutional framework to encompass all of GATT, with agreements and arrangements concluded under its auspices, and the complete results of the Uruguay Round. The WTO will monitor trade policies of its members, but enforcement of rules will continue to be more difficult for a LDC than for the US. Issues such as the liberalisation of the services sector, supervision of the phasing out of MFA, and labour and environmental codes have been placed high on the list of priorities of the WTO (see below).

Ad 10.

The Uruguay Round may be praised for its commitment to the multilateral trade system. The IMF [*1994*] added that the Uruguay Round 'has created an environment conducive for tackling future challenges in trade policy'.

IV. CONSEQUENCES OF THE URUGUAY ROUND

What is the impact of the Uruguay Round on the international trading system? We would like particularly to assess the outcome of the Round for developing countries. However, it is extremely difficult to predict the consequences of

GATT for developing countries. Research in general points to positive effects for the world economy. Between US$200 and 270 billion of additional trade would be generated. The additional cost of protectionism for developing countries (at US$45 billion) is a multiple of the development aid available each year [*Goldin and Van der Mensbrugghe, 1993*].

Several publications have tried to assess the implications of the Uruguay Round for developing countries [e.g. *UNCTAD, 1990*] or of Europe 1992 [*Schuknecht, 1993*]. UNCTAD Trade and Development Board [in: *GO Between 46, 1994*] already noted that the tariff cuts agreed in the Uruguay Round will erode the value of trade preferences for developing countries under the GSP.

Schuknecht [*1993*] tries to measure the trade effects of Europe 1992 for developing countries, looking at factor market adjustments, sector specific production effects and welfare effects. He concludes that the EU has adapted an array of protectionist policies towards the rest of the world, while liberalising trade internally. The following protectionist measures are all highly politicised, according to him: voluntary export restraint agreements, national measures under article 115 of the Treaty of Rome, anti-dumping actions and price undertakings.

The International Monetary Fund [*IMF, 1994*] argues that the Uruguay Round could benefit all countries and reduce trade conflicts and protectionism. It notes that 'given the fairly long implementation period, any transition costs are likely to be felt gradually, providing time to exploit the opportunities opened up by the Round'.

However, LDCs are likely to face problems in adjusting to the results of the Uruguay Round as a result of the erosion of their preferential margins. LDCs may also have difficulties in effectively implementing the agreements and actively pursuing their interests within the framework of the WTO.[9] Some of these countries may also have to incur higher costs for imported foodstuffs.

V. ISSUES FOR THE FUTURE

Third World countries have an interest in maximising their gains from the multilateral trade system. This requires that their interests are adequately represented in the new monitoring and enforcement bodies. One problem is the unequal distribution of the benefits of the boom in the second half of the 1980s. East Asia benefited in particular, while a number of African and particularly LDCs continued to suffer from stagnation and recession.

The question remains of what the future role of the United Nations Conference on Trade and Development (UNCTAD) will be. Its Trade Development Board (TDB) has suggested that UNCTAD could play a major role in providing technical assistance to LDCs which will strengthen their

institutional and human resource capacities, and their information management. More concretely, UNCTAD should continue to provide background
work and build consensus on trade and economic policy issues before they
become negotiable in WTO.

There is still a dispute between textile importing and exporting countries.
The issue concerns membership of the textile monitoring body. Exporting
countries fear that the monitoring body that will oversee the changes would
interpret the rules in favour of importing countries, unless they have a
majority of seats on it. They are demanding six of the ten seats in this group
as well as the chairmanship. On the other hand, the importers, for example, the
EU, are insisting that the seats be divided equally between importers and
exporters.

The Uruguay Round is a blow for a number of other trade schemes. The
advantages of the Generalised System of Preferences (GSP) will diminish for
developing countries. They will face a decline of benefits from the GSP, under
which industrialised countries allow specified imports with little or no duties.
The tariff cuts will erode the value of trade preferences for developing
countries under the GSP.[10]

VI. THE ALTERNATIVE: REGIONALISM

Evidence of growing regionalism is given by Page (in Chapter 5). She shows
the increasing importance of regional trade blocs, besides global agreements
such as the Uruguay Round of GATT. The NAFTA agreement in 1994, just as
the creation of the Single European Market (SEM between 1988 and 1992),
has given a push to other regional trade blocs to get moving. The fact that
these processes have taken place simultaneously have made the conclusion
of the Uruguay Round more difficult. MERCOSUR (the custom union comprising Brazil, Argentine, Paraguay and Uruguay) became effective as of
1 January 1995 (the world's second largest), while on that date the Andean
Pact (Bolivia, Colombia, Ecuador, Peru and Venezuela) entered into their own
free trade agreement (see Chapter 2).[11]

Trade will increase because of GATT, the extension of the European Union,
NAFTA and ASEAN.[12] However, these developments do not benefit a number of African countries, whose share in world trade is actually declining. This
partly reflects the frustration with multilateral organisations: the Uruguay
Round has had to counter the wave of bilateral and regional trade agreements.
There is certainly the risk that a number of small countries will be left out if
the world opts for a few important regional blocs.

Regionalism is often presented as conflicting with multilateralism. The IMF
[*1993: 114*] concludes, for example, that 'it is clear that from a global perspective, full multilateral free trade would be preferable'. The report points to

8

the case that regional trading blocs may shift their priority to narrow regional concerns. Bhagwati (in De Melo and Panagariya (eds.) [*1993*]) also fears that the formation of trade blocs hampers world-wide trade liberalisation. Alternatively regional integration can be viewed as a complement to multilateralism, or a first step in the direction of operating on a liberalised world market. A number of arguments will be given in the first five chapters for and against regionalism.

Some look at regionalism and multilateralism as two complementary approaches [e.g. *Han, 1992*]. It would be a threat if the trade blocs which have been created should compete so much with each other that they would oppose a multilateral agreement. However, such has not been the case. Instead, it can be seen as a first step towards freer global trade. Fishlow and Haggard [*1992: 4*] rightly conclude that the US remains a truly global player. However, with a diversified trade and investment structure, the US is, in effect, a member of several regions at the same time. The country exploits this situation by being involved in regional trade associations within North America, with Latin American countries and Asian countries, besides a large number of bilateral arrangements.

One argument in favour of intensifying regional trade preferences is the absence of an effective multilateral trading system which would stimulate faster integration on a world scale. According to Conklin [*1991: 381*]: 'the extent and nature of free-trade arrangements will be determined by the degree to which potential signatories have common producer and citizen interest[13] ... such commonalities of interest are most extensive among countries that are geographically close'. Free trade requires harmonisation of government policies, not the elimination of them. This is also an argument for considering regional integration efforts as a first step in the direction of world-wide trade liberalisation. If, at the same time, certain issues are settled at the multilateral level (such as property rights and guarantees for capital movements) multilateral agreements may in fact stimulate regional blocs to become more active on a world scale. Two-track negotiations may be inevitable!

Others argue that regionalism can play the function of a laboratory, where experience is gained with competition in the world market [*Hormats, 1994*]. Officially GATT has criteria for the approval of custom unions (article XXIV); in practice these were all approved and no supervision has taken place to assess the real functioning of these regional efforts to integrate. Stare [*1993: 7–8*] describes in the case of Slovenia the advantages of regional integration in the EU. It is argued that multilateralism is dangerous for small economies in transition, but Slovenia would like access to the enlarged SEM. It is more important for such a small country to have access to this nearby developed market rather than to opt for multilateralism, as will also be argued in the next section.

The situation will become more complicated when the interaction between the three large economic blocs, NAFTA, the EU and East Asia, is taken into consideration. If each bloc focuses on its region this could divert trade to regional markets. Irwin (in De Melo and Panagariya (eds.) *1993*]) points to the role of one dominant country in the world. If there is such a 'hegemon', it is likely to be liberal because it gains by free trade, and because it has the power to enforce it. He doubts, however, that the US can play such role in the present world trade system. It should be noted that even when regional integration has taken place in the form of some Free Trade Association (FTA), trade between blocs will still continue.

The Asian countries have given priority to successfully concluding the Uruguay Round instead of concentrating on regional integration. Regional institution-building has not been as important in that region as in Europe and North America. In fact, the success of these countries is based on a world-wide trade strategy. No regional bias in trade among East Asian economies can be found.

VII. THE SITUATION IN CENTRAL AND EASTERN EUROPE

The collapse of trade links that existed under the Council for Mutual Economic Assistance (CMEA) forced the Central and Eastern European Countries (CEEC) to open up their economies, and to search for new markets for their products. These countries generally want to establish close links with the EU. Proximity to the Western European market and a reasonably developed infrastructure are natural conditions favouring increased trade between the two parts of Europe. Page (in Chapter 5) shows that the EU is becoming less important in world trade, which may be taken as an indication for the fortress Europe point of view. Chapter 3 deals with trade relations within the EU and between the EU and Eastern Europe in more detail, while Chapter 4 looks at the relations between the EU and the African, Carribean and Pacific (ACP) countries.

The EU has an association agreement with six Central and Eastern European countries: Bulgaria, the Czech Republic, Hungary, Poland, Romania and the Slovak Republic.[14] The EU, being a powerful partner in these deals, has tended to resort to protectionism in certain sectors. In negotiations it has not given up, for example, its right to impose anti-dumping and countervailing measures on low-cost imports. The association agreements are sometimes considered a second class substitute for EU membership. They set down a ten-year timetable for dismantling trade barriers for industrial products. However, they also contain protective elements. Limits remain on exports of 'sensitive' goods such as chemicals, clothing, farm products, footwear, iron and steel and textiles.

The EU has also started a special programme (PHARE) with Bulgaria, the Czech Republic, Hungary, Poland, Romania and the Slovak Republic[15] and, under the TACIS programme, assistance is provided to the former Soviet Union countries. On 1 January 1995 FTAs between the EU and the three Baltic republics (Estonia, Latvia and Lithuania) came into effect as a first step towards eventual accession.

While previously facing more trade barriers than other developing countries, Eastern Europe now benefits from more trade concessions than most developing countries. Kovacs [*1993: 4–5*] describes the East–West trade patterns as a dramatic reorientation in foreign trade of the CEEC, intensified by numerous association and other co-operation agreements. On the other hand intra-East European trade is decreasing in importance. Because of low wages, labour-intensive products (such as textiles and clothing; see also Chapter 11) dominate the exports. Kovacs also discusses the foreign trade prospects for the CEEC, looking at trade performance as well as the development of trade policies in these countries. He concludes that increased exports to the West have not yet been accompanied by a shift in the commodity structure of exports. Primary goods and fuels still play a relatively large role in the exports to Western markets. Manufactured products account for a 65 per cent share of the exports of the CEEC, with a relatively higher share of semi-manufactures, some consumer goods and a smaller quantity of engineering goods of higher quality. The bulk of Eastern Europe's imports from the West consists of manufactures (81 per cent in 1991).

The case of most Eastern European countries can be summarised as preferring multilateralism, but being forced to opt for regional trade agreements. Trade with the former Soviet Union republics is no alternative for these countries; while the advantage of Western Europe is that an important and rich market is within reasonable distance, connected by a relatively good infrastructure. Wages are still low and the EU programmes mentioned help them to develop their economies and to attract foreign investors. Unfortunately they face protectionism, presented sometimes as green and sometimes as red. They would prefer multilateralism but opt for regional integration. It would be desirable if the EU were to take a more liberal stand towards these countries, which would like to recover as quickly as possible from years of communism.

VIII. THE AGENDA FOR THE WTO

The WTO has been inaugurated in January 1995. Although China's membership is not settled yet, one may speak of a new era. The East Asian economies have shown that benefits can be derived from openness to international trade and finance [*World Bank, 1993b*]. Stable macroeconomic conditions and an equitable international trading system were essential elements for the development of these countries. The East Asia miracle study of the Bank points to the factors which helped the eight countries studied to achieve more than twice as much growth between 1961 and 1990 than other developing countries. Sound macroeconomic policies and keeping their economy open to foreign technology helped. Crucial were the high levels of domestic saving and heavy investment in education and development. Part of this investment (presently about five per cent) is financed by international capital. Although small on a worldwide scale, in specific dynamic countries such as the so-called second tier newly industrialising countries (Indonesia, Malaysia and Thailand) the percentage is much higher. The question remains as to what extent their success can be repeated in other parts of the world, notably in Africa and some of the LDCs. The Uruguay Round creates new opportunities, but it also poses challenges.

The Uruguay Round creates new opportunities for trade for other countries, too. It also poses challenges for developing countries. It presumes, for example, the existence of domestic institutions and resources, which may be wanting in many developing countries. The LDCs are likely to face particular problems in adjusting to the results of the Uruguay Round. In the first place they face difficulties because of the erosion of preferential margins.[16] The LDCs can also be expected to incur higher costs for imported foodstuffs.[17] The main beneficiaries will be the more advanced developing countries, which have more to gain from tariff cuts and liberalisation of the agricultural, textile and apparel trade [*IMF, 1994*].

The first issue to be discussed in the framework of the WTO is further market liberalisations, particularly in specific areas such as, for example, steel and the production of civil aircraft. Other issues to be discussed are further harmonisation (of government policies, taxes and technical standards (see Chapter 7), rules of origin and intra-regional trade.

Secondly, the agreed liberalisation of the agricultural sector is very limited. Because of the Uruguay Round, protection of Western markets may go down from 99 to 95 per cent, according to Van Rooy [*1994*]. There is still the risk that countries protecting their farmers may simply replace their quotas with prohibitive tariffs; further, anti-dumping measures may still be used for protection [*IMF, 1994*]. These are arguments in continuing attempts to liberalise agricultural exports.

Trade and the environment is another issue which is rapidly climbing the international trade agenda. At the close of the Uruguay Round a decision was taken, for example, to establish a Committee on Trade and Environment within the WTO. UNCTAD also decided to establish an *ad hoc* Working Group on Trade, Environment and Development, with particular emphasis on the special circumstances of developing countries [*Go Between, June 1994*].

Negotiations on the service sector have not ended. These negotiations in some service sectors will continue for an unspecified length of time, even after the signing of the agreement. Generally the weak obligations in the GATT are seen as an indication of limited commitments to trade liberalisation in services [*FT, 5–10–1994*]. Western countries are striving for an agreement which would allow foreign financial institutions, including banks, securities firms and insurance companies, to establish and operate on terms no less favourable than those applied to domestic institutions.[18]

National competition and investment policies influence trade. As traditional trade barriers are lowered, attention is shifting to the impact of these policies. Calika and Ibrahim [*1994*] conclude that 'Competition policy issues need better definition and analysis before multilateral approaches can be formulated to tackle emerging trade frictions in this area. Openness and nondiscriminatory treatment of foreign direct investment will be critical in maximizing the global gains from an international specialization.'

There is also the challenge of integrating new competitors in world markets. A number of problems and prospects of creating a level playing field with, for example, Brazil and China as new competitors can be mentioned. Harmonisation is already one of the most difficult things within the EU, let alone trying to achieve it on a world scale. On the other hand developing countries often do not have the money to subsidise their exports and, hence, will certainly be in favour of eliminating such subsidies.

Labour and environmental standards will need to be developed. The first question here is: who needs them? In particular, the OECD countries argue in favour of internationally accepted standards concerning labour conditions and the environment. The social consequences of internationalisation are increasing unemployment and income differences. These could possibly come with a social crisis in the West, as demonstrated by the student unrest in France in March 1994, or the hostile reactions to migration to the EU from Eastern Europe and Third World countries.

IX. PART I: REGIONALISM VERSUS MULTILATERALISM

In this book we want to go beyond the Uruguay Round and ask questions about:

- the issue of bilateralism or regional groups versus world wide trade agreements (Chapters 2, 3, 4 and 5)
- green protectionism (Chapter 6)
- the issue of standardisation (Chapter 7)
- the issue of intellectual property (Chapter 8)
- the consequences of disarmament for international trade (Chapter 9)
- the effect of the multi-fibre arrangement (Chapter 10 and 11)

- the need to add social clauses to the international trade agreements (see Chapter 11)
- the role of agricultural commodities in world trade, illustrated by coffee (Chapter 12)
- the impact of the new common agricultural policy of the EU (Chapter 13)

Part I concentrates on regionalism versus multilateralism. In Chapter 2 Schultz provides an overview of recent developments in the world trade system, namely, the formation of different Free Trade Associations (FTAs) in Africa, America and Asia. He provides the main arguments in favour of multilateralism and discusses reasons for, and the potential dangers of, regionalism. He is in favour of multilateral negotiations since they hold a better prospect for general trade liberalisation than bilateral FTAs. According to him, the fallback position should not be bilateral trade agreements, but rather a GATT-plus approach. In that case like-minded parties, ready to reduce trade barriers and to adopt new trading rules, would go beyond GATT. He suggests a Most Favoured Nations approach where the benefits would be restricted to the participants, but access for other parties is possible on the basis of reciprocal commitments.

Stevens discusses in Chapter 3 the implications of regionalism for the multilateral system. The paper discusses the effects of Europe 1992, the results of the Maastricht treaty, of creating the European Economic Area (EEA) and agreements with Eastern Europe. Stevens concludes that the EU's structure of non-reciprocal trade agreements is conflicting with the multilateral system, a point taken up in Chapter 4. However, the fact that multilateral agreements provide an inadequate regulatory framework for cross-border flows of investments and services remain an argument for regionalism as illustrated by the SEM. According to Stevens, the multilateral trading system should not give way to a set of regional economic clusters, since developing countries have an interest in the discipline imposed by the multilateral system.

In Chapter 4 Van Dijk discusses the relations between the EU and the ACP countries. Although Stevens is right that developing countries have an interest in experiencing the discipline imposed by the multilateral system, he finds that the Lomé convention in fact protects ACP countries from the vageries of the world market. The multilateral framework may be an inadequate regulatory framework for cross-border flows of investments and services, special regulations for former colonies does make it more difficult for them to compete at the world market. The discussion about the dollar versus ECU bananas has made this point very clear.

Page deals in Chapter 5 with the issue of regional groups in multi-country organisations. She points to organisations of developing country integration and analyzes the role of these regional groups in multi-country organisations such as GATT. She argues that regional agreements may be a problem if legal arrangements conflict with those of multilateral organisations.

X. PART II: SPECIFIC ISSUES ON THE TRADE AGENDA

Wiemann discusses in Chapter 6 green protectionism as a threat to Third World exports. The OECD countries take environmental threats more and more seriously and put their industries under pressure to invest in cleaner products and production methods. Developed and developing countries have to adjust to a set of eco-policies in the OECD. Eco-standards can become trade barriers for developing countries' exports. However, if they are complemented with the necessary efforts in the field of development co-operation they can also be used as a leverage to enforce stricter environmental controls on developing countries' industries. A case study on India is presented to show how industries there are coping with the new challenges of green consumerism and new legislation on environmental standards.

Technical standards are non-tariff barriers and the application of these standards may become a protective tool against imports from developing countries. The GATT Standards Code was adopted in 1980 as an attempt to develop international rules for the standardisation process. The Code was revised during the Uruguay Round and now allows trade restrictions by countries adversely affected by low environmental regulations. The chapter investigates theoretically what the expected consequences and problems of implementing harmonisation are. The harmonisation process is modelled, allowing different types of asymmetries between the countries concerned. The author argues that the chosen procedure for implementing harmonisation is important and that the adjustment costs are different in developed and developing countries.

The adaptation and use of new technologies is important for the economic growth of developing countries. Sideri presents in Chapter 8 the issue of intellectual property in much detail. Intellectual Property Rights (IPR) are important, since innovations are costly and often the result of time and resource-consuming Research and Development (R&D) activities. Sideri sketches the role of GATT for the harmonisation of IPR protection, noting that the Uruguay Round may set a multilateral framework for the conditions of international competition in the next century. After summarising the theory of intellectual property, and reviewing the arguments used to plea for stricter IPR protection in LDCs, he concludes that stricter IPR protection may be recommended for Newly Industrialising Countries (NICs) and some more advanced LDCs only.

Van Rompuy analyses the consequences of disarmament for international trade, using a general equilibrium model in Chapter 9. He shows that certain sectors and countries bear a more than proportional burden, due to world-wide defence cuts. Secondly, he finds that it is necessary to distinguish between the short and long-term consequences of these cuts. Finally, government assistance is necessary for these sectors and countries (or regions) which are severly affected because, otherwise, conversion will be very problematic.

Brugnoli and Resmini deal in Chapter 10 with the restrictiveness of the multi-fibre arrangement on Eastern European exports to the EU market. Quota developments are reviewed for the period 1988–97 and the restrictiveness of the MFA is analysed for the period 1988–92. It is concluded that the MFA is less restrictive on Eastern Europe than other authors have suggested. The short-term impact of the MFA on trade flows is marginal for a number of reasons given in the text.

In Chapter 11 Barba Navaretti discusses the effects of trade policy on foreign investment in the textile and clothing industry, taking the perspective of restructuring European firms and deals in particular with Germany and Italy. If trade barriers are lowered, incentives to set up production facilities elsewhere increase. The impact of trade policies on the cost of redeployment is analysed, evaluating the costs and benefits of the phasing out of the MFA. It is argued that protection is, in fact, not beneficial to European producers, because it increases the cost of redeployment and introduces a bias in favour of high quality firms. The bias introduced by the MFA bilateral quantitative restrictions is partially offset by the Outward Processing Trade (OPT) regulation. Because OPT quotas have gradually increased in the second half of the 1980s and national regulations have loosened, redeployment has become less expensive. Redeploying firms have been able to improve their competitive position and the quality of their products. This illustrates the positive effects of gradual dismantling of quantitative trade restrictions in the industry.

Coffee is an interesting case of a commodity which used to be supported at the international scale by means of the International Coffee Agreement (ICoA). In Chapter 12 Mori analyses the relationship between the negotiations on trade in agricultural products within the Uruguay Round and the negotiation process for a new ICoA. The difficulties of ICoA renegotiation were related to an uncertain future of protectionism in agricultural trade. If liberalisation of agriculture had failed, the ICoA would have been renegotiated. Now that liberalisation has been achieved, consumer countries oppose market support pacts for commodities and commodity producers are more inclined to accept this point of view. According to the author, the national schemes for commodity price stabilisation are increasingly important when the future of ICoA is uncertain.

Finally, Passarelli discusses in Chapter 13 the impact of the new Common Agricultural Policy (CAP) of the EU on the competitive strategy of third countries. He uses game theory to explain some aspects of the international negotiations for the liberalisation of agricultural trade flows. The first model predicts the improvement of the foreign welfare as the guaranteed price of the product rises. The second game predicts a positive impact of increasing compensation on the foreign country's welfare. Passarelli concludes that the recent reforms of the CAP, based to a larger extent on deficiency compensation, have played an important role in releasing the Uruguay Round from its impasse in 1992.

XI. CONCLUSION

This book is the result of the activities of the EADI Working Group World Trade and Commodity Policies. Professor dr. Sandro Sideri is the convenor of this Working Group. First drafts of most chapters have been discussed during the VIIth General Conference of EADI, which took place in Berlin from 15 to 18 September 1993. They have been revised since in the light of the discussions and to take into account recent developments, such as the completion of the Uruguay Round of GATT. The editors wish to thank the participants of the Working Group, a number of anonymous referees and Ms. A. van den Berg for skillfully handling most of the text processing.

NOTES

1. The Punta del Este declaration in 1986 stressed that the Uruguay Round should try 'to halt and reverse protectionism and to remove distortions to trade' [*GATT, 1986*]. It should bring about further liberalisation and expansion of world trade.
2. The growing importance of financial services and international capital flows is very clear. Total net capital flows to developing countries have increased 30 per cent in 1992 and 13 per cent in 1993 despite the economic recession [*World Bank, 1994*]. International competition leads to a continuing restructuring and relocation of economic activities. This pushes down wages in developed countries.
3. Regionalisation is used in this book for the process of spatial concentration of economic activities [*Van Dijk, 1993*].
4. In the literature different stages of integration are distinguished [*Nielsen et al., 1991*]:
   - free trade area: no visible trade restrictions;
   - custom union: the same, plus a common external trade policy;
   - internal commodity market: the same, but also no invisble trade restrictions;
   - common market: the same, plus free movement of factors of production (namely capital and labour);
   - monetary union: the same plus a common currency;
   - economic union: the same plus a common economic policy.
5. The previous (Tokyo) Round had taken six years, but was less ambitious than the Uruguay Round.
6. It covered 15 separate issues and involved over 100 contracting parties (117 plus

17

the EU). It was concluded on 15 December 1993.

7. By the Trade Development Board (TDB) of UNCTAD, reported in *Go Between*, June 1994.

8. For example, statement by the minister of trade of the Netherlands [*Van Rooy, 1994*].

9. This point is made by the NGOs, *Go Between*, June 1994.

10. UNCTAD has made several proposals to maintain the value of the GSP to developing countries, including one to establish a GSP systems for trade in services, and another to set up a Green GSP under which environmentally friendly export products would receive extra preferences, *Go Between* 46, June 1994.

11. Interesting developments are agreements between different regional groups. NAFTA is considering linkages with MERCOSUR and also the EU plans a free trade zone with MERCOSUR.

12. The ASEAN countries are under pressure to speed up their economic integration process, *Financial Times*, 22 Nov. 1994.

13. The participating countries should have the same view on the role of the government in the economy. In particular they should agree on the need to regulate certain sectors (for example, the financial sector) and on the policy of subsidising technological development and education and training.

14. Besides an association agreement with Cyprus, Malta and Turkey.

15. Yugoslavia was originally part of PHARE's effort to support the process of economic reconstruction in the countries of Central and Eastern Europe.

16. Some countries in North Africa and the Caribbean which rely overwhelmingly on preferences on industrial products could especially be adversely affected by the Uruguay Round.

17. Large importers of food might be hurt, but the agricultural sector in other countries could thrive as world market distortions are reduced [*IMF, 1994*].

18. The principle of equal competitive opportunity was stressed for the financial sector by S.E. Katz, *Wall Street Journal of Europe*, 11 Oct. 1991.

REFERENCES

Calika, N. and A. Ibrahim (1994): 'Uruguay Round Outcome Strengthens Framework for Trade Relations' in IMF Survey, 14 Nov.

Conklin, D.W. (1991): *Comparative Economic Systems*, Cambridge: Cambridge University Press.

De Melo, J. and A. Panagariya (eds.) (1993): *New Dimensions in Regional Integration*, Cambridge: Cambridge University Press.

Dijk, M.P. van (1993): 'Industrial Districts and Urban Economics Development', *Third World Planning Review*, Vol. 15, No. 2 May.

Fishlow, A. and S. Haggard (1992): *The US and the Regionalisation of the World Economy*, Paris: OECD.

GATT (1986): *Ministerial Declarations of the Uruguay Round*, Geneva: GATT Secretariat.

Goldin, I. and D. van der Mensbrugghe (1993): *Trade Liberalisation: What's at Stake?* Paris: OECD.

Grilli, E.R. (1993): *The European Communtiy and the Developing Countries*, Cambridge: Cambridge University Press.

Han, S.T. (1992): *European Integration: The Impact on Newly Industrialising Economies*, Paris: OECD.

Hettne, B. and A. Inotai (1994): *The New Regionalism*, Helsinki: UNU WIDER.

Hormats, R.D. (1994): 'Making Regionalism Safe', *Foreign Affairs*, Vol. 73, No. 2.

ICDA (1994): *Update on Trade Related Issues*, Brussels: International Coalition for Development Action.

IMF (1993): *World Economic Outlook*, Washington, DC: IMF, May.

IMF (1994): *World Economic Outlook*, Washington, DC: IMF, Oct.

Kovacs, Z. (1993): 'Emerging Central and Eastern Europe: A New Phenomenon in World Trade in the 1990s', Paper presented at the EADI General Conference in Berlin.

Nielsen, J.U., Heinrich, H. and J.D. Hansen (1991): *An Economic Analysis of the EC*, London: McGraw-Hill.

OECD (1992): *Employment Outlook*, Paris: OECD.

Page, S., Davenport, M. and A. Hewitt (1992): *The GATT Uruguay Round: Effects on Developing Countries*, London: ODI.

Paridon, C.W.A.M. (1993): 'Buitenlandse economische betrekkingen van Nederland: strategische ontwikkelingen en overwegingen', *Internationale Spectator*, Jan.

Piore, M. and C. Sabel (1984): *The Second Industrial Divide*, New York: Basic Books.

Reich, R.B. (1991): *The Work of Nations. Preparing Ourselves for 21st Century Capitalism*, New York: The Free Press.

Schuknecht, L. (1993): *Trade Protection in the EC*, Philadelphia, PA: Harwood.

Sideri, S. and J. Sengupta (1992): *The 1992 Single European Market*, London: Frank Cass (EADI Book Series 13).

Stare, M. (1993): 'The Importance of Multilateralism in International Trade for Smaller Economies in Transition: The Case of Slovenia'. Paper presented at the EADI General Conference in Berlin.

Thurow, L. (1992): *Head to Head*, New York: Warner Books.

UNCTAD (1990): *Trade and Development Year Book*, Geneva: UNCTAD.

UNCTAD (1991): *Trade and Development Year Book*, Geneva: UNCTAD.

UNCTAD (1994): *The Outcome of the Uruguay Round: An Initial Assessment*, Geneva: UNCTAD.

Van Rooy, Y. C.M.T. (1994): 'The Consequences of GATT for Developing Countries' (in Dutch), Speech delivered at the Dutch chapter of SID meeting, Amsterdam, 9 Feb.

Wolveren, K. van (1990): *The Enigma of Japanese Power*, New York: Vintage Books.

World Bank (1993a): *World Development Report*, New York: Oxford.

World Bank (1993b): *East Asian Miracle*, New York: Oxford.

World Bank (1994): *Debt Tables*, New York: Oxford.

PART I

2

Regionalisation of World Trade: Dead End or Way Out?

SIEGFRIED SCHULTZ

INTRODUCTION

The merging of countries by forming free trade zones and customs or even economic unions is a phenomenon which is currently on the agenda all over the world. There is talk of the 'globalisation' of markets, but at the same time there is increasing regionalisation.[1] Concern about the efficacy of the GATT process has led some countries to divert their negotiating capacity more on such arrangements than on their serious involvement on the multilateral level. It has clearly been seen in recent years that there is a close – negative – interaction between progress in the GATT and progress on regional economic integration.

With regard to the coverage, in the majority of agreements it was mainly the 'first freedom' which was exchanged, that is, for trade in goods, through complete abolition of tariffs, and also of quotas, after a certain transition period. First, within the European Community, now the European Union (EU), and subsequently in the treaty with EFTA on the European Economic Area (EEA), all four freedoms were agreed on: those for goods, services, capital and people, although with exceptions, especially for agriculture.

The recent proliferation of regional integration arrangements and proposals, and the difficulty of concluding the Uruguay Round, have fuelled fears that international trade is becoming more of a regional affair in ways that will reduce global welfare. 'There is a debate between those who take the view that there is a constructive and creative tension between regional economic integration and multilateral liberalisation, and those who take the opposite view that regional integration efforts can be corrosive and even cancerous to the multilateral system' [Smith, 1993: 98–9].

Over the years, the GATT system has been eroded by excessive use of rights, and disregard of obligations emerging from the set of rules originally agreed on. So GATT was seriously weakened in dealing adequately with the changing patterns of world trade and retaining control of the policy tools resorted to by national governments or regional blocs in pursuit of their policy objectives. Thus the multilateral trading system is considered to be jeopardised by the creation of regional trading blocs – a move which seems to be brought about by the following reasons [*Schott, 1989b: 1*].

First, due to concerns about the effectiveness of GATT rules and procedures (complexity of talks, cumbersome decision-making process, consensus rule, tardy implementation, soft enforcement), the founding of regional units has been promoted as a complement, if not a substitute, for multilateralism. It is in this context that charges are brought forward against exceptions to agreed rules (Multi-Fibre Arrangement: MFA), the vagueness of language with respect to regulations affecting sensitive items (agriculture, subsidies), and the inventiveness with regard to 'new instruments' and their proliferation (voluntary export restraints). Most of this, it is alleged, runs counter to the spirit, if not the letter, of the GATT treaty.

Second, the increased weight of the EU, as the core unit of the EEA on the one hand, and Japan on the other, have brought about the relative decline in the role of US exports on a world-wide scale. This restructuring among the main actors in world trade may have an impact on the kind of trading system.

Third, an excessively long period of multilateral talks in the Uruguay Round has only brought limited results. The thrust of protectionism has not been curtailed, and the erosion in multilateral trade disciplines will probably continue. No halt is being put to the renaissance of unilateral actions.

Fourth, the completion of the Single European Market (SEM) and the signing of the North American Free Trade Agreement (NAFTA)[2] have given support to the positive connotation of regional trading blocs. Considerations of regional arrangements in East Asia and the Pacific area have been promoted. This is adding to the concerns of third countries and causing them also to propose new or seek membership of existing regional integration agreements.

II. MOTIVATIONS FOR REGIONAL INTEGRATION

Both developed and developing countries pursue various forms of regional integration for a variety of reasons, the 'ideal' sequence being free trade area (FTA), customs union, common market and economic union. Because they have different roots, regional arrangements may also evolve in their own way and hence will have varying implications for non-partner countries. The range of motivations behind regionalism is wide; these motives can be observed frequently:

- There is an implicit assumption that, at least temporarily, national economic welfare will be advanced more thoroughly by means of regional co-operation than by multilaterally agreed liberalisation. The welfare gain is supposed to be brought about by reallocation of factors of production as well as by economies of scale and specialisation and subsequent price cuts.
- Besides the static component of welfare gains there are expectations of a rise in total productivity through increased competition, growing investment and higher income in the longer run (dynamic component).
- Considering trade-creating versus trade-diverting [*Viner, 1950*] and suppressing effects, on balance the net impact of lowering of barriers to market access on partners of regionalisation is expected to be positive.
- Transaction costs, carrying a strong element of distance, may play an important role in favour of the regional orientation of economic activity. This applies to the gathering and dissemination of information, communication and transportation. Cultural affinity may have a dampening effect on transaction costs.
- Beyond trade policy considerations, factors such as supporting macroeconomic policy reforms or inviting foreign direct investment may also be on the mind of those pushing ahead with integration.
- Besides expected economic gains there are also political motives behind promoting regional integration. Political considerations have often outweighed other factors in decisions to accede to the terms of the agreements. A dominant theme in this context is the affiliation with a dominant power and the hoped-for increase in political stability and security in the respective region. More weight of negotiating power in trade talks and in the context of disputes may be another case in point.
- The obvious weakness of the present world trading system, and the tardy progress to change it, provide a good breeding ground for seeking trade liberalisation in regional integration schemes. In effect, regional negotiations may be less hampered than GATT negotiations by members enjoying MFN benefits while escaping obligations ('free-riding'), by parties taking advantage of consensus rules to block progress until their demands are met ('foot dragging'), and by the least willing participant determining the pace of negotiations ('convoy effect').

III. REVIVAL OF REGIONALISM

The recent wave of regional arrangements has a predecessor in the 1960s, which, except for industrialised countries, more or less failed. Developing countries in particular had high expectations which were not realised.

'Regional trade did not offer a viable alternative to trade with industrialized countries and could not offset the disadvantages of an excessive import substitution policy applied in most member countries of regional groupings' [*Langhammer and Hiemenz, 1990: 73*].

The revival of regionalism since the 1980s is fed by somewhat different reasons. However, the present regionalism will probably last longer because the United States (US) changed camps. Having been sceptical about partial solutions before, the US altered its basic stance [*Bhagwati, 1992: 12*] and developed a preference for playing the regional card. After giving consent to the foundation and expansion of the EU on political grounds and the establishment of the admittedly special relationship – FTA with Israel, the FTA with Canada marked a distinct change. Now, the extension to NAFTA has taken place. And the Enterprise for the Americas Initiative envisages one or several FTAs embracing North and South America;

Numerous proposals for new arrangements have been put forward in recent years, especially in the Pacific and North American regions. Over the last five years or so proposals have been made for new bilateral regional trade agreements between the US on the one hand, and Australia, ASEAN, Japan, Korea and Taiwan on the other. There have also been proposals for multi-nation Pacific groupings. These began with the proposal for a FTA involving five developed Pacific countries. More recently, Malaysia has proposed an East Asian economic group including the ASEAN countries and possibly Japan and other Asian countries. For a brief survey of the objectives and achievements of the main regional agreements see Tables 1 and 2.

TABLE I

MAJOR REGIONAL TRADE ARRANGEMENTS

Name [1]	*Objectives/Instruments*	*Implementation Record*
Central American Common Market (CACM) Signed: 1960; effective: 1961; revised: 1991 Population: 25 million	Customs union, industrial integration. Elimination of tariffs and quantitative restrictions (QR), no foreign exchange constraints in intra-trade. Adoption of common external Tariff (CET).	Initially on schedule; most restriction lifted by early 1970s, deterioration in 1980s (new QR). CET 1986, not effective in all member countries.
Latin American Integration Association (LAFTA/LAIA) LAFTA signed: 1960; effective: 1961; replaced by LAIA: 1980 Population: 375 million	Free Trade Area (FTA) and industrial planning. Facilitation of bilateral co-operation. Regional and bilateral tariff preferences. Clearing and credit schemes.	Bilateral trade agreements. In 1987, about 40% of intra-LAIA imports eligible for preferences. Intra-regional trade expanded mostly for manufactures.

TABLE I (cont.)

Name [1]	Objectives/Instruments	Implementation Record
Andean Pact (AP) Founded: 1969; modified: 1988; revised: 1989 Population: 90 million	Customs union gradually, regional industrial co-operation. Establish FTA by 1992; common market by 1993, phase out exceptions by 1995. Harmonise macroeconomic policies.	Several postponements. Internal customs tariffs eliminated; no common external tariff. Policy of joint industrial projects abandoned.
European Community Founded: 1958; European Union (1993) Population: 340 million	Free movement of goods, services, and factors of production by 1993. Common external tariff. Exchange rate arrangements.	1968 removal of tariffs and QR ahead of schedule; common external tariff ahead of schedule. Internal Market completed 1993.
European Free Trade Association (EFTA) Founded: 1960 Population: 32 million	Eliminate all tariffs on manufactures by mid-1967.	Achieved on schedule. More highly integrated with EU than among themselves.
Economic Community of West African States (ECOWAS) Founded: 1975 Population: 180 million	FTA and customs union. Original targets for liberalisation and CET by 1990. Target to eliminate non-tariff barriers (NTB) by 1995. Enhance labour and capital mobility.	Poor progress of liberalisation retarded by QR. Structural imbalances due to heterogeneous membership. No freedom of labour mobility.
Southern African Development Coordination Conference (SADCC) Founded: 1980 Population: 80 million	1. Reduce economic dependence (in particular on South Africa); 2. Concerted action to realise economic liberation; and 3. Coordinate and secure external support.	Successful in achieving 2 and 3.
Preferential Trade Area for Eastern and Southern Africa (PTA) Founded: 1981 Effective: 1984 Population: 220 million	FTA, elimination of tariffs, reduction of NTB; mfn treatment, common external tariff. Ultimate target: African common market (model: EC).	Tardy progress on tariffs, covering limited range of commodities. Reserve Bank of Zimbabwe acts as multilateral clearing house.

Name [1]	Objectives/Instruments	Implementation Record
Gulf Cooperation Council (GCC) Founded: 1981 Population: 22 million	Political coordination and customs union; harmonisation of policies. CET and customs union originally by 1986; altered to 1983.	1982: Virtual elimination of customs tariffs. 1983: Unification of tariff schedules, liberalisation of trade in services. Customs union not yet achieved.
Association of South East Asian Nations (ASEAN) Founded: 1967 Population: 310 million	Preferential trading arrangements. FTA, regional industrial co-operation. Industrial joint ventures	FTA repeatedly postponed. Industrial co-operation scarcely implemented, some joint ventures. Failure in reducing NTB.
North American Free Trade Agreement (NAFTA). Extension of US-Canadian FTA (1989) concluded in 1991; amended in 1993 Population: 370 million	Gradual elimination of customs duties. Initial intention to establish FTA by end of 1992, postponed to Jan. 1, 1994.	Treaty renegotiated (pollution control, labour rights). Supplementary agreements concluded.
Mercado del Cono Sur (MERCOSUR) Founded: 1991 Population: 190 million	Elimination of internal customs tariffs and NTB by 1994. Final target: common market (model: EC), with joint parliament.	No visible progress. Decision on establishment of common external tariff postponed until June 1994.
South Asia Association for Regional Cooperation (SAARC) Founded: 1983 Population: 1,125 million	More active co-operation in the economic, social, cultural, technical, and scientific field ('collective self-reliance').	Poor record (due to rivalry between India and Pakistan). Technical cooperation programmes. Annual summits with emphasis on changing subjects.
Asia Pacific Economic Cooperation (APEC) Founded: 1989 Population: 1,950 million	Loose coalition to, *inter alia*, advance liberalisation in a GATT-consistent manner. Assist members in promoting trade, investment, and improve information flows. Few formal ties.	Slow progress due to heterogeneous membership. Reluctance of some Asian countries to fully support the US-initiative.

TABLE I (cont.)

Name [1]	Objectives/Instruments	Implementation Record
ASEAN Free Trade Area (AFTA) Founded: 1991 Population: 320 million	Establishment of FTA within 15 years, begin- ning Jan. 1993. AFTA is to lay foundation for a single ASEAN market.	As yet, the engine of growth of ASEAN coun- tries has been extra- regional trade. AFTA may serve as a safety net.
Australia-New Zealand Closer Economic Relations Trade Agreement (ANZCER- TA) Signed: 1983; effec- tive: 1983; modified: 1988 Population: 20 million	Elimination of all tariffs by 1 January 1994, all QRs by mid-1995. Elimination of all direct export subsidies and incentives by 1987.	Broadly on schedule with elimination of all QR and liberalization of trade in services.

1) See Table 2 for membership.

Source: de la Torre and Kelly [*1992*]; Handbuch für Internationale Zusammenarbeit, Nomos, Baden-Baden (loose-leaf compilation); Informationsdienst (Informating Service), Institut der deutschen Wirtschaft, Vol. 18, No 2 (Jan. 9, 1992); OECD, Regional Integration Agreements and Macroeconomic Policy Discipline, in: Anderson and Blackhurst (eds.) [*1993*] additional informa- tion from DIW.

TABLE 2

FORMAL MEMBERSHIP OF REGIONAL TRADE ARRANGEMENTS

Western Hemisphere

CACM	Central American Common Market (1960) Members (5): Costa Rica (1962), El Salvador, Guatemala, Honduras and Nicaragua
LAFTA/LAIA	Latin American Free Trade Area/Latin American Integration Association (1960/80) Members (11): Mexico and all S. American countries, except Guyana, F. Guiana and Suriname
ANDEAN PACT	Andean Subregional Integration Agreement (1969) Members (5): Bolivia, Colombia, Ecuador, Peru and Venezuela (Chile withdrew in 1976)
MERCOSUR	Members (4): Argentina, Brazil, Paraguay and Uruguay (1991)
NAFTA	Members (3): Canada, Mexico and USA (1991)

Europe

EC/EU	The European Communities (1958)/European Union (1993) Members (12): Belgium, Denmark (1973), France, Germany, Greece (1981), Ireland (1973), Italy, Luxembourg, the Netherlands, Portugal (1986), Spain (1986) and the United Kingdom
EFTA	European Free Trade Association (1960) Members (7): Austria, Finland (1968), Iceland (1970), Liechtenstein (1991), Norway, Sweden and Switzerland
EEA	EU plus EFTA (1994)

Africa

ECOWAS	Economic Community of West African States (1975) Members (16): Benin, Burkina Faso, Cape Verde, Côte d'Ivoire, The Gambia, Ghana, Guinea, Guinea-Bissau, Liberia, Mali, Mauritania, Niger, Nigeria, Senegal, Sierra Leone and Togo
SADCC	Southern African Development Coordination Conference (1980) Members (10): Angola, Botswana, Lesotho, Malawi, Mozambique, Namibia (1990), Swaziland, Tanzania, Zambia and Zimbabwe
PTA	Preferential Trade Area for Eastern and Southern Africa (1981) Members (19): Angola, Burunda, Comoros, Djibouti, Ethiopia, Kenya, Lesotho, Malawi, Mauritius, Mozambique, Namibia, Rwanda, Somalia, Sudan, Swaziland, Tanzania, Uganda, Zambia and Zimbabwe

Middle East

GCC	Cooperation Council for the Arab States of the Gulf; also: Gulf Cooperation Council (1981) Members (6): Bahrain, Kuwait, Oman, Qatar, Saudi Arabia and the United Arab Emirates

Asia and the Pacific

ASEAN	Association of South East Asian Nations (1967) Members (6): Brunei, Indonesia, Malaysia, the Philippines, Singapore and Thailand
SAARC	South Asian Association for Regional Cooperation (1983) Members (7): Bangladesh, Bhutan, India, Maldives, Nepal, Pakistan and Sri Lanka
APEC	Asia Pacific Economic Cooperation (1989) Members (17): ASEAN plus Austrilia, Canada, China, Hong Kong, Japan, Korea (Rep.), Mexico, New Zealand, Papua New Guinea, Taiwan and USA; Chile is a candidate
AFTA	ASEAN Free Trade Area (1991); Members: see ASEAN

TABLE 2 (cont.)

Functional Groups according to stage of economic development

NIE	Newly Industrialising Economies: Hong Kong, Korea (Rep.), Singapore and Taiwan
NNIE	Next-tier NIECs: Indonesia, Malaysia, the Philippines and Thailand

Source: See Table 1.

Over the years, a number of high-ranking conferences with substantial documentation have been devoted to the subject of FTAs and regional integration schemes. The respective studies go substantially beyond statistical analyses of data showing time trends in regional and global trade patterns. However, the studies differ both in their methodological approaches and the particular results that they generate. By and large, empirical evidence of the actual performance is sketchy and inconclusive [cf., *inter alia*, Pelkmans. *1992: 6, 8*].

In a recently concluded study different approaches have been compiled and analysed [*Srinivasan et al., 1993*]. Summarising the main findings, with respect to developing countries it is emphasised that the establishment of FTAs and integration schemes has been supported by factors which are not properly reflected in the accompanying analyses.

> A key one is the search for safe-haven trade agreements by smaller countries, which now, more than ever before, wish to secure access to the markets of large neighbouring trading partners because of their fear of higher trade barriers in the future (the insurance value of secure access to a larger market). A second is the frustration felt by larger countries with progress toward new multilateral liberalisation and their belief that their threatening to negotiate (or actually negotiating) regional agreements may force otherwise reluctant larger powers to make concessions multilaterally [*1993: 73*].[3]

With regard to growth of intra-regional trade, for the period 1980–91 it can be observed that this trade has gained weight almost exclusively in developed countries (see Table 3). The growth in intra-regional *exports* as a percentage of total exports of the region (the same applies to *imports)* has been particularly perceptible with the EU while the rise of the region's share in the world market has been moderate. In the case of EFTA the descending ratios are a reflection of falling membership. Among the developing countries most of the integration schemes mentioned here register, after an initial rise, a slackening of the regional component of trade. The outward-oriented approach of the Newly Industrialising Countries (NICs) is clearly shown by the doubling of their share in world exports in the period under consideration.

28

TABLE 3

REGIONAL TRADE SHARES

INTRA-REGIONAL TRADE AND WORLD TRADE OF REGIONAL GROUPINGS

		1980	1985	1986	1990	1991
North America	a	27.8	39.8	38.3	35.6	34.3
	b	16.4	17.5	16.2	16.3	16.5
	c	28.2	30.5	28.2	30.7	31.0
LAFTA/LAIA	a	14.5	9.0	11.6	11.4	11.0
	b	4.5	4.8	3.6	3.5	3.7
	c	13.7	13.1	13.3	13.2	12.2
EC	a	58.1	56.4	58.7	62.8	63.8
	b	39.5	37.7	42.3	42.9	41.6
	c	55.9	57.5	62.2	62.7	62.2
EFTA	a	15.5	14.4	15.4	14.1	13.1
	b	6.3	6.2	6.9	7.0	6.6
	c	14.1	14.8	14.9	14.2	13.5
ECPWAS	a	11.0	5.5	7.3	5.1	6.0
	b	0.4	1.1	0.6	0.7	0.6
	c	3.0	7.3	6.5	6.4	6.5
PTA	a	11.6	5.8	6.2	8.0	7.8
	b	0.3	0.4	0.4	0.3	0.3
	c	5.4	4.5	5.1	5.3	5.3
GCC	a	3.1	5.6	10.1	9.2	9.1
	b	8.9	3.3	2.3	2.5	2.4
	c	9.8	7.5	10.9	14.5	11.4
SAARC	a	5.6	5.4	4.4	3.8	5.0
	b	0.6	0.7	0.7	0.7	0.8
	c	3.2	2.4	2.2	2.4	4.0
ANZCERTA	a	7.0	7.6	7.5	8.2	8.2
	b	1.5	1.6	1.4	1.5	1.5
	c	7.4	7.0	6.9	8.4	9.3
NIES	a	7.4	6.5	6.6	7.8	8.2
	b	3.2	4.8	4.9	6.1	6.7
	c	6.1	7.1	7.1	8.0	8.2
NNIEs	a	3.3	4.6	3.9	4.3	4.1
	b	2.7	2.7	2.3	2.7	3.0
	c	4.0	6.3	5.2	4.4	4.3

(a) Share of intra-regional exports in total regional exports.
(b) Share of regional exports in total world exports.
(c) Share of intra-regional imports in total regional imports.
For membership of regional integration schemes see Table 2.

Source: IMF, Direction of Trade Statistics, magnetic tape; own calculations.

In the majority of cases there was obviously little potential for trade expansion or, even worse, the arrangements themselves became instruments of protection. Declining world market shares and low shares of intra-regional exports suggest that 'the arrangements' potential for improving efficiency through competition or technological diffusion within the arrangements was limited or non-existent [*De Melo and Panagariya, 1992b: 15*].

IV. FEATURES OF THE NEW TREND

Regional trading arrangements – bilateral as well as plurilateral – have been a fairly constant characteristic of the world trading system. The recent trend toward regionalism, however, may be qualitatively different from past efforts and does carry greater risks of becoming a substitute for, rather than a complement to, multilateralism. Apart from the potentially distorting effects of these arrangements on the allocation of world resources, elements unique to current regionalism seem to pose a greater threat to the multilateral system than earlier challenges [*de la Torre and Kelly 1992: 41–2*].

First, the renewed interest in regionalism has taken place in a weakening multilateral trading system. The GATT's inability to curb rising protectionist pressures since the end of the Tokyo Round has created frustration with the sluggishness of the international negotiations and raised concerns about the GATT's effectiveness and ability to adapt to the emerging trade issues of the 1990s – among which problems posed by high-technology industries and by firms engaged in trade and investment in goods and services on a global scale rank highly. Thus, doubts have arisen about the political will of the major players to strengthen the GATT's credibility. In this context, regionalism has been advocated as an *alternative* to multilateralism.

Second, thorough and successful regional initiatives by major industrial countries have created the perception that preferential trading arrangements are here to stay. Prominent examples in this context are 'EC 1992' and the US–Canadian FTA. The fact that both were initiated at about the same time seems to confirm a trend toward a fragmentation of the multilateral trading order into a tripolar system of trading areas, centred around the United States, the European Union and Japan (although the latter is not part of a trade block). The accords in favour of the EEA and NAFTA have heightened this perception.

These concerns became more serious with the shift in the trade policy perception of the United States 'from a virtually one-track approach emphasizing non-discrimination to a multitrack approach comprising unilateralism, regionalism, and multilateralism' [*de la Torre and Kelly 1992: 41–2*].[4] Certainly, the US started out with regional initiatives as *complements* to multilateralism. However, this stance since the mid-1980s gradually gave way to the readiness to settle for bilateral or plurilateral arrangements as an *alternative* course of action.[5] Furthermore, the EC's move to establish bilateral preferential trading arrangements with a number of countries pointed in the same direction.

Third, the new kind of preferential trading arrangement is characterised by the fact that reciprocal trade preferences are increasingly requested also from Third world countries while previous arrangements generally took the form of one-way preferences.

V. REGIONALISATION, GLOBALISATION AND MULTILATERALISM

While liberalisation steps became smaller in the 1970s and 1980s, the process of integration of the major economic regions of the world gained momentum. This process seems to go on, notably in North America and Europe as the core units. It may also become more important in the Asia-Pacific region. Questions arise with regard to the future of these arrangements and their likely impact on trade and investment patterns, as well as on the evolution of the multilateral system in coming decades [*OECD, 1992: 17–19*].[6]

Concerns have been expressed about the increased regionalisation of the trading system. The preferential liberalisation features of such agreements could be a major source of trade diversion which may well offset their trade-creating effects. Theoretically, regionalisation could have adverse spillover effects since it may induce outsiders who bear the brunt of trade diversion to retaliate by seeking preferential trade agreements among themselves so as to offset their loss of markets and strengthen their bargaining power. This process of competitive regionalisation may undermine the multilateral system and could turn the world into one of hostile economic blocs and discriminating trade regimes similar to those that prevailed in the 1930s. In reality, however, the bargaining power of the affected countries outside the emerging groupings is quite limited.

FTAs are by definition discriminatory. They affect the multilateral system in a number of ways. One concern is that they could lead to retaliatory actions or even to trade wars. Larger countries or blocs could start off trade wars at the expense of small countries. Another aspect is the possible spread of preference to third countries. These systemic effects may be the most serious consequence of the spread of regional arrangements. As a consequence, one would have to resist them on the argument that regional negotiations will lead to a weaker set of multilateral trade institutions and will produce exclusive and inefficient solutions.

In fact there is the risk that the formation of trading blocs could force business to adopt strategies considered to be sub-optimal from a global welfare perspective. In particular, private foreign direct investment is determined, at least in part, by market access rather than efficiency considerations. Moreover, trading blocs may be tempted to use their bargaining power to gain concessions from others. This power play could significantly underline the operation of the rule-based multilateral system of trade, investment and technology. As in the 1930s, it might lead to the establishment of a series of discriminatory bilateral agreements between groups of countries which would not only hamper and distort trade flows, to the detriment of all parties involved, but also serve to heighten confrontations since players excluded from particular bilateral agreements are eager to obtain the same market access concessions as their rivals.

The opposing position can be described as welcoming regional and plurilateral strategies as perhaps the best way of fostering global liberalisation, given the growing obstacles which had slowed down multilateral negotiations to almost a complete halt and which are not likely to disappear overnight. In contrast to multilateral negotiations, regional agreements are said to be attractive because they make negotiations more manageable: a relatively small number of like-minded countries is involved, which reduces the likelihood that liberalisation will be prevented by a persistent player. Moreover, the free-rider problem implicit in the MFN principle is eliminated. Through gradual enlargement and mergers (e.g. EU plus EFTA = European Economic Area; EEA), regional approaches could contribute to liberalisation on a wider scale. Indeed, given continued protectionist tendencies and the cumbersome progress of negotiations in the GATT context, regional liberalisation could prove essential for further trade liberalisation in the future.

Defenders of regionalism contend that a division of the world into a few blocs will lead to a more liberalised world trade faster – and with greater certainty – than the multilateral process. Unfortunately there are two sides to the issue. A small number of blocs can make the approach to a co-operative solution faster and more certain. But the larger the blocs and their market power, the greater the temptation to impose restrictions on trade outside the bloc [*de Melo and Panagariya, 1992b: 8*].

The reinforcement of multilateral trade liberalisation may be brought about in a number of ways. Regional arrangements can act as a model for multilateral trade liberalisation, especially in areas of non-tariff measures and services trade where the GATT record was poor [*Lloyd, 1992: 29*]. By including on their agenda areas not covered by multilateral negotiation, such as standards and government procurement, the regional approach can serve as a catalyst in the pursuit of removing market fragmentations. The costs of concluding agreements may be lower on the regional level with few countries and more homogeneous cost structures than in negotiations with world-wide participation. Consequently, the approach would seem to be to encourage regionalism for these reasons [*Srinivasan et al., 1993: 75*]: 'liberalizing the

32

dynamic component of global trade, frustration with the multilateral process, and the chance that bilateral negotiation will reignite multilateral negotiations'.

One of the key questions is the effect which the creation of large groupings of countries may have on the balance between liberal and protectionist forces. Country groupings may result in a more liberal attitude to the extent that protectionist arguments originating in one country are likely to have less weight at the regional level than in the purely national context. However, powerful cross-national coalitions can still materialize (for example, with regard to agricultural policy in the EU), and a weak decision-making process at the regional level (e.g. unanimous voting) may provide opportunities for blocking liberalisation. In the final analysis, however, the net outcome will be determined by two effects: the trade creation and economic dynamics from intra-regional liberalisation, and the level of (effective) protection *vis-à-vis* the outside world.

Over the longer term, much will also depend on the way the business community responds. While further regional integration could affect the decisions of firms related to the localisation of their activities, business is nevertheless increasingly adopting a global approach to its operations. Global supply and demand considerations, new patterns of co-operation and competition and, in particular, the concern of business about access to technology wherever it may be obtained are likely to make contributions towards liberalisation.

The globalisation process, initiated by rapid diffusion of computer and telecommunication technologies [cf. *Oman, 1993: 62*] and carried out by transnational corporations, has extended the limitations of nationally-based policies and increasingly confronts governments with the need to liberalise and harmonise policies, standards and regulations with other countries, including trade and trade-related areas. Harmonisation and liberalisation in response to the challenges posed by globalisation is partly being conducted in the context of regional arrangements. Increasingly, however, the process of globalisation calls for multilateral solutions. The ongoing process of globalisation of investment and production is likely to lessen the impact of regionalism.

There seems to be a fairly widespread consensus in the science community that an overall assessment on whether the formation of blocs leads to trade creation or trade diversion cannot seriously be made yet, more research is needed [cf., *inter alia, Krugman, 1992: 29*]. Existing empirical evidence is limited with respect to coverage and thus inconclusive. Whether the emergence of regional trading blocs leads to more or less effective global negotiations is an open question. With regard to the other key aspect of the regionalism–multilateralism debate, that is, the 'value' of regional blocs, it looks like they are a reasonable answer to the prevailing difficulties of multilateralism.

VI. COMPATIBILITY WITH GATT RULES

By their nature, arrangements which provide trade preferences to members of a regional grouping are not consistent with GATT Article I. According to this Article trade concessions awarded to one member country are to be extended to all GATT members (MFN principle). This rule of non-discrimination is the cornerstone of GATT. FTAs conflict with this principle.

Although GATT founders obviously judged multilateral trade liberalisation to be fundamental, they also intended to capture the trade-creating benefits of bilateral and regional liberalisation efforts. At the same time, however, clauses were inserted in GATT to control and minimise the trade diversion likely to result from those arrangements. Article XXIV permits departures from the MFN obligation provided that the FTA or customs union meets three conditions: (1) duties and other restrictive regulations are eliminated on 'substantially all' trade between partner countries; (2) the general incidence of duties and regulations affecting third parties is no higher after the establishment of an agreement than it was before; and (3) the agreement contains a plan and schedule for its complete formation within a reasonable period of time.[7] Although the intent of these rules is sometimes interpreted as meaning that an FTA should be trade-creating, there is no guarantee that this will be the case. 'However, the presumption that an FTA must be more trade-creating than trade-diverting has been incorporated into GATT working party reviews of FTA notifications, and is now generally considered the key standard by which to judge the value of FTAs to third countries' [*Schott, 1989a: 24*].

For several reasons the original concept has been diluted and, in fact, turned almost upside down. Due to political considerations, free trade areas (e.g. EFTA) and customs unions (e.g. the EU) have been permitted or tolerated by GATT members, although these agreements did not fully meet the conditions required by Art. XXIVs.[8] It seems to have become standard procedure to insist that new FTAs be 'GATTable'. Of all the GATT articles, 'this is one of the most abused, and those abuses are among the least noted' [*Patterson, 1989: 361*]. In addition, preferential treatment between and for developing countries has become an accepted norm in GATT law[9]. Under the Enabling Clause (1979) regional arrangements involving developing countries are excluded from the requirement to meet the formal criteria of Article XXIV. Regional arrangements among these countries are permitted as long as they facilitate trade, do not create 'undue difficulties' for the trade of other countries, and do not act as an impediment to the reduction or elimination of trade barriers on a MFN basis. Formal procedures have not been established to ensure that these conditions are met.

Because most GATT members are today involved in some form of preferential trading arrangement, there is a tendency among industrialised countries to refrain from openly criticising preferential trading arrangements involving other GATT members. Previously the major critic of discriminatory arrangements, the US has become a user of Article XXIV. There is a general understanding that in the past regional arrangements did not hinder multilateral liberalisation. This assessment also refers to the drastic cutting of import tariffs *vis-à-vis* third countries and the gradual reductions of formal quantitative restrictions on most manufactures. Except for the EU's Common Agricultural Policy,

> regional arrangements cannot justifiably be blamed for the proliferation over the past fifteen years of non-tariff measures (such as voluntary export restraint arrangements, countervailing and antidumping measures, and orderly market arrangements). These reflect a resistance in industrial countries to structural adjustment required by changes in comparative advantage and have not been confined to members of regional arrangements [*de la Torre and Kelly, 1992: 44*].

In order to adjust international trading rules on the basis of past experience, one important element in their further development should be the extension of Art. XXIV of the GATT treaty [*Nunnenkamp, 1993: 198*]. The suggested innovation refers to insert stipulations which make it possible (i) to reject new preferential trade arrangements on the grounds of non-liberal accession rules and (ii) to provide for compensation of non-member parties which are negatively affected by the formation of a regional trade arrangement. These components are considered to be essential in order to reconcile both regionalism and multilateralism.

VII. OUTLOOK

The GATT was highly successful in its *early* days both because the negotiating mechanisms followed were especially well suited for reducing the high tariff levels which existed at the end of the Second World War and because the hegemonic behaviour of the US in its international economic relations served to minimise the adverse effects of certain flaws in the GATT. The increase in the number of negotiating parties, the greater use of bilateral deals to achieve trade policy goals, and the increased willingness to take unilateral action against 'unfair trading practices' all indicate that the GATT may no longer be facilitating increases in world trading welfare to the extent it did earlier [*Baldwin, 1993: 388*]. These policies weaken a central principle of the agreement, the resolving of trade disputes and achieving trade policy goals by means of multilateral procedures. It remains to be seen what the envisaged successor, the World Trade Organisation (WTO), will attain in this respect.

The prospect that the global trading system is becoming more regionalised refers to the enlargement of existing regional clusters (NAFTA, EEA) as well as to the proliferation of more regional arrangements. Along with this comes the fear of more exclusive forms. 'Hence, concerns over regionalism in the 1990s reflect increases in the coverage of countries in existing regional schemes [as well as increases] in product and area coverage such as services and investment provisions' [*Srinivasan et al., 1993: 73–4*].

The pertinent issue from the viewpoint of global welfare thus seems not to be whether the world's trade is becoming more or less regionally focused. 'Rather, the key issue is simply whether overall world trade is becoming more or less liberal and predictable (and thereby more or less conducive to global investment and employment growth)' [*Anderson and Norheim, 1993: 21*]. Regionalisation in the 1990s is likely to continue to generate a wide range of reactions for some time. As was suggested by Hamilton and Whalley [*1992: 22*], the 1990s may reveal a trading system which progressively devolves towards two separate sets of disciplines: *multilateral* disciplines dominated by large power negotiations between American, European and Pacific groupings led by the US, the EU and Japan; and a second tier of *regional* agreements which apply to trade between dominant and smaller powers whose trade is largely with one of the former. These may show great variety due to the differences in country composition and institutional structures.

VIII. CONCLUSIONS

With regard to the likely future of the world trading system a few conclusions can be drawn from the facts touched upon above and from the positions of the main players involved.[10]

The future of the trading system should be tied to a GATT reinforced and strengthened by prospective reforms in key areas such as the pace of negotiations, and the scope and coverage as well as the enforcement of rules. The WTO is supposed to be instrumental in this respect.

Neither the US nor the EU formally surrendered the position that their trade and related economic policies are focused on multilateralism. In fact, this is the course to be preferred since multilateral negotiations basically hold a better prospect for general trade liberalisation than bilateral FTAs.

As long as the idea of multilateral talks does not cease to exist FTA negotiations could undermine the trading system: the pursuit of more FTAs would send clear signals that the prospective partners were disillusioned with the multilateral process. This perception might trigger a defensive reaction from trading partners, leading them to turn away from further GATT talks and instead try to secure trade preferences in the main markets through FTA arrangements.

If, however, the multilateral process of negotiations would turn out to be too clumsy to produce truly multilateral results, the main industrialised trading areas, in particular the NAFTA and the EEA, tired by the delays on the multilateral level, will without formally disengaging from this system enter into trade pacts with (groups of) countries prepared to do so.

As an alterative to the multilateral process the preferred fallback approach would not necessarily be bilateral agreements. Rather, an approach similar to the 'GATT-plus' concept in which like-minded parties, ready to reduce trade barriers and adopt new trading rules that go beyond the GATT, might be pursued on a conditional MFN basis. The benefits would be restricted to the participants; access for other parties should be open on the basis only of reciprocal commitments.

NOTES

1. With regard to terminology, *regionalisation is* interpreted here as a process of spatial concentration of economic activity which can be empirically observed and where geographical proximity is an important element, while *regionalism is* the 'philosophy' of actively pushing ahead economic coherence by regional grouping. In a somewhat different approach it is advocated [*Lorenz, 1991,1993*] that the former be considered as the outcome of a 'natural' location phenomenon leading to closer economic ties while the latter is seen as the creation of preferential trading arrangements.
2. The earlier outline of a NAFTA (in 1967) has been less narrowly geographically defined, that is, it was supposed to be the North *Atlantic* FTA, including the UK.
3. In this context an interesting case in point is the desire of developing countries to lock in domestic policy reforms by signing international agreements, and regional arrangements made easier to negotiate than multilateral arrangements have been considered to be suitable for this purpose.
4. After supporting the formation of the EC on political grounds, since the establishment of the FTA with Israel (in 1985) a growing trend towards reciprocal and preferential arrangements was discernible.
5. This was in evidence in public statements by George Shultz (in 1985) and James Baker III (1988) on the course of US foreign trade policy.
6. Here and in the following, this source has been drawn on fairly extensively.
7. It should be noted that GATT also grants exemption to the MFN rule for historical arrangements such as the Commonwealth.
8. Since 1948, around 70 FTAs and preferential trade agreements have been reviewed by the GATT under the provisions of Article XXIV. Only four agreements – the South African – Rhodesian Customs Union (1948); the Nicaragua–El Salvador Agreement (1951); Nicaraguan participation in the Central American FTA (1958); and the Caribbean Common Market (1973) – were declared fully compatible with Article XXIV requirements. However, no agreement has been declared as being incompatible with GATT rules. As a result of these precedents, countries are perceived to be able to derogate from MFN obligations in FTAs without regard to the effects on third countries.
9. Preferential treatment is considered to be justified with the 'infant industry' argument. It suggests that developing countries might have comparative advantages in

some industries but do not have the resources or time to build them up. In order to avoid inefficient allocation of resources, these industries need to be protected temporarily against imports from established industries abroad. Implementation is difficult, since the distinction between infant and inefficient industries is almost impossible.

10. For an in-depth discussion of the listed items see, *inter alia*, Schott [*1989a; 1991*]; parts of his conclusion are being taken up here.

REFERENCES

Anderson, K. and H. Norheim (1993): 'History, Geography and Regional Economic Integration', in Anderson and Blackhurst (eds.) [*1993*].

Anderson, K. and R. Blackhurst (eds.) (1993): *Regional Integration and the Global Trading System*, Harvester Wheatsheaf, Hertfordshire, U.K.

Baldwin, R.E. (1993): 'Adapting the GATT to a more Regionalized World: A Political Economy Perspective', in Anderson and Blackhurst (eds, 1993).

Bhagwati, J. (1992): *Regionalism and Multilateralism: An Overview*, Columbia U., Discussion Paper Series, No. 603; New York.

Genberg, H. and F. Nadal de Simone (1993): 'Regional Integration Agreements and Macroeconomic Policy Discipline', in Anderson and Blackhurst (eds.) [*1993*].

Hamilton, C. and J. Whalley (1992): *The Future of the World Trading System*, Washington, DC: Institute for International Economics.

Hoekman, B.M. and M.P. Leidy (1992): 'Holes and Loopholes in Regional Trade Arrangements and the Multilateral Trading System', *Aussenwirtschaft*, Vol. 47, No. III (Oct.); St. Gallen or Anderson and Blackhurst (eds.) [*1993*].

Krugman, P. (1992): 'Regionalism vs. Multilateralism: Analytical Notes', World Bank and CEPR, Conference on New Dimensions in Regional Integration, Session IV, Paper No. 7, Washington, DC.

Langhammer, R.J. and U. Hiemenz (1990): *Regional Integration among Developing Countries – Opportunities, Obstacles and Options*, Kieler Studien, No. 232, Tübingen: Mohr.

Lloyd, P.J. (1992): 'Regionalisation and World Trade', *OECD Economic Studies*, No. 18, Spring.

Lorenz, D. (1991):, 'Regionalisation versus Regionalism – Problems of Change in the World Economy', *Intereconomics*, Vol. 26, No. 1, Hamburg: Weltarchiv.

Lorenz, D. (1993): 'Europe and East Asia in the Context of Regionalization: Theory and Economic Policy', *Journal of Asian Economics*, Vol. 4, No. 2.

Melo, J. de, Panagariya, A. and D. Rodrik (1992a): *The New Regionalism: A Country Perspective*, Centre for Economic Policy Research, Discussion Paper Series, No. 715, London.

Melo, J. de and A. Panagariya, (1992b): *The New Regionalism in Trade Policy*, Washington, DC: World Bank; London: Centre for Economic Policy Research.

Nunnenkamp, P. (1993): 'The World Trading System at the Crossroads: Multilateral Trade Negotiations in the Era of Regionalism', *Aussenwirtschaft*, Vol. 48, No. II, Chur/Zurich: Ruegger.

Oman, Ch. (1993): 'Globalization and Regionalization in the 1980s and 1990s', *Development and International Cooperation*, Vol. IX, No. 16.

OECD (1992): 'Long-Term Prospects for the World Economy', OECD Forum for the Future; Summary of a conference held in June 1992, OECD/GD (92)68, Paris.

OECD (1993): *Regional Integration and Developing Countries*, Paris.

Patterson, G. (1989): 'Implications for the GATT and the World Trading System', in Schott (ed.) [*1989a*].

Pelkmans, J. (1992): *Regionalism in World Trade, Vice or Virtue?*, Centre for European Policy Studies, Working Document No. 74, Brussels.

Schott, J.J. (ed., 1989a): *Free Trade Areas and US Trade Policy*, Washington, DC: Institute for International Economics.

Schott, J.J. (1989b): 'Is the World Devolving into Regional Trading Blocs?' (manuscript), Institute for International Economics, Washington, DC.

Schott, J.J. (1991): 'Trading Blocs and the World Trading System', *The World Economy*, Vol. 14, No. 1.

Smith, M.G. (1993): 'The North American Free Trade Agreement: Global Impacts', in Anderson and Blackhurst (eds.) [*1993*].

Srinivasan, T.N., Whalley, J. and I. Wooton (1993): 'Measuring the Effects of Regionalism on Trade and Welfare', in Anderson and Blackhurst (eds.) [*1993*].

Torre, A. de la and M.R. Kelly (1992): *Regional Trade Arrangements*, International Monetary Fund, Washington, DC, Occasional Paper, No. 93.

United Nations (1990): *Regional Trading Blocs: A Threat to the Multilateral Trading System?*, 1990, ST/ESA/219; New York.

Viner, J. (1950): *The Customs Union Issue*, New York.

3

Bilateralism versus Multilaterism: Changes in EU's Trade Policy for Europe

CHRISTOPHER STEVENS

I. INTRODUCTION

One of the motives for launching the Uruguay Round was to 'defend' multi-lateralism from the spread of bilateral and regional responses to trade issues. There were more than a few hints from the United States of America (USA) that the North American Free Trade Area (NAFTA) and the Enterprise for the Americas Initiative (EAI) were an 'insurance' against the failure of the Round to produce the desired results. The General Agreement on Tariffs and Trade (GATT) has entered the fray with a recent panel ruling that the Lomé Convention and, by implication, the European Union's (EU's) entire structure of non-reciprocal trade agreements, is in conflict with the multilateral system. The EU's initial response is that it will contest this view vigorously.

The Uruguay Round has been completed 'successfully', but as is demon-strated by the USA's threat of action against Japan under Super 301 before the formal signing ceremony, this does not mean an end to unilateralism. What are the regionalist challenges that the multilateral system has to face, and how far does the Uruguay Round deal go in meeting them? This chapter reviews the status of current EU regional initiatives that have implications for the multi-lateral system. It covers the Maastricht Treaty, the European Economic Area (EEA) and the Nordic enlargement of the Community, and the 'Europe Agreements' with the East European states. The final section considers the implications of regionalism for the multilateral system.

Any lingering doubts that there may have been on the persistence of region-alism must have been reduced by recent events, both in Europe and elsewhere.

- While the Single European Market (SEM) remains uncompleted much of the task set by the EU Commission has been completed and the remain-der is in process.
- The EEA has been agreed, the European Free Trade Association (EFTA) members have applied for full membership of the EU and terms have been agreed with three of them, subject to referenda.

- Agreements have been negotiated between the EU and six East European states to foster economic exchange in the short term. These may lead the way towards full integration in the longer term.
- The list of Mediterranean states that have expressed an interest in joining the EU now includes Turkey, Cyprus, Malta, Morocco and the Gulf Co-operation Council members. Although no early start to membership nego-tiations is in prospect, economic integration has been fostered in some cases by partial free trade and customs union accords.
- The NAFTA has been signed even though ratification has been delayed by the change in the US government. Other countries in the region have expressed an interest in joining. The Clinton administration has professed itself open to the extension of the agreement to the rest of the region, with Argentina, Chile, and Venezuela having been mentioned as potential candidates.

Even though these arrangements are claimed by their participants to be com-patible with existing multilateral institutions, they have their origins in a sharp change in the pattern of world production and finance away from the model assumed by the current regulatory structure. By the end of the 1980s the volume of goods and services bought by foreign affiliates totalled an estimated US\$ 4.4 trillion, almost double the level of world exports minus intra-firm trade [*UN, 1992: 2*]. Foreign direct investment (FDI) and its associated flows of capital, technology, training and trade have become the primary means by which a growing number of countries are integrated into the world economy. At the same time there has been an increase in the share of world trade occurring within rather than between regions. By the end of the 1980s intra-regional trade accounted for 61 per cent of EU, 41 per cent of Asian, and 35 per cent of North American trade in goods [*UN, 1992: 34*].

A distinction has been drawn between 'policy-led' and 'investment-led' integration, which may have different implications for the multilateral system. The former are programmes in which policy measures (typically to reduce barriers to trade) initiate the process of economic integration. An essential feature is that the institutional framework for integration precedes actual inte-gration. Investment-led integration occurs when the activities of firms serve as the principal force for regional integration because transnational corporations perceive advantages in integrating their operations across countries.

In practice the dividing line between these analytical categories is not clear cut. Often policy and investment initiatives move in parallel: the reduction of trade barriers leads to an increase in intra-regional trade which encourages firms to make cross-border investments that, in turn, lead to pressure for policy changes to harmonise standards etcetera.

There is a certain temporal correlation, for example, between the Single

European Market initiative and the level of investment in Europe. In four of the six years prior to 1986 the rate of gross fixed capital formation in the EU was lower (often markedly lower) than the Organisation for Economic Co-operation and Development (OECD) total; in each of the six years from 1986 it was comfortably higher. At least part of the increase in European FDI is likely to have been associated with the SEM, and designed to take advantage of the expected new opportunities.

Both the US–Canada free trade area and the NAFTA have been associated in time with investment surges. In the four years 1983–86, Canadian investment flows to the USA averaged US\$ 15.5 billion; in the four years 1987–90 the average was US\$ 26.9 billion. In the case of US investment in Canada, the increases were from US\$ 47.2 billion to US\$ 63.6 billion [*Hufbauer and Schott, 1992: Table 4.1*]. A similar pattern appears to be emerging in US–Mexican investment relations.

II. THE MAASTRICHT TREATY

The Maastricht Treaty, like the SEM, alters the way in which the 12 EU member states and the Union institutions relate to each other. A set of trade, finance and political arrangements has grown up over the past three decades to accommodate relations between these 13 actors and the rest of the world. These arrangements are now being changed.

The present pattern of Europe's relations with the countries of the South has been woven from 12 bilateral sets of policies and a thirteenth, partly cross-cutting, Union-level set. The balance between the bilateral and Union levels is established by the distribution between them of those powers that are most relevant to developing countries. Maastricht may alter this balance and, hence, the policy environment for developing countries. The extent of Union-level relations has been limited by the characteristic of the EU Commission that it does not possess the full array of attributes of a nation state. It cannot conduct a normal foreign or defence policy; even its responsibilities on debt are limited. The European Economic Community (EEC) Treaty contained three provisions that conferred power expressly on the EEC to make agreements with countries outside the EU. These were:

- Part IV of the EEC Treaty (Articles 131–136) which provided for aid to Overseas Countries and Territories (OCT). The practical importance of these Articles declined as the process of decolonisation progressed.
- Article 113 provided the legal basis for the Community's common commercial policy. It entitled the EEC to grant trade preferences, to make available export credits and to administer the Generalised System of Preferences (GSP).

- Article 238 enabled the EEC to conclude with a third party (a state, a group of states or an international organisation) an association agreement involving reciprocal rights and obligations, such as the Lomé Convention.

The principal direct implications for developing countries of the Maastricht Treaty are that it establishes a new legal framework for Union action and, in so doing, establishes a common framework for European policy towards developing countries. The elements of this common framework refer largely to aid but also include a potentially very important provision on the coherence of aid and other policies. Its indirect effects, therefore, could be greater if it opens the way for a more coherent EU development policy.

None of the provisions of the old EEC Treaty gave the Community institutions any exclusive rights to deal with developing countries. Nor did they specify any development goals for EU-developing country relations. The Maastricht Treaty confirms the first of these characteristics and alters the second. Articles 130u–y of the Maastricht Treaty cover development co-operation. They confirm the legal basis for any division of responsibility between the Union institutions and the member states, and they introduce for the first time the objectives of Union development policy.

Unlike many of the powers covered by the Maastricht Treaty, development co-operation is not one that is to be handled at either the member state or the Union level. The term *subsidiarity* that has figured prominently in so much debate on distribution of responsibilities between Union and national instruments, has no place in development co-operation. Rather, the appropriate term is *complementarity*. That is to say, the 12 member states and the EU institutions run 13 parallel development co-operation policies with no areas of activity (apart from trade and agriculture) reserved exclusively for one tier or the other.

Although this merely confirms the practice that has grown up over the past three decades, the Maastricht Treaty goes further than its predecessors by suggesting how these thirteen parallel policies should cohabit. The aims of all thirteen shall be to foster:

- the sustainable economic and social development of the developing countries, and more particularly the most disadvantaged among them;
- the smooth and gradual integration of the developing countries into the world economy;
- the campaign against poverty in the developing countries;
- the general objective of developing and consolidating democracy and the rule of law, and that of respecting human rights and fundamental freedoms.

The part of the Maastricht Treaty with potentially the greatest trade implications for developing countries is Article 130v; this states that the objectives of development policy should be taken into account 'in the policies that [the Union] implements which are likely to affect developing countries'. If this requirement is actually implemented, it would mean that the implications of trade, agricultural, financial and other Union policies affecting developing countries should be designed to ensure the sustainable economic and social development of the poorest countries and the poorest people within them.

What such declarations will mean in practice remains to be seen. However, the first steps are being taken to improve the co-ordination and coherence of European policies affecting developing countries. The EU Development Council requested the Commission to produce by May 1993 a review of past practice on policy co-ordination, a review for a more systematic approach to operational co-ordination, and a review for the integration of the various Union aid instruments. Of even greater potential importance, the Commission was to produce by November 1993 a report on the link between development co-operation policy and other Union policies. These reviews may lead to a change in EU practice, with implications for developing countries. They need to be monitored with care. A recent report by the United Kingdom (UK) House of Lords has argued that the EU 'Council must exercise more effective control of the [aid] programme in order to achieve an integrated and coherent policy ...' [*House of Lords, 1993: para. 65(h)*]. The need for policy oversight of other aspects of development co-operation is no less important.

III. THE EUROPEAN ECONOMIC AREA AND A FUTURE ENLARGEMENT

The agreement between the EU and EFTA states (except Switzerland) creating the European Economic Area has potential implications for third parties with respect both to its provisions and to the fact that it is likely to be a precursor of the accession to the European Union of the EFTA states, three of which have now concluded terms with the EU subject to referenda. The EEA builds upon the free trade agreements concluded between each of the EFTA countries and the European Community in 1972 and 1973. There will be a transition period for some elements of the package. These vary in length but most will be concluded by 1996.

The EEA is not a customs union and so it does not involve completely free exchange of all goods and services and nor does it involve the systematic adoption of common policies towards third parties. However, it does involve some liberalisation of trade between the European countries and, hence, it will have implications for countries outside the European area, including those in the developing world.

It continues a process that has been under way for many years. The extent of the liberalisation achieved on this occasion has been limited by two factors: trade in industrial products is aready largely unrestricted (except for a very small number of sensitive items); and neither side has yet been willing significantly to liberalise trade in temperate agricultural goods. The broad scope of the EEA is presented in Table 1, which classifies the relevant aspects of the four freedoms according to the degree to which they have been increased in the EEA.

TABLE I
THE COVERAGE OF THE FOUR FREEDOMS IN THE EEA

Degree of change over the status quo ante

Major	Limited	Nil
Internal changes:		
– Government procure-ment	– Liberalisation of a few, selected temperate and processed agricultural products	– Liberalisation of indus-trial products
– Competition policy		– Quantitative restrictions and non–tariff barriers
– Rules of origin		– Customs borders
– Standards		– Agricultural policy
– Free movement of workers		– Value added tax admin-istration
– Free movement of capi-tal and investment		
– Free right of establish-ment		
– Free movement of ser-vices		
Changes in external rules:		
– Establishment of bank-ing services	– Co-ordination clause on shipping	– Tariff and non-tariff barrier system
– Use of third country inputs in rules of origin	– Standards testing by third countries	– Trade (including trade preferences schemes)

The EEA covers: the free movement of specified goods, the free movement of capital and services subject to some restrictions, the free movement of persons, and a set of 'horizontal and flanking policies'.

The Free Movement of Goods

Tariffs: In principle the agreement covers all goods but in practice there are *ad hoc* restrictions for some agricultural and fisheries products. The EEA builds upon existing EFTA-EU agreements in the sense of extending the number of products covered (particularly in the area of processed agriculture, agriculture and fisheries, since most industrial products were already subject to free trade) and by reducing non-tariff barriers to trade such as technical standards and onerous rules of origin.

For processed agricultural products a new regime has been established for calculating the import levy which will tend to reduce the trade tax payable compared to the present arrangement. In addition, and of direct potential interest for developing countries, intra-EEA trade taxes have been removed on a range of agricultural goods. These include tomatoes, cocoa paste, butter and powder, coffee and tea and their extracts, and various other agricultural goods exported by developing countries. The provision appears to have been of most interest to Switzerland, which is the largest EFTA exporter to the EU of these products, but has since decided not to join the EEA. None the less, a significant cross-border trade in the beverages does occur between Austria, Sweden and the EU. Moreover, while the liberalisation may have been agreed with the interests of specific EFTA countries in mind, its existence has resulted in a larger market for third party suppliers.

Non–tariff measures: The EFTA states have agreed to accept existing EU rules on technical standards. These cover a wide range of product groups, the most important of which are foodstuffs, household goods, building materials, electrical machinery and equipment, pharmaceuticals, handling and lifting equipment, automobiles and chemicals.

The EU's rules rest on two principles: mutual recognition of national rules in most cases, and harmonisation of legislation in areas of health, safety and environmental protection. At the end of any transition period for implementation of the EEA, therefore, a third party good that meets the technical standards of any of the signatory states will be acceptable in all others.

The implications for third parties, therefore, are very similar to those of the SEM. The mutual recognition principle will tend to enlarge market opportunities for competitive suppliers and, by the same token, increase competition for the less competitive. The impact of harmonised standards will depend on their level compared with pre-existing national standards. Since there is a tendency for standards to rise to the highest prevailing level, it may be assumed that raising will be more common than lowering. But the implications for developing countries even of raised standards will depend on commodity and country characteristics.

The EU has agreed to negotiate with non-EEA countries that are signatories of the GATT code on technical barriers to trade a mutual recognition agreement, enabling designated bodies and laboratories in each country to carry out on their own territory the tests required by the other party and to provide the certification valid in the other party. Under the EEA agreement the EU has indicated that where it makes such mutual recognition agreements it will do so on the basis that the third party concerned will conclude a parallel agreement with the EFTA states.

The rules of origin, which determine whether or not a product is eligible for any preferences agreed under the EEA, have been modified. There are four substantial changes as well as a number of procedural ones.

- Cumulation: there is now full cumulation within the EEA, which is considered as a single entity for origin purposes. Hence, all working or processing operations carried out anywhere in the zone contribute to the acquisition of EEA originating status. This should facilitate the acquisition of originating status by producers within the EEA. Under the present situation each of the seven trading partners concerned is able to use materials from any of the other six without prejudicing the originating status of the end product, but only if they have acquired full originating status in that country. Hence, it is not possible for one part of the processes required for originating status to be undertaken in one state and the rest in another. Under the new regime this will be possible.

- General tolerance: there is now a general tolerance of non-originating materials. Provided that these do not exceed ten per cent of the ex-works price of the product concerned they do not prejudice the granting of originating status. However, an important exception to this rule is that the tolerance does not apply to the clothing and textiles sectors.

- Relaxation of the territorial principle: under the existing rules goods must be worked within the territory of the EFTA countries and the EU, and products may not leave this territory in the course of production without prejudicing originating status. Under the EEA a limited derogation has been agreed which makes it possible to send products outside the EEA in the course of production and to re-import them after processing in a third country without any detrimental effect on the acquisition of originating status. However, the derogation applies only if the total value added through such extraterritorial operations does not exceed ten per cent of the ex-works price of the product.

- Alternative percentage rules: in order to simplify the application of the rules producers of chemicals and plastic products (Harmonised System Chapters 28, 29, 31–38, 39) may elect to apply a value-added rather than a change-of-tariff-heading rule in order to acquire originating status.

These changes may affect third parties in several ways. First, to the extent that they make it easier for EEA member states to produce domestically (albeit from imported inputs) goods that can be sold competitively on other members' markets, it may result in some diversion of trade from third parties. On the other hand, any changes that make it easier to use non-originating inputs (such as the general tolerance rule) or to undertake certain processes in third countries (such as the territoriality derogation) increase the opportunities for using materials from developing countries. It is unfortunate, therefore, that the territoriality derogation does not apply to the clothing and textile sectors, which are the ones in which benefits for developing countries would be most likely. Given the existing pattern of outward processing, the countries most likely to be affected positively or negatively are likely to be primarily those in eastern Europe and the Mediterranean.

Public procurement has been opened up. Firms in the EEA can submit tenders to public sector organisations in any of the contracting parties. Hence, developing country firms that are established in any of the EEA states will have greater potential opportunities for public-sector work.

An area of trade policy that is of growing concern for some developing countries is the use of anti-dumping actions in a contentious fashion. The EEA does not have any direct implications for this area of trade policy. Anti-dumping policy is an area in which autonomy is specifically retained by the contracting parties.

The Free Movement of Capital and Services

Two elements of the EEA agreement liberalizing capital and services may have implications for certain developing countries. These concern provisions for financial services and for external transport.

The EU's banking and insurance directives allow the Union to negotiate with third countries to obtain effective market access for European institutions and to suspend or limit concessions to third countries if they restrict European institutions. It was agreed in the EEA that, as far as possible, a common third country regime should apply for the whole of the region. Hence, an authorisation granted in the EU or in an EFTA state to a third country financial institution will normally be valid throughout the whole EEA. However, the EU retains the right to suspend or limit authorisations which have been granted by an EFTA state to a third country financial institution. As in the case of the arrangements for goods, the possibility is opened up, therefore, of improved access to some of the more restricted EEA national markets. However, this possibility may be limited in practice by the EU's retention of its right not necessarily to accept agreements negotiated by the EFTA states.

No formal common positions have been adopted on either maritime or air transport. Indeed, in the case of aviation no special provisions are foreseen in the EEA agreement. However, as regards maritime transport it is foreseen that there will be close co-ordination between the Union and EFTA states in all cases where the EU intends to undertake actions against third countries and their shipping companies. Nonetheless, the agreement does not place any obligation upon the EFTA states to follow the EU line.

The Free Movement of Persons

The EFTA states have agreed to take over Union arrangements which provide for the free movement of workers, the right of establishment, mutual recognition of diplomas and social security. These arrangements apply only to citizens. Hence, they will not necessarily affect the rights of migrant workers or visitors from third parties. Nonetheless, to the extent that they are accompanied by the removal of police controls at frontiers, the effect will be similar to that of the SEM. In other words, movement between countries will tend to be easier but there may be offsetting reinforcements to the external barriers to the movement of people.

Horizontal and Flanking Policies

The EEA agreement covers some areas of co-operation outside the four freedoms. In some cases, these may have implications for developing countries. For example, the EFTA states will participate in the implementation of the EU's Third Framework Programme of Union activities in the fields of research and technological development. There is scope for third parties to participate as members of the research consortia active within these programmes. The Third Framework Programme specifies that, subject to certain conditions, programmes are open to interested parties in non-member states with which the Union has concluded economic and technical co-operation agreements. These include most developing countries.

The Enlargement of the EU

The EEA has been seen by all parties as a precursor of accession to the EU by the EFTA states, although this is not certain to occur. The potential implications for third parties of a new, 'northern' enlargement of the EU would be greater than those of the EEA, but probably less substantial than the SEM given the relatively small size of the EFTA markets. The total gross domestic product (GDP) of EFTA (minus Switzerland) in 1991 was US$639.5 billion compared to the US$6,251.7 billion of the EU, or about ten per cent.

There are three main ways in which a northern enlargement might affect third parties for good or ill. The actual impact will depend not only on the way in which EFTA and EU policies change to take account of the enlargement but also on the characteristics of the third party. According to their production and export situation some states may tend to benefit, some to lose, and some to do both in relation to different products from the same changes.

The three sets of effects are:

• Enlarged market: goods and services that can be sold in one national market will be saleable in all after enlargement. This increase in the size of the market could be of value to third parties that are able to increase the volume of competitive exports and widen the geographical spread of their sales. This potential is more likely to be realised if exports are currently constrained by demand rather than supply factors. On the other hand, for those states that have no prospects of increasing substantially the volume of competitive exports, the removal of internal barriers to trade within the EEA may result in increased competition on their traditional markets without any offsetting gains.

- Trade policy harmonisation: the EFTA states will have to alter their trade policies in order to conform with those of the EU. This will alter the terms of access for third parties on to the EFTA markets favourably (if the current policy is less liberal than that of the EU) or unfavourably (if the reverse is the case).

- Increased efficiency and growth: the complete removal of barriers to trade between the EEA states may be expected to increase competition and, hence, efficiency. As in the case of the SEM, this may result in some trade diversion but this may be offset by trade creation from the consequential increase in European income.

The implication for developing countries of trade policy harmonisation are the most easy to identify at this distance from enlargement. The EFTA countries' GSPs will be replaced by the Union system of preferences. Similarly, the EFTA countries will adopt Union levels of protection in the clothing and textiles sectors.

Even in the area of trade policy, however, the extent to which EFTA policies will change is not entirely clear because the EU is in the process of revising its GSP and because the successor regime for the existing MFA is not yet known. However, some deterioration of access is a potential danger. Since Sweden has already lifted all import restrictions on clothing it follows that any post-MFA IV restrictions that the EU imposes will result in a deterioration in the terms of access at least to the Swedish market. The other EFTA states have restrictions on clothing imports, but these tend to bear on a more limited range of textile and clothing categories and affect fewer developing countries than do those of the EU. The number of MFA bilateral agreements with quantitative restrictions of the EFTA states range from seven for Finland and Austria to 18 for Norway; the EU, by contrast, has 30 such agreements, together with an exchange of letters for ten other states.

Whereas the EFTA states have one system for all developing countries (or in some cases two, since least developed countries are given special treatment), the EU's system provides significantly different levels of preference under its various agreements. In those cases where the main suppliers to the EFTA markets are countries in the upper echelons of the EU's pyramid (that is, in Africa and the Mediterranean) the enlargement of the EU will tend not to result in any change in access terms. By contrast, in cases where the major suppliers to the EFTA markets are in the lower levels of the EU's pyramid (that is, Asia and Latin America) enlargement is likely to result in a deterioration in their access terms. This opens up the possibility that enlargement will have differential effects on different developing countries: the losses for those countries low in the EU's pyramid may be offset by market gains by those higher up.

<h2 align="center">IV. EASTERN EUROPE AND THE EU</h2>

While, in the long term, growth in eastern Europe is likely to be a positive-sum game benefiting most parts of the world, in the short to medium term there are likely to be both positive and negative effects. These will include both trade creation and trade diversion, increased global demand for savings, and a potential diversion of OECD resources that may affect developing countries whether or not this is dubbed as 'aid'. The trade creation and diversion effects are likely to be the most pervasive and complex in the early stages. They may include increased competition on OECD markets (especially the EU) from east European exports, increased demand in eastern Europe for both primary and manufactured products from developing countries, and a shift in demand in eastern Europe away from imports from those developing countries which used to engage in barter trade in favour of other sources, possibly other developing countries.

This section is not concerned primarily with these effects arising from the change in economic system in central and eastern Europe or with trade between these countries and developing countries. Rather, it is concerned with one aspect only of many changes affecting the former centrally planned economies – the change in their terms of access to the EU market. Trade policy changes in the EU will be important because eastern Europe's exports have tended to be of goods for which protectionism is high, and because the region has been near the base of the EU's hierarchy of trade preferences. Hence, there is scope for changes in EU trade policy to result in significant improvements in the competitiveness of east European exports on the European markets (in addition to any improvement resulting from the change in economic system).

Although the task of assessing the incidence of protection on east European exports under the old regime is not straightforward it is clear that the region was near the base of the EU's pyramid of privilege. Until the revolutions, Poland, Romania, Czechoslovakia and Hungary, as signatories of the GATT, were supposed to benefit from MFN treatment (although they did not always do so), but only Bulgaria and Romania (with Yugoslavia) benefited from the EU's GSP.

51

The New Trade Regime with the EU

There has been a rapid evolution of policy governing trade between the EU and eastern Europe since the change of political and economic system. The GSP was quickly extended, first to the countries of eastern Europe and more recently to the Baltic states, the Commonwealth of Independent States (CIS) and Ukraine. Association agreements were subsequently negotiated and signed with Poland, Hungary and Czechoslovakia on 16 December 1991, with Romania on 1 February 1993, and with Bulgaria on 8 March 1993.

All quantitative restrictions have been abolished on industrial imports into the EU except for textiles and coal, and tariffs have been reduced to zero on more than half of imports. The remaining tariffs on industrial imports except for textiles are scheduled to be reduced to zero during a transition period. There have also been some EU concessions for agricultural products. The elimination of quantitative restrictions on textiles will be linked to the results of the Uruguay Round. Further concessions on agricultural products will be applied on a reciprocal basis and trade in processed agricultural products and fishery products is governed by specific provisions.

Under the agreements that came into force in 1992 the transition period for the removal of tariffs on industrial imports is scheduled to be completed by the beginning of 1998, except for textiles which will last another year. In May 1993, however, the European Commission and the six East European states reached agreement on a package of measures including a shortening of the transition periods and more flexible treatment of sensitive goods. These proposals, which have not yet been approved by the EU Council of Ministers, would allow customs duties on most industrial goods to be reduced to zero by the end of 1994, agricultural concessions to be introduced six months earlier than planned, industrial import quotas to be replaced by ceilings, and agricultural import quotas to be raised by ten per cent. Duties on steel imports would be abolished by the end of the fourth year, subject to a new agreement with eastern Europe controlling trade in this product.

For their part, Poland, Hungary and Czechoslovakia will be liberalising their import regime for the EU, but over a longer transition period. Poland will abolish all trade barriers on industrial imports over seven years (except for motor vehicles, which have a ten-year transition period), while Hungary and the Czech and Slovak Republics will do so over nine years.

Although these agreements represent a liberalisation of trade, significant restrictions on products of importance to eastern Europe do remain. The extent of the residual restrictions will depend upon the EU Council's response to the latest Commission proposal. However, most agricultural products will continue to be excluded or heavily restricted and quantitative restrictions are retained for textiles, steel and coal. Union steel quotas have replaced national quotas for some products. The EU has also imposed anti-dumping duties on steel products, not only from eastern Europe but also from the CIS and the Ukraine.

Trade Competition with Developing Countries

Improved access will not by itself result in increased exports; there must be in addition a responsive supply of competitive goods. On the whole, eastern Europe's exports to the European Community stagnated or declined during the second half of the 1980s. What evidence is there that the economic reforms have resulted in an increase in exports in advance of the improved market access?

A first answer to this question is provided in Table 2 and Figure 1. These identify what appear to be the fastest growing East European exports to the EU with direct implications for developing countries. They are derived from an analysis of EU import statistics for the period 1989–92 designed to throw light on the new products emerging in the course of the economic restructuring.

TABLE 2
FAST-GROWING EAST EUROPEAN EXPORTS TO THE EU

Product group	Main competitors
Chemical products (superphosphates, polystyrenes and articles of plastics)	Brazil, China, Hong Kong, Israel, Malaysia, Morocco, Saudi Arabia, Singapore, South Korea, Taiwan, Thailand, Tunisia
Leather (chrome-tanned bovine leather, grain splits of bovine leather)	Argentina, Bangladesh, Brazil, India, Indonesia, Pakistan, Paraguay, South Africa, Thailand, Uruguay, Zimbabwe
Wood and paper (parquet, builders' joinery, paper/paperboard)	Brazil, Indonesia, Malaysia, Singapore, South Korea, Thailand
Clothing	Numerous
Parts of footwear (uppers and insoles)	India, Tunisia
Metal products (articles of iron or steel, unrefined copper)	Chile, China, Mexico, Namibia, Peru, South Africa, Taiwan, Zaïre
Miscellaneous manufactures (machine parts, injection/compression moulds, motor vehicles and parts/accessories, etc.)	Argentina, Brazil, China, Hong Kong, Israel, Malaysia, Mexico, Philippines, Singapore, South Africa, South Korea, Taiwan, Thailand, Turkey

FIGURE I

EU IMPORTS OF SELECTED PRODUCTS FROM EASTERN EUROPE

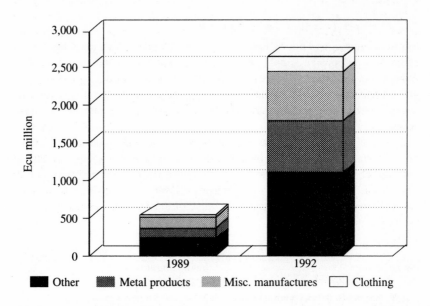

Data were collected on two groups of items imported from the Europe Agreement states. The first included all product groups (four-digit Combined Nomenclature) from the principal agricultural and industrial chapters that experienced current value growth between 1989 and 1992 of 200 per cent or more and had a value in the latter year of ECU 25 million or more. The second was of items (four-digit) imported in 1992 but not in 1989 with a value of ECU 10 million or more. EU trade statistics were then analysed in relation to each of the items (eight-digit) in these two groups with a 1992 value of ECU ten million or more to identify the level and source of imports from developing countries. These cut-off points were selected for purely pragmatic reasons to limit the analysis to the more substantially traded products.

The figure and table illustrate broad features of the 66 products identified through this sifting process. The figure shows how rapidly EU imports of these products from eastern Europe have grown. In 1989, they represented only 4.7 per cent of imports totalling ECU 12.1 billion; by 1992 this share had almost tripled to 13.9 per cent of an ECU 18.9 billion total.

In the table, the disparate list of items has been regrouped into broad product categories of particular interest to developing countries to make them more digestible. It confirms expectations of the type of products in which competition between eastern Europe and developing countries is most likely, at least in the short term. Metal products and miscellaneous manufactures are the most substantial both in terms of the value of EU imports and the range of eight-digit items imported. The developing countries that export the same products to the EU, and which may face increased competition, are mainly higher – and middle – income states (such as Turkey, Thailand, and Brazil), but they also include some of the poorest (such as Bangladesh and China).

A word of caution: these patterns are still very volatile. A similar exercise conducted with 1991 trade data produced a rather different picture. EU imports of clothing and footwear did not figure prominently in the selected basket, although by 1992 they had made their appearance. At the same time a group of products that were prominent in 1991 had virtually disappeared from the growth product list by 1992. These are fresh and processed agricultural products. Three groups of fresh agricultural products (including vegetables, apples and cherries) saw a 333 per cent increase in the value of EU imports between 1989 and 1991, but then a 59 per cent fall in 1992. Was this because of supply problems or because the EU raised the common agricultural policy draw bridge?

V. IMPLICATIONS FOR WORLD TRADE INSTITUTIONS

The countries of the EEA, NAFTA and the Japan–East/South East Asia region account between them for more than four-fifths of world production and exports. The question whether bilateralism and regionalism are supportive of a world trade system needs to be asked with such magnitudes in mind. In a very real, practical sense these three regions *are* the world trade system. What they do cannot avoid influencing the framework within which all other states have to operate. This is a reality which applies regardless of whether the European, North American and Asian states are operating inside or outside the formal multilateral framework.

None the less, there is a crucial difference between the actions of, say, the USA, the EU or Japan inside and outside the GATT framework. Inside this framework not only is there a set of rules to prescribe permitted action *vis-à-vis* other traders but, equally important, there are other powerful trading parties that exert pressure on all parties to abide by such rules. Within each region, by contrast, the EU/USA/Japan are dominant and to a significant extent set the rules.

How well does the Uruguay Round agreement address the perceived problems of the multilateral system? One of its main innovations is the extension of the institutional framework for trade. The replacement of the GATT Secretariat with a World Trade Organisation (WTO) reflects both the broadening of the scope of the new agreement and the desire to strengthen the monitoring of trade policy. The Uruguay Round establishes a WTO as a single institutional framework to encompass the GATT, all agreements and arrangements concluded under its auspices, and the complete results of the Round.

The WTO will be inaugurated by early 1995. It will be headed by a Ministerial Conference meeting at least once every two years. Day-to-day operations will be overseen by a General Council, which will also act as a Dispute Settlement Body and a Trade Policy Review mechanism. Its permanent staff will replace the GATT Secretariat.

The General Council will spawn a host of specialist subsidiary bodies such as the Council for Trade in Goods (which will, *inter alia*, oversee the phase-out of the MFA), a Safeguards Committee (to oversee operation of a revised Article XIX), a Council on Services, and a Council for Trade-Related Intellectual Property Rights (TRIPs).

Although the detailed *modus operandi* of the WTO is yet to be agreed, the key principles are:

- membership of the Councils will be open to all signatories of the agreement;
- when there is no consensus, some decisions can be taken by qualified majority (mostly three-quarters or two-thirds) but others require unanimity;
- voting will not be weighted;
- the WTO will not itself take sanctions against transgressors, but will authorise aggrieved parties to withdraw MFN treatment from them.

The WTO is evolutionary rather than revolutionary. It has a much more limited remit, for example, than the ill-fated International Trade Organisation (the intended third pillar of the post-war economic institutional framework, alongside the International Monetary Fund and the World Bank).

The scope for the WTO to reinforce developing country interests, or impose on them unwanted policies, depends on the structure of decision-making and enforcement. The use of qualified, unweighted majority voting means that the developed countries cannot force upon developing countries as a whole unwanted decisions. The OECD states form only one-fifth of the signatories. But developing countries can only defend their perceived interests if they are aware of what is being discussed. Poorer developing countries will have to concentrate their resources, giving priority to the WTO, join with others and seek technical assistance to ensure that they are adequately represented in key councils.

The enforcement of rules will continue to be asymmetrical because it will be undertaken by aggrieved parties imposing penalties on transgressors. In a dispute, for example, between USA and Bangladesh the imposition of penalties by Bangladesh on US exports will have far less impact than penalties imposed in the opposite direction.

There are other innovations in the Uruguay Round agreement, but their sharp edges have been worn away by seven years of negotiation. Temperate agriculture, TRIPs and services are all areas of trade that have been brought for the first time (or more fully) into the GATT framework of rules. But the Round represents only the first step in what will be a continuing process. For the time being, barriers to trade will be higher in these new areas than in the GATT traditionals of manufactures and non-temperate primaries, and rules less clear cut. In other areas, such as trade-related investment measures (TRIMs), the agreement does little more than to legitimate existing illegal barriers and give their perpetuators a transition period within which to remove them.

Hence, the successful completion of the Round has not removed the pressure on multilateralism. One of the motives for initiating regional agreements appears to be that the multilateral system is perceived to provide an inadequate regulatory framework for cross-border flows of investment and services. Effective regional integration typically requires agreement (explicit or implicit) on a much broader range of issues than does trade liberalisation, as is evident from the EEA. On this view, the world community will never be willing to move as fast or as far into sensitive new areas of regulation as will those states that are involved in close cross-border invest-ment and trade.

There is no intrinsic reason why regional agreements should be in con-formity or in conflict with multilateral undertakings and aspirations. Various NAFTA provisions in areas outside trade in goods have been drafted in con-formity with US proposals to the GATT Round. But, by the same token, unless such care is taken there is a danger that they will not be in conformity. Not all regional accords have been approved under GATT Article XXIV, a point brought home with force by the recent GATT panel verdict on the Lomé Convention. It is particularly difficult to establish the relationship between regionalism and multilateralism in areas which are not yet subject to GATT procedures or in which GATT rule-making is at an early stage of development. Yet this may be precisely the type of situation that is likely to occur most frequently as regional integration develops in investment and services.

Rules of origin, for example, may encourage bilateral trade. There has been a proliferation of differing origin rule systems for the various free trade and preferential areas (which were excluded from the Uruguay Round agreement on origin rules). The USA and Canada each have six different sets, and the EU has no less than fourteen! An export that meets one set of rules may not meet another. Each exporting state must organise separately its production in relation to the requirements of each of its trade partners. This will tend to restrict the number of markets to which even middle-income states can export.

Differing technical standards tend to have the same effect. To the extent that regional integration results in common standards it will reduce the problem within the integrated markets. But it will not affect the problem between different regional schemes.

In conclusion, therefore, it would appear that the successful completion of the Uruguay Round has not neutralised regionalist pressure, and that the compatibility of the more intense rules in regional accords and multilateral standards cannot be taken for granted. Developing countries, because they are characterised in the main by their economic weakness and marginal position in world trade, have an interest in the discipline imposed by the multilateral system. Participation in a regional group, while it may involve significant advantages in terms of access to markets, technology and capital, also has the in-built tendency to increase vulnerability. They have reason to be concerned, therefore, if the multilateral trading system gives way to a set of regional economic clusters.

REFERENCES

House of Lords (1993): *EC Development Aid*. Select Committee on the European Communities, Session 1992–93, 21st Report (HL Paper 86), London: HMSO.
Hufbauer, Gary Clyde and Jeffrey J. Schott (1992): *North American Free Trade: Issues and Recommendations*, Washington, DC: Institute for International Economics.
UN (1992): *World Investment Report 1992*, New York: United Nations.

4

The EU's Trade Policy for the ACP Countries: Is It Conflicting with Multilateralism?

MEINE PIETER VAN DIJK

I. INTRODUCTION

The fall of the Berlin Wall in 1989 and the recession of the early 1990s meant that the countries of the European Union (EU) were preoccupied for some time with three major issues: how to deal with Eastern Europe and the countries of the former Soviet Union; what the implications of the Maastricht Treaty are and how to avoid more unemployment. In the meantime the EU market has been fundamentally transformed through the completion of the Single European Market (SEM) project, and the creation of the European Economic Area (EEA). At the same time the EU was negotiating with four EFTA countries for membership.[1] These preoccupations pushed developing countries to the periphery of the EU's immediate interest. The Lomé IV treaty had been signed in 1989 and would give some respite for at least five years (for the financial part). It would take ten years before the following convention was on the agenda again.

In this chapter the EU policies with respect to developing countries and in particular the so-called ACP (African, Caribbean and Pacific) countries will be reviewed. The history of the EU's co-operation policy, shaped by the Lomé conventions, will be reviewed in the third section of this chapter. We will focus on the dilemma formulated in Chapter 3: the EU's structure of non-reciprocal trade agreements conflicting with the multilateral trade system. The effects of the EU's trade and aid policies for developing countries will be analysed using empirical material from Africa. Special attention will be paid to STABEX, the export earnings stabilisation scheme of the EU. European development aid will be reviewed briefly and an example of distortions introduced by the EU trade policies will be given (as in the case of bananas). An effort will be made to appraise the Lomé convention and the STABEX instrument. However, before drawing some conclusions the question will be posed: what is wrong with the EU's trade policies with respect to the ACP countries?

II. THE EU'S GENERAL SYSTEM OF PREFERENCES

The EU's common commercial policy regulates uniform tariffs, trade agreements and protection measures. The desire for special and differential treatment of developing countries has led to the creation and adoption of Part IV of the GATT in 1965. At the second UNCTAD conference in 1968 the principle of preferential tariff treatment in favour of developing countries was officially accepted, resulting in the Generalised System of Preferences (GSP).[2] Negotiations leading to the adoption of the GSP lasted almost ten years [*Sampson, 1990*]. Most developed countries started offering GSP schemes in the early 1970s.[3] As early as 1971 the EU granted GSP status to developing countries.[4] This status provided tariff preferences to all Third World countries, although there were a number of exceptions and safeguard clauses.[5] The unique characteristic is the one-way nature of the concessions. These developing countries are not required to grant reciprocal tariff concessions for EU products.[6] They are only obliged not to discriminate between EU countries and to apply to them import arrangements which are at least as favourable as those applied to other countries (the Most-Favoured Nation, MFN clause).[7]

The objective of the EU's trade policy has always been to open its markets to products from developing and, in particular, ACP countries. Its trade policies take a development perspective. For that reason a general system of zero duties is in place. It applies for products imported from EFTA countries (reciprocal elimination of tariffs and quantity restrictions; QRs), ACP countries (unilateral), Mediterranean countries (elimination of tariffs and QRs, except certain textiles) and other developing countries (unilateral tariff concessions under GSP and the Multi-Fibre Arrangement; MFA).[8] These countries have usually concluded preferential agreements with the EU, in particular, the southern Mediterranean and the ACP countries.[9]

Under GATT third countries used to pay an average 24 per cent on imports to the EU using the MFN clause. Developing countries under the GSP would only pay ten per cent, while the ACP countries under Lomé would pay no import duties at all. Successive rounds of GATT have led to a reduction of the MFN tariffs and, hence, to an erosion of the preferential margin of the GSP and the special preferential treatment of ACP countries.

According to UNCTAD [*1994*] these 'protected trade flows' used to represent $77 billion in 1992 or 20 per cent more than in 1991. At that time they made up almost 40 per cent (39 per cent) of total trade and it is expected that this figure will go down to 32 per cent when the Uruguay Round becomes effective [*Jeune Afrique, 2 June 1994*].

III. THE LOMÉ CONVENTIONS

The Lomé conventions are considered the main instrument of the EU's policy with respect to an important group of developing countries, the ACP countries. The Lomé convention is an integrated trade and aid instrument and sometimes considered a step in the direction of a New International Economic Order (NIEO) [e.g. *Stevens, 1990*]. Negotiations for the funding of the second five years of Lomé IV should have finished in the first half of 1995 (the European Development Fund; EDF 8), but were delayed because of disagreement on the available financial support. After almost 20 years it is worth looking at the functioning of the Lomé convention and of the role of STABEX, one of its major financial instruments.

The idea behind the EU's trade policy is that in particular the former colonies of the EU members (most ACP countries being ex-colonies of European countries) need to be helped to expand their exports. The main instruments of development aid are STABEX and SYSMIN.[10] For some products (sugar and beef, for example) specific preferential measures apply. Quotas can be exported to the EU free of custom duty.[11] Given the outcome of the Uruguay Round, the importance of the Lomé IV agreement for trade between the ACP and Europe will diminish. Africa is losing part of its preferential treatment because tariffs will go down for all developing countries as a consequence of the Uruguay Round. Hence, some people have questioned whether there will be a Lomé V.[12]

EU–ACP co-operation began in 1958 when the six members of the then European Community unilaterally granted aid to the overseas countries and territories placed under their jurisdiction. This was when the first European Development Fund came into being [*CEC, 1985*]. In 1963 the first Yaoundé convention was negotiated between the EU and 18 newly independent countries and the second Yaoundé convention ran from 1969 to 1975 [*EID, 1986*].

On 1 February 1975 the first Lomé convention was signed by 45 ACP and nine EU countries [*Courier No. 120, 1990*]. At the same time a number of instruments were put in place: trade arrangements, financial and technical assistance and a stabilisation system (STABEX). 380 million European Currency Units (ECU) were available for STABEX for a five-year period.[13] The latter was considered one of the major innovations in international relations. Twenty-nine products are mentioned in the convention as eligible for STABEX, while the number of products covered by the scheme increased to 49 under Lomé IV.

The French attached a lot of importance to STABEX because it allowed support of tropical agricultural exports from the former French colonies. The former British colonies were accommodated through the special undertakings on sugar (and rum and bananas, also called rum and bananas protocols). The first Lomé convention was renewed in 1979 for a further period of five years. The raw materials crisis and the definition of a new world economic order within the United Nations encouraged Europe to take more ambitious co-operation initiatives. However, Lomé II did not live up to expectations, according to an evaluation by the EU [*CEC, 1985*].

No link could be established between the Lomé policy and the lack of economic progress in many ACP countries; the achievements were not impressive. Community aid accounted for only a modest share of about ten per cent of external contributions in the ACP countries and several other factors turned out to be more important. The EU Commissioner at that time, Mr E. Pisani, spelt out his ideas for Lomé III in a memorandum, stressing dialogue, food strategies, rural development and a concern for effectiveness [*Van Dijk, 1983*].

The Lomé III convention was signed on 8 December 1984 and covered the period 1985–90. New features include the accent put on agricultural and rural development, increased development of fisheries, promotion of private investment, aid for refugees and social and cultural co-operation. The number of articles of the convention increased from 191 in Lomé II to 294 in Lomé III [*CEC, 1985*], the first part conveying the spirit, summarising its objectives and principles. Agricultural and rural development was the cornerstone of Lomé III.

In 1989 negotiations for Lomé IV took place. By then 12 EU members were negotiating with 66 (68 including Haiti and the Dominican Republic since 1989 and 69 including Namibia after its independence). The convention was signed on 15 December 1989 in Lomé, after 14 months of negotiations. Lomé IV concerned a ten-year period, but the financial protocol was only valid for five years. Hence new negotiations started in May 1994.

The new Lomé convention will cost the EU 12 billion instead of 8.5 billion ECUs, an increase of 40 per cent in nominal and 20 per cent in real terms. Trade arrangements will provide preferential access for a larger number of products as well as improved rules of origin and general principles for commercial co-operation. New STABEX and SYSMIN conditions are designed to help ACP countries to face the instability of world commodity markets; also new are the elimination of requirements to replenish STABEX resources and the transformation of SYSMIN into subsidies. Lomé IV will also include a mechanism to support the structural adjustment of economies in the ACP area. Concerning the foreign debt of ACP countries the convention does not suggest concrete solutions. After all, it is only a very small amount that the ACP group owes to the EU, representing only 1.2 per cent of their total debt servicing costs. This is due to the concessional nature of the EU's aid.

Developing countries consider the provisions under Lomé IV for the establishment of a trade development service an important trade safeguard, given the Uruguay Round and the Single European Market in 1993. It 'will ensure that the ACP states improve their competitiveness on the EU market' [*Courier, 1990*]. The Lomé conventions for the ACP countries comprise the most comprehensive effort in their economic development. The compromise in trade preferences is more advantageous than that of the EU's GSP, the STABEX scheme and development aid. The latter two instruments will now be discussed.

IV. STABEX

STABEX was first introduced under Lomé I with the objective of providing funds to ACP countries to cover shortfalls in earnings brought about by fluctuations in prices or the output of agricultural products to EU countries. STABEX is a system for stabilising export earnings from agricultural commodities.[14] Finished products are excluded, just as minerals, for which a special mineral facility (SYSMIN) has been created. STABEX has an annual disbursement profile.

A country is eligible for STABEX funds if in the year prior to that of application the commodity represents five per cent of a country's total export earnings. Secondly, a country is eligible if there has been a drop in earnings of at least 4.5 per cent compared to an average of the last six years, minus the lowest and the highest figure, preceding the year of application. Countries have to submit a request for STABEX funds before 31 March of the following year, and provide very detailed statistical information.

A country has to prepare an annual report to show how STABEX funds have been used, and the Commission of the European Community (CEC) has also to prepare a report [e.g. *CEC, 1992; 1993*]. According to the latter source, in 1991 1,062 million ECUs were necessary for STABEX. Thirty-five ACP countries benefited from 67 transfers. Total financial resources for that year were only 391.5 million ECUs (40.9 per cent of needs). In 1990 transfers were less concentrated on a small number of countries than in 1988 and 1989. During the last three years income losses due to very low coffee and cocoa prices on the international market accounted for the biggest share of the transferred amounts. Resources transferred for these two products accounted for 81.7 per cent (64.1 for coffee and 17.6 for cocoa).

In the 20 years of its existence STABEX has undergone a number of changes. In the first place the number of products and countries concerned has increased substantially, and the rules of the game have changed several times. With Lomé IV the obligation to repay STABEX funds during a good year has been discarded; also the minimum dependence threshold of export earnings as a condition for eligibility of transfers has been gradually reduced. Under Lomé IV export earnings on each product covered must represent at least five per cent (one per cent for LDCs, landlocked or island countries) of total export earnings from all products.

Secondly, a number of new non-ACP producers of agricultural export products has appeared in Asia and Latin America. The use of new varieties and sometimes plantation production has made competition in these markets tougher for ACP countries. Combined with the general trend of declining raw material prices, requests for STABEX funds have all but increased. In 1981 and since 1987 the amounts allocated to STABEX have not been sufficient to cover total demand. Roughly 12 per cent of the total EDF was used for STABEX during the successive five-year Lomé conventions, and funding for the period 1985–90 amounted to 9.25 billion ECUs.

Initially the EU did not question the use of STABEX transfers. Later the ACP countries were obliged to make an *ex-post* declaration of use [*Hewitt, 1990*]. Subsequently the procedure has become more complicated. At present a memorandum of understanding needs to be signed, specifying the use of STABEX funds. Since Lomé IV, transfers should be specified within a Framework of Mutual Obligations (FMO or COM in French), to be agreed between the ACP country concerned and the European Commission in each case. Within the FMO a number of conditions is specified, which need to be respected before the money is disbursed. Funds will be used either for the sector recording the loss of export earnings, or for diversification purposes.

Conditionality has become more important since Lomé IV, as shown by the use of frameworks of mutual obligations. Previously a memorandum of understanding could be signed and a country was able to use the funds for almost any purpose. Conditionality is thus to some extent in conflict with the nature of a convention, which normally implies that a country is entitled to certain financial allocations.

V. EUROPEAN DEVELOPMENT AID

Under the Lomé convention the ACP countries also receive a substantial amount of aid. EU aid is programmed over a generously long period of five years. ACP states need to prepare a five-year indicative programme (financing under the EDF is for five years), containing medium-term development projects, disbursable over a period ranging from two to almost ten years, with a five-year maximum commitment period. Since Lomé III the use of funds is determined by programming missions. The usual project aid objectives are development and recovery rather than short-term stabilisation, which is the focus of support for adjustment programmes [*Marin, 1992*].

Hewitt [*1990: 141*] remarks that the objectives of European development aid and the STABEX interventions can be complementary, particularly in the agricultural sector. The question of general complementarity can also be posed. Is the EU's trade policy complementary to its aid policy? When conditions are imposed under STABEX and conditional support is given under the structural adjustment facility of the EU, the question then is to what extent are all these conditions complementary? Since Lomé III a higher proportion of programme aid is going to agricultural and rural development, reinforcing the complementarity of aid and the use of STABEX funds. Since Lomé IV the issue of general complementarity has become very relevant. The EU Delegation in a country concerned has to oversee the ambit of the conditions imposed by the EU and may stop or delay parts of, or all, the aid provided.

In May 1994 the mid-term review of Lomé IV was begun. The aim of the review was to set a new overall budget for the period 1995–2000. It also provided an opportunity for the ACP and EU countries to amend certain provisions of the convention. A clear trend was that the EU would become more businesslike. Typically the NGOs characterised the Commission's proposals for the mid-term review of Lomé IV as a 'use it or lose it approach' [*Randel and German, 1994*].

An example of the businesslike attitude of the Commission can be given. During the mid-term review a general conditionality was suggested. This would allow stopping disbursements in cases of non-respect of the democratisation process or in cases of bad governance. The Commission would also tend to abolish the fixed amounts allocated to each country and to open the possibility of diverting National Indicative Programme (NIP) allocations to other purposes. In the end the EU would no longer be legally bound to disburse the full amounts committed.

A key outcome of the revised Lomé IV convention was that each ACP state would draw up a new National Indicative Programme (NIP) mapping out the country's five-year development priorities. Work on defining these priorities would start immediately after renegotiation of the financial protocol in 1994.

VI. AN EXAMPLE OF DISTORTIONS: BANANAS

In the case of bananas, the attempted integration of the two EU regimes (concerning the so-called ECU and dollar bananas) has shown the problem of trying to serve the interests of ACP countries, while respecting trade agreements within the framework of GATT. Certain EU countries import cheap dollar bananas, while others import the more expensive ECU bananas. In aiming to remove obstacles to the EU internal market, the SEM policy has stipulated that as of 1 January 1993 bananas may be moved freely from countries importing dollar bananas to countries buying ECU bananas. The EU has thus chosen to replace national curbs by EU curbs. However, the solution taken favours bananas from ACP countries and the overseas territories of France, Portugal and Spain over cheaper dollar bananas from Latin America [*Financial Times, 20 Jan. 1995*].

The issue has received much attention because Latin American countries (non-ACP members) have complained to GATT that their access to the European market has been hampered by Lomé preferences. Although the dispute has focused on access for Latin American bananas, the complaint has widened, and a dispute panel of GATT has ruled that Lomé preferences have generally contravened free trade conventions (*Africa Recovery*, December 1993).

The consequences of the EU policy are that a country such as Cameroon continues to increase rapidly its banana production on large-scale plantations. Ironically these are owned by some of the same banana companies that are active in Latin America trying to get preferential access to the EU in this way. At the same time Cameroon tends to neglect its traditional smallholder coffee and cacao production. Due to lack of production or low world prices of these products the country is compensated for, anyway, through the STABEX scheme; the otherwise not competitive bananas may be sold in the protected EU market since Cameroon has a quota. Clearly the quota-based regime is contrary to the spirit of GATT, which does not want protectionism.

Imports of so-called dollar bananas under the rules of GATT would have saved the EU US$2.3 billion a year in artificially inflated prices.[15] Ironically most of the extra cost is in monopoly profits for European companies that market bananas. Borrell [*1995*] states that the EU system severely distorts competition, encourages black marketeering, restricts the growth of the EU banana market, discriminates against efficient producers and robs inefficient ones of incentives to raise productivity and cut costs.

VII. APPRAISALS OF LOMÉ

Much has been written about the intentions of the Lomé conventions: the spirit of Lomé or the Lomé ethos. The convention is based on principles of equality, partnership and consultation. As early as 1972 the desire was to institute a comprehensive world-wide development co-operation policy that materialised in the Lomé I convention. High expectations were aroused in the 1970s that Lomé I to IV may not have fulfilled. Three aspects dominate the debate: conditionality in general, respect for human rights in particular and the view on trade.

Conditionality was included only since Lomé IV because of the framework of mutual obligations which needed to be signed for the use of STABEX funds. The term 'mutual obligations' is an euphemism for conditionality. EU Delegates prefer to speak of mutual obligations rather than conditionality. In practice, when some of these 'obligations' are not respected, disbursements may be stopped for shorter or longer periods.

For the first time, the Lomé III convention makes a reference to human rights, although the ACP countries resisted such a move, as this would allow the EU to block aid if these rights were not respected. In the present negotiations for the EDF the issue is back on the agenda, however. As summarised in *Africa Recovery* (December 1993): 'ACP countries could soon be forced to prove their democratic and free market credentials before getting further aid from the EU.' Again the ACP countries have signalled their objection to any moves to increase EU influence on domestic economic policy; they stress instead joint verification and joint decisions in such key areas as human rights.

The spirit of Lomé with respect to trade can be described as 'an opportunity for a group of industrialized and developing countries to break out of the impasse created in the global negotiations to establish a regional arrangement that would incorporate a number of the items on the NIEO agenda' [*Stevens, 1990: 77*]. We will return to the NIEO idea, which seems to be a relic of the 1970s.

Several efforts have been made to assess the results of the different Lomé conventions [*CEC, 1985*; *Faber, 1983*; *Randel and German, 1994*]. However, all these appraisals take a different approach and study different questions. The CEC [*1985*] mainly describes the changes over time. Faber [*1983*] asks the question whether STABEX has led to an effective stabilisation of export revenues in the countries concerned. Randel and German [*1994*] blame the Commission for not making poverty reduction a priority and not addressing the issue of lack of institutional capacity in ACP countries.

Criticism of the conventions has ranged from 'Lomé is neo-colonialism' to 'the EU's structure of non-reciprocal trade agreements in conflicting with the multilateral system'. Lomé can certainly be characterised as a political convention. The convention creates extreme favourable conditions for a limited number of former colonies, which will subsequently have a hard time to compete at the world market because they have not adjusted their production structure as most other (non-ACP) countries have done. They will have to adjust one day however, if only because the European countries themselves have had to adjust their production, given the larger (in terms of number of countries) and freer SEM (since 1992). Secondly, the decreased importance of benefits, given the Uruguay Round has lowered all tariffs, will force them to adjust. Finally, growing internationalisation or globalisation of their economies will require agricultural adjustment to keep exports competitive. The Lomé approach cannot be globalised, however, without some ACP countries losing some of their benefits.

Another point of criticism of Lomé is that it is beneficial for the EU, since most of the ACP countries are among the least developed in the world and pose little competitive threat to EU industry and agriculture [*Matthews, 1985*]. This argument has become less valid as the number of countries and products has increased. However, there are no real 'tigers' among the ACP countries and manufactured exports are treated differently, anyway. South Africa can be a potential strong exporter. This may explain why it has taken some time for the EU to come to a trade agreement with that country.[16]

VIII. APPRAISAL OF STABEX

The history of STABEX is that ever more countries and more products have been included. Already in 1981 the total amount available was not sufficient to satisfy all claims. This was again the problem in 1987. Ever since, the resources made available for export stabilisation funds have proved consistently inadequate to cover the demand. Questions are being asked about the effectiveness of STABEX as an instrument.

Another way of assessing the impact of STABEX is to look at its effects on trade shares. STABEX was part of the EU's effort in boosting the ACP group's share of international trade. The EU is the ACPs' main trading partner, with EU imports still predominantly in raw materials, often unprocessed. Almost 70 per cent of ACP exports to the EU are made by just eight members of the 66-country group [*Stevens, 1990*]. Eight principal products account for over 70 per cent of the total export by value. STABEX is thus a very partial scheme [*Hewitt, 1990: 140*], as far as the number of products and countries are concerned. Within STABEX only a limited number of countries and a few products receive most of the funds. The question raised then is why help these ACP countries more than other developing countries?

In most African countries the share of trade to Europe decreased in the 1970s. If it went up in the 1980s, this was often because less foreign exchange was available and it was easier to get credit from the former colonial power. From the European point of view, trade with Africa (where most of the ACP countries are located) is becoming less and less important. Its trade share has gone down from six to three per cent of total trade during the last 15 years.

Is the increase of STABEX requirements due to falling prices or quantities, or to target products losing their competitiveness, or a combination of all these factors? In 1991 67.5 per cent of all STABEX funds went to coffee and 15.9 to cocoa, which was certainly linked to the falling world market prices for these two commodities at the time.[17] In the same year Ivory Coast received 18.8 per cent of the total funds and Cameroon 13.9. Ethiopia came in third place with 13.4 per cent, while the other countries received six per cent or less. Strange enough, it pays for a country like Cameroon to neglect coffee and cacao production since the country is compensated through STABEX anyway. Growing bananas is more interesting for Cameroon, given the quota allocated to that country by the EU. However, these ECU bananas are not competitive with the dollar bananas in the real world.

Does STABEX provide the ACP countries with genuine protection against the instability of export prices or does it simply protect sectors which are economically inefficient in these countries? Does it involve only financial support to the government, or does it mean going against the market and the philosophy of the time: a withdrawing of government, deregulation, privatisation, liberalisation and more competition? There is certainly evidence that African farmers did not receive the message at the end of the 1970s that an oversupply of coffee and cacao on the world market was pushing prices down and that they would have to adjust their production patterns, for example, by diversifying their production. These sectors have consequently been protected much too long.

Are countries receiving STABEX funds doing better? Have these funds led to an increase of production? In a country such as Cameroon one notes that when STABEX funds increased (1989, 1990 and 1990) coffee as well as cocoa production decreased. STABEX may have compensated (partially) for the conjunctural price fluctuation, but it did not help with structural factors such as an overvalued Franc CFA, increased production costs, increased international competition, neglect of these sectors by governments and limited availability of necessary inputs (such as fertilisers and pesticides) in a country.

Does STABEX really introduce distortions? Yes, at the macro level because a government is forced to use the money in favour of the sector, or for diversification, but not necessarily for the best purpose, from an economic point of view. It also leads to distortions at the micro level in the sense that farmers receive the wrong signals. After years of bad prices they may still continue to produce certain crops, because the government supports the producer or input prices with STABEX funds. In that case STABEX disbursements lead to long-term distortions instead of pushing for agricultural adjustment.

Increased stability? According to Burger and Smit [*1992*] the revenues of countries receiving STABEX funds are not more stable than those of other countries. They tend to be higher, however, because of the larger grant element in STABEX transfers. The question needs to be asked as to whose earnings are stabilised: those of the government, the farmers or the intermediaries? At present only a limited number of countries also have an internal stabilisation system that should benefit the farmers. In practice these systems often benefit the traders in particular. The trend is to do away with such internal stabilisation schemes in the framework of liberalisation and structural adjustment policies. In such a case only government export revenues are stabilised by the availability of STABEX funds, a system originally designed to stabilise an ACP's country's export earnings. However, in the course of time, the EU has added to the expectation that STABEX would also benefit farmers, which may have been wishful thinking.

The attention of the EU has shifted from a concern over stabilising foreign exchange revenues for the country to using STABEX funds in the framework of structural adjustment.[18] In a number of countries systematic efforts will be made to tie in STABEX funds with structural adjustment programmes [*Marin, 1992*]. It means STABEX funds will become more and more integrated in regular EU aid programmes, which may be the best solution.

One may look at the effectiveness of STABEX as such, or at the complementarity with other instruments of the EU's trade and development policies (for example, structural adjustment). Sometimes STABEX funds are considered as a NIP plus, as extra money becoming available for the indicative programme. The question is, however, whether the money will not be more effectively spent as part of the NIP, which would allow:

- less distortions;
- better planning (with known amounts) in advance;
- better prioritisation (the funds could be used for top development priorities in the country); and
- multi-annual commitments that are not possible with STABEX funds.

IX. WHAT IS WRONG WITH THE EU'S TRADE POLICY

What is wrong with the EU trade policy with respect to the ACP countries? We will summarise our critique under the following four considerations:

(1) the underlying philosophy of Lomé is different from what the multilateral trade agreements want to achieve: non-reciprocal with a development perspective versus becoming more competitive in world markets;
(2) the advantages for the ACP countries are diminishing;
(3) the wrong incentives are given to farmers; long-term distortions are created while adjustment is delayed;
(4) EU's trade policies are an example of regionalism and not of multilateralism.

Ad 1. The underlying philosophy of Lomé is different from what the multilateral trade agreements want to achieve.

The GATT trade rounds have stressed elimination of trade barriers by pushing reciprocity, which is different from the principles of EU's trade and aid policies for developing countries. These are based on the one-way nature of concessions (the GSP), and on helping basically former colonies (selectivity), excluding other developing countries. Given reciprocity has become more important after the Uruguay Round, the one-way concessions become less relevant. Secondly, the Lomé convention means going against the market and the philosophy of the 1980s, a withdrawing government, more deregulation, privatisation, liberalisation and more competition. The philosophy of Lomé is based on protectionism and as such may have had its longest time.

Finally, Stevens' [1990] argument that Lomé gives an opportunity to break out of the impasse in global negotiations to establish a regional arrangement, incorporating elements of the NIEO agenda, is no more relevant. First, the impasse of the Uruguay Round has been broken and secondly, nobody discusses the NIEO agenda any more; it remains a relic of the 1970s.

Ad 2. The advantages for the ACP countries are diminishing.

As mentioned, successive rounds of GATT have led to a reduction of import tariffs and, hence, to an erosion of the preferential margin of the GSP and the special preferential treatment of ACP countries. UNCTAD [1994] has calculated that the tariff cuts agreed in the Uruguay Round of global trade talks will lead to big reductions in the value of special trade preferences for developing countries and thus erode their competitive advantage. Preferential tariff margins on imports will be cut by about 23 per cent in the EU, 15 per cent in Japan and nine per cent in the US. Trade covered by the GSP will shrink by some 17 per cent, because of new zero duties agreed in the Uruguay Round. UNCTAD [1994] also notes that the preferential share of exports from developing countries to preference – giving countries will drop from 39 to 32 per cent.[19]

Secondly, the wrong incentives are given to producers. The bananas and STABEX examples have shown that the EU trade policy may lead to the wrong signals to the farmers in the ACP countries and introduces long term distortions. The ACP countries benefit from favourable access to the European market, as was shown by the example of the bananas. These countries will have a hard time, however, to compete at the world market, because they have not adjusted their production structure as did the other (non-ACP) countries. They will have to adjust one day, however, when multilateralism becomes more and more important. The EU missed an opportunity to rationalise and improve its distortionary bananas policies. According to Borrell [1995] ACP producers would be better off if the EU abolished its banana policy and gave them direct aid instead.

As mentioned, the Lomé convention and, particularly, the export revenue stabilisation scheme (STABEX) and quota system (for sugar, etc.) may lead to a situation where a country concentrates on growing bananas in plantations (benefiting from the quota system), while neglecting small farmers' coffee and cacao growing, the traditional strongholds. Such, for example, is the case in Cameroon [*EIU, 1994*].

Ad 3. Lomé causes the wrong incentives, introduces distortions and delays adjustment.

STABEX has been conceived as an instrument of protection. When the UK joined the EU, STABEX intended to give the same protection to exports from former French colonies as the British had given quotas to their sugar producing colonies.[20] It now gives the wrong signals to farmers. A convention is by definition an agreement between governments. However, the money is spent in the government sector and this may not always be the most appropriate use. The EU would like to change this and tell ACP countries 'to encourage the growth of their private sector and make sure that local entrepreneurs can get access to EU funds' (*Africa Recovery*, December 1993). The tradition is not easy to change, however.

Lomé in fact protects ACP countries from the vagaries of the world market and makes it more difficult for them to be integrated at a later stage. The EU as a regional block should still decrease tariffs and eliminate other barriers at the multilateral level, if only for non-ACP developing countries.

Another question is why Lomé should last as an exclusive club (selectivity). Pooley has suggested that if there is a Lomé V, it will be a more generalised one, because there is no reason to exclude countries such as Bangladesh [*Financial Times, 3 Nov. 1994*].[21] The Lomé approach can not be globalised, however, without some ACP countries losing some of their benefits.

Ad 4. EU's trade policies are an example of regionalism and not of multilateralism.

Does regionalism challenge the multilateral system? Yes, in the case of the EU–ACP agreement. The Lomé conventions have been called a model for North–South co-operation. However, the number of problems in implementing the convention has increased and, hence, people have become doubtful about its future. An aid-freeze has been suggested because the use of Lomé IV funds has been too slow (*Africa Recovery*, December 1993). The discussion on the democratic and free market credentials has shown the problems of mixing trade, aid and diplomacy. Commissioner Marin has argued that the Convention can only survive by adjusting to post-cold war realities. For him, this means that, to receive aid, the EU will have to give a definite seal of approval to adjustment policies, good governance and democratisation. It will suspend it for governments accused of human rights violations. This implies a system of step-by-step aid disbursement.

The ACP countries can be considered an annexure of the EU and, as such, as part of one of the three major trade blocs in the world: NAFTA, the EU and an Asian trade bloc. In such a model there is an argument for the ACP countries to be associated with the EU, in which case they do not have to stand alone. If the final objective is to achieve a multilateral trade agreement, this association does not make sense.[22]

X. CONCLUSIONS

The approach behind the trade policies of Lomé conflicts with the multilateral system. In the first place, the EU's structure of non-reciprocal trade agreements is contrary to the spirit of GATT. Secondly, the system favours a limited number of countries which happen to have relations with a number of European countries. No additional aid, no such favourable access to European markets, and no STABEX and SYSMIN funds are available for a number of Asian and Latin American developing countries.

In the third place, considerable trade gains for developing countries can still be achieved if tariffs are reduced further. The different Rounds of GATT and, in principle, the EU trade policy are directed at doing away with protection. However, the gains of Lomé for certain countries need to be balanced against the losses for other countries.

In the fourth place, the trade policies and, in particular, STABEX go against the market and, as such, are conflicting with the multilateral approach which stresses the advantages of competition. Lomé and, particularly, STABEX are protecting weak sectors in ACP countries and stimulate the production of goods (bananas and sugar, for example) which would otherwise not be economically competitive. They have often delayed timely adjustment.

In the fifth place, the EU-promoted trade instruments require an important role for the government. STABEX, for example, requires government intervention to assess the needs and to spend the funds in the sectors concerned. This goes against the market and, more specifically, it goes against the philosophy of the 1990s, which is one of liberalisation and the decreasing role of government. Many governments in the Third World are not even capable of playing such an important role in the economic process, anyway.

Finally, the trend world-wide is to disentangle trade and politics and, hence, the satisfaction of finishing the Uruguay Round successfully, or achieving NAFTA.[23] The EU's trade and aid policies are still very much interwoven and serve economic and political purposes. The question has been asked whether there will still be a Lomé V.[24] Probably the political element of the convention will be saved, but the corresponding trade and aid policies may be changed drastically, given the realities of the 1990s.

NOTES

1. With Austria, Finland, Norway and Sweden, but not with Switzerland. Only Norway voted against membership in November 1994.
2. In total there are 16 different preferential schemes, benefiting over 160 countries. Trade under these schemes has risen more rapidly than trade in general over the past 20 years.
3. Developing countries have long complained that the GSP is too restricted in scope and operation. Only half dutiable exports by beneficiary countries are covered, and

only half of these actually receive GSP treatment [*Financial Times, 18–5–1994*].
4. The European GSP allows [*Cuyvers, et al. 1994*]:
   - duty free entry for industrial products (except for some primary products), with product/country specific limitations for sensitive products using so-called fixed duty-free import amounts and tariff ceilings,
   - reduction or abolition of duties on certain agricultural products, and import limitations by tariff quotas for some products like pineapples, coffee extracts and unmanufactured tobacco,
   - duty-free access for textiles and clothing from GSP beneficiaries with whom MFA agreements are concluded. These agreements provide for tariff quotas and tariff ceilings.
5. The significant exceptions are agricultural and textile products. Preferential import arrangements only apply to goods actually produced by the partner country (rules of origin).
6. The establishment of GSP required a waiver of the Most Favoured Nations clause in UNCTAD [*Sampson, 1990*].
7. Except ACP or other developing countries.
8. This summary is taken from Nunnekamp [*1993*], who adds that for other industrialised countries there are tariffs (and some QRs against Japan), while in the case of the CMEA there were tariffs and QRs.
9. The EU has signed over 20 bilateral and multilateral agreements since the EU has a predisposition to favour formal trade and cooperation agreements. According to Stevens [*1990: 78*] these establish the legitimacy of the EU as opposed to national action.
10. SYSMIN is a special system somewhat similar to STABEX to help ACP countries whose economies depend on mining products. It will not be discussed here.
11. Only ten per cent of the variable levy is due provided the remaining 90 per cent is charged as an export tax in the country of origin and the proceeds are used to develop the local beef economy.
12. For example P. Pooley, director general of the development directorate of the CEC (*Financial Times, 3* Nov. 1994).
13. The ECU is valued at Dutch Guilder 2.11, while the dollar was DG 1.69, both on 20 January 1995.
14. Two other forms of stabilisation can be distinguished: deals between producers and consumers or between producers only; and loans from the IMF under the Compensatory Financing Facility.
15. This is US$700 more than the national trade restictions it replaced 18 months ago according to Borrell [*1995*].
16. South Africa is not yet one of the ACP countries, but still negotiating. It does benefit from the EU's GSP, however.
17. 4.3 per cent went to cotton; the other commodities received less than two per cent.
18. In Cameroon, for example, the agreed structural adjustment programme for the agricultural sector hopes to use unused 1990 STABEX transfers, most of the 1991 transfers and all of the 1992 funds.
19. UNCTAD [*1994*] has called for increased preferential margins and duty-free treatment for Third World goods.
20. The quota system is, in a sense, less distorting. Once the country has reached its quota it will only be able to sell for (undistorted) world market prices.
21. It is also suggested that a new accord would seek to differentiate between countries of different development levels, and differentiate one region from another.

22. There is a trend of collaboration between the EU and regional blocks such as SADCC and ECOWAS, which could go at the expense of Lomé.
23. President Clinton's decision not to apply the human rights criterion to China any more (summer 1994) can be seen in this light.
24. For example, in the NRC Handelsblad (28 Jan. 1989).

REFERENCES

Borrell, B. (1995): 'EU Bananarama 111', Washington, DC: IBRD Policy Research, Working Paper 1386.

Burger K. and H.P. Smit (1992): 'Stabiele prijzen blijven droom', *Inzet*, Dec.

CEC (1985): *Lomé III, Analysis of the EEC–ACP Convention*, Brussels: Commission of the European Communities.

CEC (1992): Report from the Commission on the Operation in 1991 of the Export Earnings Stabilization System under the Fourth Lomé Convention, Brussels: Commission of the European Communities.

CEC (1993): *Financial Cooperation under the Lomé Convention*: Review of Aid, 1992, Brussels: Commission of the European Communities.

Cuyvers, L., de Lombaerde, P. and D. van den Bulcke (1994): *The Effect of the EU Single Market on ASEAN: Trade and Investment Issues*, Antwerp: CIMDA.

EID (1986): *Ten years of Lomé, A record of EEC–ACP partnership 1976 to 1985*, Brussels: CEC, Europe Information Development.

EIU (1994): *Cameroon*, London: Economist Intelligence Unit.

Faber, G. (1983): 'De effectiviteit van STABEX tijdens Lomé I', Economisch Statistische Berichten, 16 June.

Hewitt, A.P. (1990): 'STABEX: The Scope for Alternative Schemes', in Kiljunen (ed.), [*1990*].

Kiljunen, K. (ed.) (1990): *Region-to-region Cooperation between Developed and Developing Countries*, Aldershot: Gower.

Marin, M. (1992): 'Le rôle de la Commission dans l'Appui au processus d'ajustement structurel', Brussels: Commission of the European Communities.

Matthews, A. (1985): *The Common Agricultural Policy and the Less Developed Countries*, Dublin: Criterion Press.

McAleese, D. (1993): *Africa and the European Community after 1992*, Washington, DC: IBRD-EDI.

Nunnekamp, P. (1993): *The World Trading System at the Crossroads*, Kiel: Institut für Weltwirtschaft.

Randel, J. and T. German (eds.) (1994): *The Reality of Aid, 1994*, London: ICVA/ EUROSTEP/ACTIONAID.

Sampson, G.P. (1990). *Trade Expansion through the Generalised System of Preferences*, in Kiljunen (ed.) [*1990*].

Schuknecht, L. (1993): *Trade Protection in the EC*, Philadelphia, PA: Harwood.

Stevens, C. (1990): 'The Lomé Convention', in Kiljunen (ed.) [*1990*].

Stevens, C. (1995): Chapter 3 in this collection.

UNCTAD (1990): *Agricultural Trade Liberalization in the Uruguay Round, Implications for Developing Countries*, New York: United Nations.

UNCTAD (1994): *The Outcome of the Uruguay Round: An initial Assessment*, Geneva: UNCTAD.

Van Dijk, M.P. (1983): *More Food, Self Grown: The NGOs and the Plan Pisani*, Oegstgeest: CEBEMO.

5

The Integration of Regional Groups into Multi-Country Organisations

SHEILA PAGE

I. THE 'NEW' REGIONALISM?

Three trade issues of the second half of the 1980s and the first years of the 1990s suggest that the multilateral organisations, particularly those dealing with trade, will need to adapt to new types of member and to a new international economic structure:

- in some regions or sub-regions, the share of intra-regional trade has increased strongly;
- the number of active regional trading areas has increased at an unprecedented rate;
- the EC, unlike previous regional groups, in some circumstances behaves within international organisations as one member or negotiator, rather than a group of members with certain common or collective interests.

If the first trend proves to be more than a normal response of fast-growing countries which happen to be neighbours, and if the second proves to be more than an expression of regional good will or a temporary bargaining counter in the face of the attempts by more economically powerful countries to bargain bilaterally, and if the new organisations follow the example of the EC, then the world-wide multilateral organisations will face a new type of member, which is neither a traditional country nor simply a very large country. They will also need to operate in a different type of international economic system: with a smaller number of larger actors; potentially, a different spread of country or national interests in different areas; and possible conflicts within as well as between negotiating parties.

These changes pose a range of empirical, organisational and theoretical questions.

Which of the recently formed or revived regional organisations embody a significant commitment for the members to behave more collectively with respect to other countries, bilaterally or in multilateral organisations? These must be distinguished from those whose principal interest is in fostering or recognising existing regional cooperation and trade flows.

In what circumstances are regional groups likely to be effective? There are traditional answers, on questions like complementary production or common currency, but the important questions are new. The conditions to be examined could include common interests, a particular level of development, and reaction to economic pressures from other countries or groups.

How do international organisations need to adapt their formal structures or their *de facto* procedures to the fact that some of their 'members' are now themselves institutions or groups of members? Transition periods (in which groups no longer behave completely independently but cannot yet be treated as single units) may offer particular problems. There are parallel problems for the Eastern European or CIS countries which are breaking up into smaller ones. Do international organisations need to adapt to having more 'large' members, in the international trade theory sense.

What are the implications for the international economic regime more generally of a more oligopolistic structure for the world economy, replacing either single-country hegemony or (the implicit assumption of organisations like GATT) a competitive system? (This must include implications for exchange rate systems and other international interactions, as well as for trade.)

What are the implications of an increase in the role of formal blocs and of regional and multilateral policy negotiations for individual countries' development strategies?

This chapter is intended to open some of these issues for discussion. It will first discuss the broad trends in intra and inter-regional trade, and give a brief survey of the existing regional groups. It will then discuss how the long-standing trading blocs have been accommodated into the international institutions, and why the new groups will strain these arrangements.

There are analogies between the problems raised by adapting to new multi-country trading organisations operating in an administrative framework designed for individual countries and those which may come from multi-national companies operating in a framework designed for national companies. This may have implications for the regulatory (and theoretical) approach which we should use.

II. TRENDS IN REGIONAL TRADE

There have been increases in recent years in the share of intra-regional trade in all the continents, and in some sub-regions within them (Table 1). Some of these increases are in areas which have seen the introduction, or planned introduction, of trading groups, notably in Latin America, and some changes can be identified for individual trading partners in groups there (Argentina with Brazil, although not the reverse; Colombia with Venezuela). The major increases, however, have been in intra-Asian trade. But other areas have also increased their exports to Asia. This suggests that there are other motives at work. Trade within Africa, for example, has increased less than African trade with Asia. Further, all these changes among developing countries took place against a background of slow import growth in some of the industrial countries, and some of the changes, notably in Latin America, could be taken as merely a reversal of the serious contraction in intra-regional trade in the first half of the 1980s.

TABLE I

INTRA-REGIONAL TRADE BY DEVELOPING COUNTRIES
(PERCENTAGES) (SHARES OF MARKETS IN TOTAL EXPORTS)

to by	Developing		Asia		Own Region		Sub-regional partner(a)	
	1985	1990	1985	1990	1985	1990	1985	1990
Developing	30.1	33.0	10.8	21.0				
Countries								
Asia	36.7	40.1	27.6	33.4	27.6	33.4	4.3	5.1
Korea	26.4	25.9	13.8	17.6	13.8	17.6	–	0.4
Bangladesh	46.6	24.0	29.1	22.3	29.1	22.3	1.3	1.5
China	52.5	60.9	39.2	53.5	39.2	53.5		
Thailand	41.4	32.0	29.1	22.3	29.1	22.3	3.8	1.4
Malaysia	43.9	48.9	40.5	44.6	40.5	44.6	1.0	2.1
Latin America	23.5	25.2	4.3	5.0	12.7	15.9		
Mexico	9.3	9.1	1.3	1.2	5.4	6.7	60.4	70.3
Brazil	31.5	30.0	6.9	10.6	9.7	11.1	2.1	2.1
Argentina	38.3	44.5	6.5	7.0	18.7	26.3	5.9	11.5
Colombia	18.5	19.3	0.9	0.7	14.0	16.9	3.6	5.9
Africa	14.8	15.0	3.3	4.2	4.9	5.4		

Source: IMF, *Direction of Trade*; Colombian trade data.
(a) For Asian Countries: China
For Colombia: Venezuela (1991 instead of 1990)
For Mexico: United States
For Argentina: Brazil
For Brazil: Argentina

The increases in Asia are a marked reversal of trend: until 1980, the area, and especially the most successful exporters, had concentrated on increasing trade with the industrial countries. There was an increase in intra-regional trade in the first half of the 1980s, but much smaller. The Asian results are also distinctive in that they include large increases in exports of manufactures (Table 2). In the past, growth in these was even more directed to the industrial countries. The Latin American countries do not show such clear breaks. It is, however, in Asia (see next section) that there has been least enthusiasm for regional trading organisations.

TABLE 2
EXPORTS OF DEVELOPING COUNTRIES IN LATIN AMERICA
AND ASIA TO SELECTED REGIONS (PERCENTAGES)

	1985		1990	
	All developing	Asia	All developing	Asia
Latin America				
Total	19.29	2.82	21.38	4.52
Primary products	15.75	2.57	16.67	3.30
Chemicals	41.11	4.97	42.80	5.84
Machinery and transport equipment	26.56	1.42	22.88	1.87
Other manufactures	26.49	5.61	30.24	9.34
All manufactures	28.66	4.26	29.81	6.69
Asia				
Total	28.83	20.56	39.30	33.19
Primary products	34.92	29.78	41.55	35.34
Chemicals	50.90	45.19	62.95	58.45
Machinery and transport equipment	27.28	19.36	40.34	34.53
Other manufactures	22.48	13.66	35.59	29.09
All manufactures	25.40	17.03	38.90	32.77

Notes: Figures from the UN *Monthly Bulletin of Statistics.*
1985 figures for the EC exclude Portugal and Spain
For Mexico: United States

Even within Asia, it is only a few countries, notably the most advanced and China, which have shared in this change, not the new NICs (Malaysia had a small rise and Thailand a fall in Table 1) or the poorest (Bangladesh). The increase in Chinese exports to Hong Kong 'can, alone, account for virtually the entire recorded increase in the share of intra-regional trade over the last decade; but three-quarters of those exports are re-exported by Hong Kong, mostly to markets outside the region' [*Oman, 1993*]. For Korea, the increase goes against a pronounced trend in the opposite direction throughout the preceding 20 years of development, and may mean more a maturing of Korea, into a developed economy trading with its less developed neighbours, than a turn explicitly to the regional market. This suggests that a variety of what could be called 'normal special factors' are operating in the countries which have seen an increase in intra-regional trade. These are not directly related either to a specific consequence of growing regional blocks or to legal moves to create regional organisations. There are, however, some exceptions (Colombia with its neighbours) which do appear to show an increase directly following on changes in regional trading regime and where the exporters and investors participating in it do attribute the change to the policy.

Regional trade among the developed countries offers equally mixed support for the view that this is a major new phenomenon. Intra-European trade rose from the 1960s to the 1980s, a period coinciding with the expansion of membership of the EC, each stage bringing a step increase in the new members' trade with the old (and also with the emergence of two new producers of primary products which substitute for extra-regional imports: the UK and Norway for oil), but it has stabilised since then [*Oman, 1993*] (Table 3). Intra-North American trade has increased more recently. This could be described as a return to the levels of the 1970s [*ibid.*], but it does suggest some effect from the US–Canada or US–Canada–Mexico agreements, although even there it could be argued that what is happening is as much the effect on perceptions from talk of regionalism and prospects for a regional organisation as the result of NAFTA. It is too early for the tariff reductions under NAFTA (which is not yet approved and where significant reductions will not appear for up to five years after implementation) to have had a direct effect on trade. But it is arguable that the publicity given by the negotiations to the *present* (low) level of tariffs and (large) market prospects on both sides of the Mexico–US border could have increased trade.

TABLE 3
INTRA-REGIONAL TRADE BY INDUSTRIAL COUNTRIES
(PERCENTAGE SHARE IN TOTAL EXPORTS)

to by	Industrial		Asia		Own Region (a)	
	1985	1990	1985	1990	1985	1990
Industrial	72.7	76.3	9.2	9.9		
EC	77.8	81.7	4.2	4.5	54.4	60.6
North America	72.9	72.7	10.5	12.8		
Canada	87.0	91.2	3.5	4.6	75.2	75.4
US	61.4	63.9	13.4	15.5	22.2	21.1
(US to Mexico)					6.4	7.2
Japan	58.0	58.6	26.4	31.3	26.4	31.3

Source: IMF, *Direction of Trade.*
(a) For Canada: US
For US: Canada

The Colombian, EC, and possibly Mexico–US examples all show the traditional model at work: lowering barriers creates trade among the members. They do not offer support for a view that (autonomously) increasing regional flows could explain the new interest in setting up regional organisations.

It is necessary to examine the evidence for a real economic content in the pressure for regional blocks in more detail, in composition, timing and industrial responses. Such studies as Oman [*1993*] and recent work in the World Bank International Economics Department are contributing to this. What is needed is data on intra – and extra – trade for regions and for key countries within them, disaggregated by industry. It is particularly important to examine the trade of the major countries within each region or the fastest growing importers to test whether what is being observed is the appearance of new 'poles' of growth rather than regional groups. We should also consider what the potential complementarities or probable growth elasticities imply. It would be desirable to model more precisely the type of expectations suggested above, of new trading links and also the possible role of regional or third-country foreign investment.

III. THE GROWTH OF REGIONAL ORGANISATIONS

Regional organisations among developing countries have a long history of enthusiastic formation followed by dissent and either dissolution or lapsing into purely formal existence. The question we must consider is whether what is happening now is different in kind from the past. The last section suggested that the question of whether it was a response to a genuine increase in regional integration remains open. Other explanations to examine are:

(1) While trade integration may not be exceptional, the growing integration in other ways (what Oman [*1993*] has called 'deep international policy integration') may be requiring a more contractual response to any degree of regional economic integration than in the past. The EC offers the most striking example of a region which began with trading objectives and found that the elimination of trading barriers made other differences in market conditions more apparent, both as barriers to trade and as 'unfair' differences between firms in different countries. The 1992 Single European Market exercise was the response [*Sideri and Sengupta, 1992*]. The inclusion of the 'new areas', investment, intellectual property, non-trade subsidies, in the Uruguay Round of the GATT offers evidence that countries not linked in a trading organisation also now find these non-trade barriers to trade more important. But although this can explain why a smaller increase in regional trade than in the past could be enough to trigger a policy response, it cannot explain why 'no change' in trend should do so.

(2) The reduction in average external barriers means that the economic and political costs (in terms of loss of tax revenue, meeting any producer interests, etc.) of offering an elimination or reduction of the remaining MFN tariff are lower.

(3) The groups may be emerging now for reasons other than promoting trade or other regional integration. The difficulties of the Uruguay Round of trade

negotiations have led both to a search for alternative ways of lowering barriers and to a desire to create groups with greater negotiating power than any one country, particularly a developing country, would have. The increased integration of the EC under the SEM initiative also was in part an attempt to increase economic power (as well as competitiveness). It in turn inspired other groups to form in order to negotiate with it. Clearly, as in more traditional forms of protectionism, there is a risk of spiralling retaliation.

A full list of regional groups would include some which are now relics of the past and would require almost daily updating for the new alliances which are forming (particularly those linking and cross-linking the Latin American countries). But it may be useful to classify the major ones, old, newly active, and new by type to indicate how extensive the network now is. A two-way classification divides them (with considerable arbitrariness) into those which are (almost) entirely trading groups and those which go beyond this and into those which are made up of only industrial, only developing, or a mixture of countries.

Industrial Country Trading Groups

The relations, at least until recently, between the EC and EFTA; in principle, those now being formed between the EC and Eastern European countries: these are not fully reciprocal, so that in content they offer 'concessions', but they are not concessional in the sense that they can be withdrawn at the discretion of the EC: they are signed agreements. The US–Canada agreements pre-NAFTA: certainly the agreement on car trade (which pre-dated NAFTA by 20 years), but arguably also the US–Canada agreement of 1989 before it was renegotiated to include Mexico. The latter was so limited that it did not even include a clause requiring either party to consult/obtain the consent of the other before entering into an agreement with another. (It was only by request and agreement that Canada entered the US–Mexico free trade negotiations.)

Industrial Country Groups Which Go Beyond Trade

The EC is the most important example. This is not only the result of the SEM changes [*Sideri and Sengupta, 1992*]. Even in its origin it was a vehicle for state industrial planning (the European Coal and Steel Community). But the recent changes arise more from the perceived need to support trade integration with other aspects of a common market than from a commitment to public intervention. The current EFTA arrangements could be approaching this. Other examples which raise more interesting possible problems would be arrangements like the effective tying of the Austrian Schilling to the DM or Danish links to other Scandinavian countries in which countries with more limited trading arrangements (Austria, Sweden and Norway are not yet members of the EC) move further on non-trade arrangements than some with full trade links, and some members of one organisation have links with some from another.

Developing Country Trading Groups

Here the problem is to identify those which are currently effective, distinguishing them from the debris of such efforts as the Latin American Free Trade Association, which retains a shadow as the LAIA, or the various West African federations, and from the intentions of others which have signed, but gone little further (Peru in the current Andean Pact; Mexico with Colombia and Venezuela). The current candidates for serious groups are MERCOSUR; the new Andean group as far as Colombia, Venezuela, Ecuador, are concerned (both discussed above); probably Mexico–Chile; the Central American Common Market; the Caribbean CARICOM. If an Asian group (AFTA), scheduled for 1 January 1993, but not yet implemented, appears, it will be in this class.

Developing Country Groups Which Go Beyond Trade

Again many in the past, when industrial and investment coordination were hoped for (most notably the Andean Group as it was founded in 1969), but of the present: the Preferential Trade Area (PTA) in East, Central and Southern Africa, which has a payments union element. (There are also groups which have little or no trading element, such as the CFA franc area of francophone West Africa or the original foundation of ASEAN, with primarily a security focus, only later diverted to at least some intentions on trade.)

Industrial-Developing Country Trading Groups

The US–Israel Free Trade agreement, the EC–Mediterranean and EC–Maghreb agreements (the latter have limited non-trade elements but not of an extent parallel to Lomé).

Industrial-Developing Country Groups Which Go Beyond Trade

The Southern African Customs Union, SACU, if South Africa is to be considered an industrial country: for most purposes it is better treated as developing, but in the context of SACU's arrangements and the contrast with its fellow members (Lesotho, Swaziland, Botswana) it seems appropriate to put SACU here. The EC's arrangements under the Lomé Agreements (now in the fourth Agreement) with the ACP countries. This is contractual, not concessional, although it is non-reciprocal. It requires its members to consult before offering trading concessions to others. NAFTA, unusual in having more industrial country (US and Canada) members than developing (Mexico). On NAFTA's potential effects there is some literature (*Institute of Latin*

American Studies, 1993 gives an introduction to the current analysis), although much of this is rather limited or principally from the point of view of the US or Canada

It should be noted that all the industrial-developing country agreements have non-reciprocal elements. Only in NAFTA is this purely temporary, i.e. it applies to the length of transition, but not to the final outcome when the treaty comes fully into effect in 15 years. NAFTA is also exceptional in not limiting the members' right to negotiate new agreements with non members. The others normally require consultation, if not agreed amendment of the treaty. This is a logical protection of the members' interests, but it is also a potential further complication in future bilateral and multi-lateral negotiating as an increasing number of countries find themselves with one or more additional stages of consultation.

Another important point is that the groups that are now emerging do not follow a continuum: most reduce or eliminate tariffs among themselves as a first step, but, as in GATT, sometimes with special provisions for non-reciprocity by the less advanced. Some preserve special traditional ties, giving two levels of membership or even ties to non-members: in the EC; in the PTA for SACU members, and implicitly probably in any Asian group including any of the Chinas. Some may then move towards a common external tariff (some of the Latin American and Caribbean), while others move further on internal common standards (NAFTA) or financial arrangements (PTA) without a common external tariff. As all countries lower their average tariffs, because of changes in domestic policies (Latin America; perhaps in the long run the EC through reforms of the Common Agricultural Policy) or (potentially) because of a Uruguay Round settlement, the common external tariff criterion for either identifying a regional group or looking at trade diversion and creation effects may become less important than looking at a range of common standards.

IV. THE EFFECTS ON INTERNATIONAL ORGANISATIONS

Why Regional Agreements May Be a Problem

It is important to distinguish between the *contractual* agreements, which are the subject of this analysis, and *concessional* or unilateral arrangements, such as the GSP or US–Caribbean Basin Initiative (CBI) arrangements. It is arrangements which include other legal commitments among the members of the groups which pose legal and organisational problems for multilateral organisations. These may come into direct conflict with those required by the multilateral organisations: any agreements to offer better than normal trade access are *prima facie* in conflict with the GATT requirement of MFN treatment among its members, and are only legitimate if they meet one of the approved exceptions to this rule. This means that they must be, or be intended eventually to be, an arrangement for completely free trade among the members or they must be non-reciprocal arrangements with developing countries (under 'special and differential' treatment).

In negotiations or other activities of the multilateral organisation, the existence of obligations to other organisations may require consultations and agreements among the sub-group, which delay or frustrate the main body. Concessional agreements could pose the same discrimination, non-MFN, conflict, but those for developing countries are also specifically exempted. Similar arrangements for non-developing countries could be a problem. The flexible nature of the GATT definition of 'developing' has prevented this from becoming an issue up to now. (The EC's granting GSP-type concessions to the Eastern European countries could have been a problem if they had not been quickly replaced by 'association agreements' with an implied commitment to eventual admission to a common market. They do not, however, raise negotiating problems: because there is no contract, the conceding country can negotiate them away without consultation, and any GATT agreement would take precedence. There is some literature on the legal and regulatory aspects of these questions with the conclusion that present legal arrangements are already inadequate [*Qureshi, 1993*].

These trade obligations can also affect the relations of countries with other organisations. The World Bank's recommendations to individual Central American and Caribbean countries on their tariffs, for example, have already come into conflict with their obligations, to CACM and CARICOM, on a Common External Tariff (CET). There have also been problems on non-trade integration, for example in IMF exchange rate recommendations to the CFA Franc area. These conflicts have been contained in recent years because the tendencies of both the regional organisations and the World Bank have been towards lowering tariffs, and conflicts of detail have been resolved.

Few groups have yet reached the point where who speaks for the group is of major importance in negotiations. With the exception of the EC, most of the organisations have been too far from full integration or too small relative to total trade or capital flows for this to be a major issue. There have been examples, however, in specific cases: OPEC in the 1970s in both trade and lending discussions, where it spoke with one and several voices; CARICOM and CACM when regional and commodity interests coincided.

The economic effects of those organisations which are integrated and large enough to have an effect obviously impinge on other parts of the international economic system (notably exchange rate arrangements or capital flows). These effects, however, are similar to those of other 'large' countries, and are discussed below in that context.

What Has Changed?

Whatever the reason for their emergence, the number and importance of new regional organisations in the last three years has appeared exceptional at least to some members of GATT, most important, to the US, as well as to researchers, and there have been requests for GATT to examine them more carefully against the criteria for their acceptability set out in the General Agreement. This concern was partly inspired by the large number of special arrangements being made between the EC and the Eastern European countries, which raised questions of whether these would lead to more opening or more discrimination in trade, but agreements among developing countries have also been questioned for the first time. In the past these have been treated as coming under the general heading of permissible preferential arrangements, the 'special and differential treatment' for developing countries embodied in the Agreement since 1979, but the US suggested that because of its size (and perhaps implicitly because of the relatively advanced economies involved) the MERCOSUR agreement among Argentina, Brazil, Paraguay and Uruguay should instead be examined under Article XXIV, as would be necessary for an agreement among developed countries. This may be a signal that agreements among the Asian countries, which would also create large markets and involve advanced countries, would be questioned. The procedural issue is still unresolved, but it is clear that there is some belief that the number and importance of regional agreements are now such that they could change the nature of GATT or the international trading system.

The US concern may not be typical: it has traditionally been more sensitive to offering or allowing special treatment for developing countries (even in the agreement with Israel, this is offered to it on the basis that it is an 'undiversified' economy, not a developing one [*Bernal, 1993*]), but the revival of groups like the Andean Pact and CACM, and the new enthusiasm of members of MERCOSUR and Colombia, and on the other hand, the attempts by some Asian countries to achieve an AFTA do suggest that the new groups are seen as significant and potentially effective by their members. Although it remains true that some of the largest countries are outside all groups (notably India, China, and other Asian countries), enough are members of one or more that the chances that at least one of the parties in any negotiation, bilateral as well as multilateral, will have other obligations are now quite high. The probability of facing the types of problems suggested in the last section is greatly increased. There are more groups which include large countries. The EC has been joined by NAFTA, MERCOSUR, and a potential AFTA. These are clearly different in their impact from CARICOM and CACM. More are moving further into non-trade commitments, increasing the potential difficulties of links with other, non-member countries, although some have gone in the opposite direction (for example, the Andean Pact). A more general reason is that trade itself is becoming more important, in share of output, in complexity of impact on the economy, to more countries, so that any change in the trading environment has more of an impact on a larger proportion of a country's decision-makers.

However, tariffs and non-tariff barriers are much lower, so that one would expect that arrangements offering further reductions on those that remain would be seen as less potentially trade diverting, and therefore of less concern for non-members.

Experience So Far

The participation of the EC as a unit in international negotiations may have altered the nature of negotiations and may indicate how these will change if there are additional groups behaving as countries. The public evidence on the course of the GATT Uruguay Round and the role of the EC indicates that there are risks and uncertainties for other participants from a negotiating agent without full authority, and offers some examples of how this can be mitigated (or exploited) by the group negotiating as a unit, and how other participants can respond.

The legal and administrative issues of having international organisations which have other organisations as members as well as countries have up to now been dealt with on an *ad hoc* basis. Within GATT, there is no formal position for the EC, although it is accepted that one country speaks for all the members and, in practice (for example, the appraisal of country trade policies under the Trade Policy Review Mechanism), the EC is now treated as one, while all other countries are treated individually. (But the EC does have collective as well as individual membership of the EBRD, although lending functions appear much less central to its formal area of competence than are GATT's activities.) Other groups are semi-recognised for various purposes (the International Textiles and Clothing Bureau formally; those developing countries which have come to be accepted as entitled to the special provisions in the Agreement, semi-formally: they have formed a continuing group; and other interest groups formed in the Uruguay Round, like the Cairns Group for food exporters, purely informally). The Lomé group, the ACP, normally negotiates directly with the EC, and expects, more or less successfully, that the EC will represent its interests. An increased number of such groups would put pressure on such informal arrangements. Differences within the EC have already caused delays and confusion in the Uruguay Round.

Related Problems

This may not be a phenomenon peculiar to supra-national groups; it may appear with any non-centralised participant. (In previous GATT rounds, it was the difficulties posed, or used as excuses, by the US as a federal country which attracted attention.) Any increase in the number of large federal groups relative to small or medium-sized centralised economies, therefore, suggests a need for new procedures.

The other parallel is with the problems raised for international organisations by large private international bodies, notably the multinational corporations. In both cases multilateral organisations designed in principle to deal with a large number of (in theoretical terms) 'small' and similar members, must adapt to deal with a combination of large countries or companies, some cartels or cartel-like groups, and those countries or companies which remain outside groups.

The growth in the number and proportion of 'large' members raises both a negotiating and a regulatory problem. Many of the regional organisations have the explicit or implicit objective of increasing their members' bargaining power both bilaterally and multilaterally (the new groups frequently cite fears of post-92 EC...). The regulatory question posed by both the new country groups and the new companies is whether there is now a need for an additional regulatory structure for 'large' members (analogous to monopoly regulation at the national level) or a strengthening of the existing structure to deal with stronger individual members.

How Should the International Organisations Respond?

At present regional trading groups are normally examined, if at all, when they are formed, but not dealt with as units subsequently. If they become more common or more significant in their effects, a continuing surveillance and a way of both allowing them to participate as a group and allowing other countries to challenge their effects on outsiders will be necessary. This in turn will make the operations of the regional groups more complicated.

It may also increase the perceived vulnerability of all countries to policies by third-countries as well as by their trading partners. (The growth in published measurement and analysis of all trade policies, including the GATT reports on trade policies, could reinforce any such trend.) This could affect the way in which developing countries react to trade and make their own trading decisions, leading to a more preference – seeking or obstacle – avoiding approach. Even if the trade-creating effects of regional groups prove to be more important than their trade-diverting ones, the resulting increase in the number of stages of potential policy intervention: regional, multilateral, multilateral appraisal of regional, national acceptance of such multilateral appraisal, could work towards a more policy, less market orientated trading strategy. This could argue for the international agencies resisting the role of regulating other institutions.

V. REGIONS, COUNTRIES AND OTHERS

One question is how important countries or regional groups are in a world of large multinational corporations (MNCs). It is conventionally arguable that MNCs expand with regional groups and with the freeing of international trade more generally, because their trade both promotes and is promoted by such forces. An alternative view is that they could ultimately become less important in a world of fewer trade barriers, in which the significance of their firm-specific advantages, greater administrative ability to deal with tariffs or other barriers, and economies of scale in overcoming barriers or altering location, would be reduced. Similar arguments could be made on both sides for the role of regional groups.

If MNCs do become even more important players in the world economy, or alternatively if lower barriers mean that the number of linkages, not only of trade, but of investment, migration, common activities and common interests, between firms and individuals in different countries continues to increase as rapidly as it has, the 'globalisation' (including intra-regional opening) which can certainly be identified as a phenomenon of the last 40 years will continue. If so, then perhaps it is these groups, not countries or regional organisations, with which international organisations should be concerned. (There is an analogy here with countries, where initially a federal government may deal principally with the component regions or states, but eventually also and even primarily with individuals and firms.) The difficulties of describing even so common and well-studied an international activity as trade negotiations in terms of national interests have been painfully obvious during the GATT negotiations. Even economists have occasionally stumbled into describing a reduction in a country's own barriers as a concession. As the international economy impinges more and in more ways not just on each country but on each economic participant in a country, defining a national interest, and thus accepting an international forum that depends for its legitimacy on the idea that each country does have a 'national interest' becomes evidently old-fashioned.

REFERENCES

Bernal, R.L. (1993): 'The Caribbean and Hemispheric Free Trade', *The Caribbean Basin: Economic Security Issues*, Study Papers submitted to the Joint Economic Committee, Congress of the United States, Washington, DC: US Government Printing Office.
Institute of Latin American Studies 'Mexico and the NAFTA', Conference Papers, University of London, Institute of Latin American Studies, May 1993.
Krugman, P. (1992): 'Does the New Trade Theory Require a New Trade Policy?', *The World Economy*, Blackwell: Oxford, Vol 15, No.4, July.

Oman, C. (1993): *Globalisation and Regionalisation: the Challenge for Developing Countries*, Paris: OECD.

Qureshi, A.H. (1993): 'The Role of GATT in the Management of Trade Blocs', *Journal of World Trade*, Vol. 27, No. 3.

Sideri, S. and J. Sengupta (eds.) (1992): *The 1992 Single European Market*, London: Frank Cass (EADI Book Series 13).

PART II

6

Green Protectionism: A Threat to Third World Exports?

JÜRGEN WIEMANN

I. FREE TRADE AND SUSTAINABLE DEVELOPMENT

With the conclusion of the Uruguay Round of GATT negotiations and the commitments of the OECD countries to open their markets for developing countries' exports, one of the demands of the Agenda 21 of the United Nations Conference on Environment and Development (UNCED) has been fulfilled: 'The international community should [...] strengthen the international trade policies system through an early, balanced, comprehensive and successful outcome of the Uruguay Round of multilateral trade negotiations' [*UN, 1992*]. During the next decade, the Contracting Parties of the GATT will have to adjust their trade policies to the agreements of the Uruguay Round and open their markets further to imports from developing countries.

Parallel to the Uruguay Round, however, the GATT has been attacked by environmentalists for its alleged neglect of the environment. Free trade, they say, would overrule environmental standards and regulations in progressive OECD countries, and the GATT would rule out trade measures being taken against countries which run down non-renewable natural resources, extinguish endangered species or do not care for the global environmental impact of their industrialisation strategies. Trade measures might be second-best policy, but what if governments are not prepared to implement first-best policies? If other governments are not willing to enter into agreements on the protection of global commons, or if they do not keep their pledge given in 1992 at the UNCED conference in Rio de Janeiro to enforce the polluter pays principle which would mean that their producers would have to internalise external costs of production for the environment? What other means than trade sanctions would then be available to enforce more effective environmental policies on a global scale?

At the same time, environmentalists fear that developing countries are becoming the dumping ground for whatever 'ecologically enlightened' industrialised countries no longer want to have within their own borders: polluting industries, dangerous technologies, hazardous and other wastes. They see free trade and international division of labour as a soft option for industrialised countries to export their environmental sins of the past so that they need not face the necessity to invest in new and cleaner technologies which would both solve environmental problems in the North and give developing countries the opportunity to avoid some of the past mistakes of the early industrialising countries. Finally, more trade means more transport and transport itself causes environmental problems with global consequences (greenhouse effect). Therefore, it would be better, environmentalists say, to have less trade than more.[1]

Economists have argued almost unanimously that import restrictions are not appropriate or effective measures to achieve the goal of environmental (or health) protection.[2] Trade measures can produce unintentional side-effects which might be more harmful for the environment than the production of the restricted export goods. An import ban on tropical timber, for example, might not be the best protection of tropical forests because the affected groups might have to clear the forests even faster in search of new agricultural land. Moreover, protectionist measures tend to provoke retaliatory measures, and the resulting process of mutual retaliation could be harmful for the open trading system. It would be better to tackle the environmental problem directly, by international agreement on environmental policies and standards and by effective domestic environmental policies.

Some economists argue that it is not even necessary to harmonise environmental standards between countries with different preferences. If developing countries have a preference for economic growth first and environment protection later, let them have it. International trade will then lead to the relocation of production according to the preferences of different countries. Those countries which do not care for their environment will attract 'dirty' industries, whereas rich countries which value the quality of their environment higher than additional economic growth give these industries away. Both sides will be better off in the end.

Finally, international competition leads to economies in the utilisation of resources which would be beneficial for the environment as well. The ecological desasters in the former eastern bloc countries demonstrate better than any theory how the repression of markets and prices and the delinking from international trade and competition of the communist countries leads to a total neglect of the environment and to a waste of resources. Therefore, eastern bloc and developing countries must open their economies to the global markets in order to absorb the latest generations of technologies and production methods which are cleaner and more efficient than the smoke-stack industries of the past. OECD countries on their side, however, must also stick to the rules of the game. If they deny developing countries access to their markets, those countries will shift to less economical and less ecological activities for income generation. Only if the OECD countries keep their markets open can they claim to have a legitimate interest in the improvement of environmental policies and standards of developing countries.

II. ECO-STANDARDS AND INTERNATIONAL TRADE

The GATT sees itself not as an institution specifically geared to the protection of the environment. It has the mandate to make and keep international trade as open as possible and impose a certain discipline on the trade policies of the contracting parties. They should avoid protectionist measures, in particular quantitative restrictions, and they should negotiate the progressive dismantling of existing trade barriers. In case of conflict they should avoid unilateral measures and follow the GATT rules for dispute settlement. By fostering the integration of developing countries into the global trading system the GATT would contribute to the improvement of the environment as well. Prospering developing countries would be able to allocate more resources to environment protection. In addition to that, by preventing the OECD countries to resort to protectionist measures for environmental reasons the GATT would stimulate the search for better alternatives which would be both more efficient for the protection of the environment and more equitable with respect to the economic problems of developing countries, for example, financial compensation for the protection of natural resources instead of an import ban against the same resources.

The GATT does not rule out stricter environmental policies and standards in one country as compared to the rest of the world. Product standards can be imposed (see Chapters 1 and 7). Standards for Production and Process Methods (PPM), however, should not be used as a criterion for allowing imports. This would mean undue interference by the importing country in domestic policies of the exporting country, and it would lead to a mushrooming of protectionist measures because of the difficulties to monitor the compliance with production standards.[3] It is yet an open question whether the distinction between product and process standards will remain watertight in the future. There are two developments undermining this distinction. One is the opening of the GATT Standards Code to process standards which has already taken place half-way. In the final agreement of the Uruguay Round process standards which are directly associated with the product quality have already been included. The trend towards eco-labelling is pointing the same direction because eco-labels can be linked with criteria for production process methods as well. And the GATT does not interfere if, on a voluntary basis, producers provide information on the environmental quality of the production process (for example, the 'dolphin safe' label) and leave it to the consumers whether they care for this information or not.

Product Standards

Product standards and norms (for example, the German DIN norms) have always played a role in international trade. In the past, however, developing countries have been less affected, since most of the technical norms and standards applied were to the more sophisticated engineering goods where Third world countries were less competitive on international markets. With the health and eco-standards affecting more traditional sectors as well (for example, agricultural goods, leather, textiles, wood, furniture), product standards and requirements are becoming an issue of increasing importance for exports of developing countries.

Product standards are compatible with the GATT. The monitoring of compliance of imported goods with domestic product standards is not a big problem, since the product quality can be checked at the border or can be tested in a laboratory in the importing country itself. Of course, the method of control can be used as a protectionist device, if one recalls the case of the small customs office in central France checking all imported video tape recorders which was obviously meant to keep Japanese recorders out.

Details for the application of standards in international trade are codified in the GATT Agreement on Technical Barriers to Trade (TBT). This agreement stipulates that members should not use technical regulations as a protectionist device ('creating unnecessary obstacles to international trade'). Technical regulations must be necessary to 'fulfil a legitimate objective'. Legitimate objectives are national security requirements, protection of human health or safety, animal or plant life or health. The protection of the environment has been added to this list in the new agreement of the Uruguay Round. New standards must be notified to other members through the WTO, and other countries must be given time for adjustment, in order to avoid disruptive effects on international trade.

International standardisation is favoured by the TBT agreement for the same reason. The mixed results of the harmonisation of technical standards within the EU has shown, however, that it is virtually impossible even among a group of relatively homogeneous countries to agree on every sensitive regulation, and that standardisation bodies are not able to keep pace with rapid technical progress that creates a steady flow of new products and production processes for which new standards have to be worked out. It would be naive to expect that the conflict between different national standards can ever be finally solved by international standardisation.

Since there is no objection from the GATT against the introduction of eco-standards for products – provided they are applied in a non-discriminatory way to both domestic and imported products and do not create 'unnecessary obstacles to trade'[4] – developing countries will have to monitor the introduction of eco-standards on the export markets and adjust their export products if necessary. Do they also have to adjust their environmental standards for production processes? This is one of the most controversial issues in the debate on international trade and the environment.

Process and Production Methods

Industries in OECD countries with strict environmental regulations charge developing countries with unfair competition (eco-dumping) as long as their industries are not burdened with environmental costs. The GATT rules out, however, that different environmental standards and policies affecting production processes and costs are taken as another justification for protectionism. Consequently, industrialised countries cannot defend themselves against imports of products that can be manufactured at lower costs in developing countries because they do not have or do not enforce environmental regulations. The GATT uses the same argument to prevent the rich countries from defending themselves against 'social dumping', that is, against imports of Third world products which, because of low wages and the absence of social costs, are far cheaper than equivalent products manufactured in industrialised countries.

Economists tend to defend the right of every country to define its environmental policies, according to the national preferences with respect to the trade-off between industrial growth and a clean environment [*Low and Safadi, 1992*]. Differences of national preferences might not only reflect different levels of development but also different absorptive capacities of the natural environment. International trade makes it possible for every country to specialise in cleaner or dirtier industries, according to its national preferences. Relocation of polluting industries from countries with a high preference for clean environment to countries with a lower preference can improve the environmental conditions of the first countries and should be acclaimed by environmentalists.[5] In this view, there is little economic justification for international harmonisation of environmental standards and even less justification for trade measures to enforce other countries to accept one's own standards.

In fact, the GATT argument against the enforcement of unified process standards in international trade is not only based on theory but also on the very practical problem of how to monitor and enforce the compliance with these standards. Testing of products would not suffice, as in the case of product standards. The importing country or, at least, a qualified international agency would have to send technical experts to the exporting country in order to inspect and certify the environmental quality of the production process on the spot. Since this could be a very costly and time-consuming procedure it could open the door to new protectionism.

There are indications, however, that the pressure on developing countries to comply with higher environmental standards for production processes will increase. First, a protectionist coalition between industries and environmental groups in the OECD countries is raising its voice. Industries argue that they cannot bear increasing costs of compliance with stricter environmental laws and regulations in OECD countries if they are not protected against eco-dumping, that is, against imports from developing countries which are cheap because of the neglect of environmental costs. Environmental groups tend to support restrictive trade measures, for many of them regard international trade in general as harmful for both the domestic environment and the global commons. They also ask what means other than trade measures may force developing countries to comply with international environmental standards and accept the obligations of international agreements on the protection of global commons. Finally, what can be said against a coalition with protectionist interests of domestic industries if this is the only way in a democracy to win enough support for stricter environmental standards at home, and to make other countries accept these standards through the threat of trade sanctions? Environmentalists also question the ecological soundness of the relocation option, arguing that the revealed preference of developing countries for dirty industries might not reflect their true preference or interest because of the lack of information about risks involved in unregulated industrial development. Only after a major industrial accident (such as the Bhopal case in India) can they really understand what is at stake and make informed choices. Further, why should industries in OECD countries not be forced to invest in the development of cleaner technologies in order to defend their location? Cleaner technologies would provide developing countries with new options for cleaner industrial development as well. In fact, relocation of industries to escape environmental regulations has been less relevant than expected in the 1970s.

Second, at the UNCED conference in Rio de Janeiro in 1992, an international consensus was achieved on all industries both in developed and developing countries internalising their environmental costs, that is, enterprises should be burdened further with the costs of removing or reducing environmental damages (for example, investments in air filters, waste-water treatment plants, new cleaner technologies and production processes) [*UN, 1992: Chapter 30*]. The polluter pays principle is widely accepted as the best market economy instrument to make every producer interested in reducing his impact on the environment. But how may developing countries be motivated in introducing the polluter pays principle which they think might jeopardise some of the cost advantages of their exports if not by a combination of carrot, that is, technical and financial assistance, and stick, that is, the threat of restrictive trade measures in the case of non-compliance?

The question of how to reconcile these new demands with the present GATT position will become an issue for future trade talks under the auspices of the new WTO. It cannot be ruled out that major trading nations will advocate some changes toward a new compromise between free trade and stricter environmental standards on a global scale. Since the GATT reflects the interests of the world's major trading nations, and has always responded in a flexible way to their demands (for example, allowing selective protectionism under the MFA), it can be expected that a creative approach will be found to absorb the growing international concern for the environment as well.[6]

The GATT distinction between product and process standards is already blurred in the case of health standards, for example, for meat or drugs, which can only be met if these standards are met throughout the production process itself. Consequently, importing countries are already controlling the sanitary conditions of production processes in exporting countries, for example, the EU checks the sanitary quality of slaughterhouses in developing countries before issuing import licences for meat.[7] In the Uruguay Round the Agreement on Technical Barriers to Trade has been adjusted to include process and production methods which are related to product qualities [*Rege, 1994*]. The discussion about child and prison labour shows that there is a growing concern in OECD countries for the social and environmental conditions under which the exports of developing countries are produced.

In a truly globalising economy the old concept of national sovereignty will lose some of its meaning. All countries participating in global trade and competition for investment have to accept certain rules of the game. Basically, this has been accepted in the Uruguay Round with the Agreements on Trade-Related Investment Measures (TRIMs) and on Trade-Related Aspects of Intellectual Property Rights (TRIPs). From here it is a small step to envisage a similar Agreement on Trade Related Aspects of Environmental Policies (TREPs) which would define what trade measures are acceptable to achieve environmental policy objectives, and what arrangements will be necessary to avoid trade conflicts arising from different national environmental standards [*Rege, 1994: 101–2*].

III. ENVIRONMENTAL PRODUCT REQUIREMENTS IN GERMANY

The growing awareness in most OECD countries of ecological problems has been translated into changes of behaviour of citizens in their various roles, that is, as consumers, as managers or employees in industry and as political citizens.[8] Developing countries have to take account of this change in attitudes in the advanced countries in all aspects of North–South relations and, in particular, as exporters to the North. As a result of the growing concern for local and global environmental problems consumer preferences are changing. More and more consumers in Germany and other European countries are demanding that the products they consume do not cause health risks or damage the environment. The call for harmful chemicals to be excluded from production processes is no longer confined to such everyday necessities as foodstuffs and detergents, but extends to clothing and leather goods as well, and more industries will come under scrutiny in the future. Opinion polls have revealed that in the past ten years the proportion of German consumers who would buy a product labelled 'environmentally friendly' rather than another has risen from 57 per cent (1981) to 72 per cent (1991).[9] Similar trends are reported in other OECD countries.

The concern for one's health and the local environment is only the starting point. An increasing number of consumers are translating their concern for wider environmental problems into changes of purchasing behaviour. They respond quickly to the debate about the destruction of tropical forests and reduce their consumption of furniture made from tropical timber, and they refuse to buy aerosol sprays using CFCs. With new technologies available, the campaign against CFCs in refrigerators is gaining momentum. Consumer associations are taking a growing interest in information about the effects of products on the environment and health, thus enabling consumers to take ecological factors into account. In Germany, there is a long tradition of testing consumer goods by independent institutions (for example, Stiftung Warentest, a semi-official German agency for testing consumer goods). Many Germans rely on these tests as a guideline for their purchasing behaviour, especially when it comes to durable consumer goods. In view of the eco-sensitivity of consumers, the Stiftung Warentest has included the environmental impact assessment of goods and services in its testing programmes.

Government Legislation and Policy

Governments and legislatures are using their influence to reduce environmental and health hazards of industry, and to stimulate the development of clean(er) technologies. In Germany, besides the general laws and regulations concerning industrial pollution of air, water and soil, there are a number of laws and regulations affecting product quality directly. Regulations concerning dangerous substances in particular have made an impact already on imported goods from developing countries. New laws and regulations are in the making [*Heimann, 1991*]. Of particular importance for third (Third World) countries exporting to Germany is the packaging ordinance which aims at reducing and recycling packaging material as far as possible. Since the conflict about the best way to reduce the burden of packaging waste on Germany's landfill capacities has not yet been solved, exporters to Germany must be prepared to adjust to changing requirements for their packaging materials in the future.

Governments influence the environmental behaviour of industry not only by setting environmental product standards; with their large and growing share in GDP, governments and public institutions can exert their influence through the markets, provided the various public bodies follow relatively uniform purchasing instructions with respect to eco-quality. Public procurement agencies in Germany are encouraged, and even obliged, by specific regulations to take the environmental quality of the products into account and to prefer environment friendly products to others even if they are more expensive.[10] The greening of public procurement would have an increasing impact on international trade if the GATT code on public procurement were taken more seriously. Developing countries' exporters bidding for public contracts in OECD countries will have to take changes in public purchasing behaviour into account if they want to make an inroad into these markets.

Greening of Industry

Industries are responding to the increasing concern for the environment of consumers and governments. They develop and market eco-products, scan their production process for potential reductions of negative environmental impacts and promote eco-labels for their environment friendly products in order to enjoy the benefits of changing consumer preferences.[11] During the last decade, there has been a basic change in the attitude of industries toward the pollution problem. In the past, the focus was on cleaning polluted effluents and air emissions at the end of a basically unchanged manufacturing process (end-of-pipe technologies). The costs of end-of-pipe treatment simply added to the total manufacturing costs reducing the competitiveness of firms applying end-of-pipe treatment *vis-à-vis* those which did not care for environment pollution. Besides this economic disadvantage, end-of-pipe treatment created secondary problems: if the harmful chemicals and wastes retained by filters or effluent treatment plants could not be recycled and used again, they had to be disposed of somewhere, causing new environmental problems if dumped in unsafe landfill sites or in the open sea.

These disadvantages of end-of-pipe technologies, both from an economic and an ecological point of view, led to a fundamental change in the approach of industries towards the reduction of their negative impact on the environment: from end-of-pipe solutions to pollution prevention through reducing materials inputs and wastage throughout the whole manufacturing process. Firms realise that an ecological restructuring of the production process can pay if it leads to substantial reductions in input costs and that of end-of-pipe treatment. They make use of a host of new concepts and tools that have been developed during the last decade and that are propagated by a growing number of eco-consultants and writers of textbooks on eco-management, for example, eco-oriented value-chain-analysis, eco-auditing, eco-controlling and so on [*Schmidheiny, 1992*].

The greening of industries in Europe and the US will have an impact on Third World industries for at least two reasons. On the one hand, many enterprises complain about unfair competition from developing countries whose industries are not burdened with environmental costs as in the OECD countries. On the other hand, an increasing number of industries seems to be realising that an active approach towards protection of the environment can be translated into competitive advantage *vis-à-vis* developing countries if educated OECD consumers make the eco-quality an important issue for their consumption patterns. The majority of ecological requirements to be satisfied by consumers goods is not imposed by government laws and regulations, therefore, but in the form of voluntary standards and eco-labels introduced by industry itself.

Eco-labels

Consumers willing to exert an influence on industry by changing their purchasing behaviour in favour of green products need information. They can study volumes of consumer guides or consult consumer associations, but this can become a time-consuming and costly process. Products are changing, new products are being marketed at an increasing speed, and companies' environmental credibility may change as well.[12] One way out of this dilemma is to delegate the search for information on the eco-quality of products to a trustworthy institution which certifies products that meet certain eco-requirements by an eco-label. If the issuing institution has a good reputation and the eco-label is regarded as effectively distinguishing between 'good' and 'bad' products, the search costs for the green consumer can be reduced to a minimum. And if a sufficient number of consumers accepts eco-labels as a guide for their purchasing behaviour, industries will feel a strong incentive to have their products tested and apply for the label.[13] Thus the interaction between environmentally conscious consumers and industry becomes a positive feedback process where each side gains from an advancement of the other in the same direction.

Germany has a long tradition of eco-labelling. The 'Blue Angel' was introduced in 1977, is well known by most Germans today, and has a high credibility. The flexibility of awarding the Blue Angel allowed for a steady upgrading of criteria, along with the development of cleaner technologies. Now the German institutions involved (in particular the Federal Environmental Agency) fear that the harmonisation of the criteria for eco-labels on the European level will reduce this flexibility and undermine the relative success of eco-labelling in Germany.

The Blue Angel is open to products from third countries as well: 'Every manufacturer, no matter whether he is German or non-German, may design his product to meet these requirements and apply for the environmental label' – even if he is no major supplier and if those products are not widely known, or even if he has gained only a small market share. In other words, any manufacturer may be granted permission to use the environmental label as an advertising vehicle, provided his product fulfils the requirements.[14] The possibility of applying for the German eco-label is intensively used by foreign companies: 'Approximately 10 percent of all contracts completed with RAL on the use of the label were signed by foreign companies.'

However, eco-labels may become an indirect trade barrier for those exporters who are not aware of their existence: the criteria, the costs and formalities of application. Even if a Third World exporter has applied for a label, the monitoring of compliance may be more costly and time-consuming than in the case of OECD manufacturers, who have easier access to laboratories and who are under closer scrutiny of the national environmental authorities for their consumption of dangerous chemicals. This holds true in particular for eco-labels guaranteeing a certain eco-quality of the production process requiring regular monitoring of the production site itself, which would be much costlier in another country, and in a Third World country particularly.

The Single European Market and Eco-Standards

Eco-standards have played an important role in the discussion on the SEM.[15] In order to facilitate the completion of the SEM before the end of 1992, the European Commission had given up its preoccupation with harmonisation of every technical detail of standards and norms and adopted a double-track approach instead. National product norms and regulations should be mutually recognised by all other member states as far as they are not in conflict with fundamental principles of safety, health and environment. These fundamental safety, health and environment standards had to be harmonised, as before, at the Community level. To complicate the European standardisation process even more, the Maastricht Treaty on the formation of the European Economic and Monetary Union gave every member country the right to define its own environmental standards according to its national preferences. This meant that some individual member countries might move ahead by introducing stricter eco-requirements on products than other EU countries.

It is yet an open question as to how potential conflict between the principle of free trade in the SEM and the right of member countries to follow their own preferences with respect to environmental policy and standards may be solved. Can a member country refuse to accept imports from other EU member countries if they do not comply with the national product related eco-standards? As shown in at least in one case, the European Court of Justice has given priority to a national environmental regulation over that of the free movement of goods (its judgment on the Danish deposit bottle regulation). Another case could be the large discrepancy between the German limit value for PCP (Pentachlorophenol), which is 5 ppm (parts per million) and the European limit value of 1,000 ppm. For the time being, third countries have to face a market where double (or even multiple) standards prevail. Exporters will be on the safe side if they try to comply with the relatively stricter standards of, for example, Germany, because it is likely that standards at the European level will become stricter in the long run as well.

Eco-labels have also become an issue for the harmonisation efforts of the European Commission. If a national eco-label has a good reputation in the respective country and consumers are searching for goods with the label they know this can become an indirect trade barrier preventing the full integration of the European market. The EU is therefore trying to establish uniform eco-labels for the European market. This is not an easy task, since there are different approaches in the philosophy behind the labelling schemes. The German approach tries putting industries under pressure to improve their environmental performance by setting relatively high standards that are periodically raised once the majority of firms in a market has reached a certain level, and the label no longer points to the excellent firms and products with respect to eco-criteria. Compared to the tough criteria for the German eco-label, the Community approach has been much softer so far, setting relatively moderate criteria that many firms may easily comply with to make the 'European Flower' well known all over Europe. As long as there is no single EU eco-label, exporters from third countries will have to undergo the cumbersome procedure of applying for the respective eco-label in EU country individually. Obviously, it would be in their interest if they could apply for just one eco-label at the European level.

IV. CASE STUDY ON THE IMPLICATIONS OF ECOLOGICAL PRODUCT REQUIREMENTS FOR INDIA'S TEXTILE AND LEATHER EXPORT[16]

The following case study of the impact of environmental regulations in Germany on India's leather and textile exports shows how the trend towards the enforcement of eco-standards in international trade is gaining importance at the market level. Two industries relevant to India's exports (and exports of other developing countries as well) are taken to show how the changing market requirements in Germany affect India's exports and how India's exporters are reacting to the new challenge.

Leather Industry: Product Standards

Leather and leather goods were the first among India's major exports to face the challenge of new product-related health and environmental standards in a relevant export market. In 1990, a large German buyer rejected a delivery of Indian leather goods on the grounds that they were not compatible with a new regulation of the German government virtually banning the use of PCP, a toxic fungicide and bactericide used all over the world for the preservation of wood, leather and so on. There was an outcry in both the Indian leather industry and the Indian government, not so much against the German regulation which, in fact, had been approved by the German government as early as 1987, and only the resistance of the EU against the German ban on PCP causing the delay of two years before it came into effect, as against the fact that the Germans took the ban seriously, and applied it against imported goods contaminated with PCP as well.

The Germans could claim convincingly that the PCP ban was not directed against imported leather goods as such, be it from India or any other country. For decades the toxin had been used to combat fungi, weeds, pests, algae, bacteria and slugs in agriculture, industry and in households. Its harmful effects became more widely known in the 1970s and 1980s, when the use of wood preservatives containing PCP in buildings had caused serious diseases. In reaction to some spectacular cases, the limit values for PCP were reduced during the 1980s, and in 1989 a virtual ban on PCP was imposed; a limit value of 5 ppm applies to goods treated with PCP; in the EU the limit value is 1,000 ppm. In 1990 PCP was assigned to Substance Category III A 2 (clearly carcinogenic in experiments on animals), and in Sweden PCP was banned in 1977 [*Gagelmann, 1991*]. Since the PCP ban was imposed, leather goods have been tested for their PCP content on several occasions on behalf of consumer and environmental magazines. Each time the limit value was found to have been exceeded, very considerably in some cases.[17] Italy, France, Greece, India and other countries have unsuccessfully protested against the German ban on PCP.

The German ban on PCP and the consequent 5 ppm limit on goods treated with PCP retain their validity in the SEM, despite the far higher EU limit value [*Umwelt 2/1993: 72*]. This is one example of the special role of environmental standards within the SEM. It is as yet an open question whether the German authorities may restrict imports and sales of leather goods containing PCP from other EU countries or the re-export of goods from third countries. Third countries' exporters will be on the safe side, however, if they comply with the stricter German standards.

The next issue could be the introduction of eco-requirements for the production process. Problems here are manifold, particularly the treatment of effluents containing a number of chemicals (for example, chromium) used in the tanning process. Untreated effluents, liquid chemicals and contaminated sewage sludge may pollute ground water. This is especially true of developing countries where people have no other source of water and are thus exposed to major health hazards. Another problem is the discharge of tannery effluents on to surrounding fields. Case studies of this practice in India have shown that yields from polluted land have fallen by as much as two-thirds; in some areas all cultivable land is so contaminated that it can no longer be farmed. The polluted water causes a wide range of diseases, including skin diseases, gastrointestinal diseases, disturbed body growth, heart diseases and asthma.[18]

In Germany, stricter environmental laws and regulations have led to a steady decline of leather production in the 1980s, and a complementary increase of import demand. This may be good for Germany's environment, but more and more Germans ask themselves whether the export of environmentally harmful industries and production activities to developing countries can be justified from a global viewpoint. Third World action groups point to the damage certain industries such as leather tanning are causing to the environment and to the health of workers in these countries. There are reports about dirty industries in India and other developing countries even in the mass media. Rising concern for the global environment may sooner or later make consumers in Germany and other European countries demand that the products they buy from developing countries should be manufactured with less impact on the environment and fewer health risks for the workers. Even if this does not lead to new government regulations affecting imports, German importers will take into account the concern of a rising number of customers by asking more and more questions about effluent treatment or the prevention of occupational hazards in the factories of their suppliers in India. It cannot be ruled out that the leather trade will introduce an eco-label of its own, the criteria of which might extend from product quality to the environmental quality of the production process as well.

It is an open question as to whether reports on water pollution in developing countries will create sufficient political pressure for government action. At least in Germany there is not much lobbying power left with the industry concerned – leather production has declined due to increasing competition from developing countries. It cannot be ruled out, however, that the leather industry in other European countries will realise the potential protectionist effect of an eco-label indicating both the product and process quality of European leather goods in contrast with Third World imports. Developing countries' leather producers are well advised to follow closely these developments in Europe and to prepare early enough for (more efficient) effluent treatment and other methods to reduce the negative impact on the environment [*UNEP/IEO, 1991*].

Textile Industry

Textiles have not yet been directly affected by government regulation as have leather goods by the ban on PCP. However, the public debate in Germany – and in other OECD countries – has focused recently not only on the harmful effects on health and environment of chemicals used in textile finishing, but also on the considerable environmental damages from traditional high chemical-intensive cotton cultivation. Even cotton has come under attack finally. It is said to be an environmental nightmare [*Schneider, 1993, Section 9: 1, 11*]. Cotton is one of the most chemical-intensive crops affecting both soil and ground-water. This has done serious damage to the environment: the growing of cotton as a single crop and the increase in irrigation and in the use of fertilisers and pesticides have leached, salinised and eroded the soil, polluted lakes and rivers or overused them. The spraying of pesticides has also affected the health of cotton pickers. Pesticide residues have been found in raw cotton and cotton clothing.[19] Traditional cotton cultivation contaminates the soils to such an extent that cotton certified as organic has to be grown in fields where no traditional cotton growing has taken place for three years [*Schneider, 1993: 11*]. This must be reflected in eco-textile labels sooner or later. These will be given only to textiles which have been made from organic cotton and processed without harmful chemicals.

It is evident from these problems that a complete change to natural fibres would be ecologically safe only if growing conditions were simultaneously improved. However, this would require more agricultural land, since productivity might be lower if less chemical pesticides and insecticides were to be used. Competition between natural fibre cultivation and food crops could become ever stronger with a growing world population. However, it is an open question – to be resolved by sophisticated means of eco-balances or other means – whether cotton textiles are actually eco-friendlier than those made from man-made fibres. Developing countries producing and exporting cotton textiles are well advised to follow this discussion in OECD countries, for the impact on their exports could be substantial if they do not shift in time to what consumers in OECD countries regard as eco-friendly fibres and processing methods.

The other environmental problem of the textile industry is water. About 100 litres of water are used in the processing of 1 kg of textiles [*Fleckenstein, 1991: 31*]. The following stages of finishing give rise to particularly large quantities of effluent: bleaching, dyeing, mercerising, antifelt finishing, silk weighting and water-proofing. Effluent is contaminated by dyes, only 60 per cent of which are absorbed by the textiles, with the remaining 40 per cent entering the effluent [*Rosenkranz and Castello, 1989: 93*]. Synthetic dyes are not easily degradable and tend to accumulate in sewage sludge. A particularly serious problem is posed by such heavy metals as chromium, copper, tin and cadmium which are used as auxiliary agents and dyes and which enter the food chain when sewage sludge is used as fertiliser. Chromium, which is found particularly in black dyes, has a highly toxic effect on effluent bacteria (biodegradation) and fish. However, dyes containing heavy metals are dangerous not only to effluent but also to consumers, since heavy metals are released by clothing when it is worn and absorbed through the skin.

Like dyes, sizes have become a problematical constituent of effluent. Sizes are used to increase the strength of yarns for the weaving process. Substances used for this purpose, polyvinyl alcohol and polyacrylates, are not easily degradable. Organic chlorine compounds (for example, PCP, banned in Germany since 1990), which are used to prevent rotting and to accelerate the dyeing process, are particularly toxic. They are a dangerous environmental toxin and not easily degradable as a rule. A fundamental problem is raised by the lack of effluent treatment, that is, the discharge of untreated or inadequately treated effluent into rivers, lakes and the sea.

Finally, there is growing awareness that the chemical contamination of textiles can be a health risk for textile workers and consumers. Hazards for consumers include the allergies that may be triggered off by textiles and the carcinogenic substances used in the processing of textiles, and naturally arouse suspicions. Although it has not yet been proved that textiles cause cancer, the feeling that azo dyes, for example, may cause allergies or cancer has resulted in the textile industry voluntarily refraining from using these dyes. The prevention principle should thus also be applied to other dangerous substances, such as benzidine dyes, which have proved to be carcinogenic.

Consumer awareness of environmental and health problems has finally uncovered the sphere of textiles and clothing. Newspaper articles and publications of consumer associations have made consumers aware of allergenic and carcinogenic substances in garments and other textile products.[20] It goes without saying that there is a higher sensitivity over certain products such as baby clothes or underwear. However, the environmental impacts of textile production, the pollution of rivers and ground-water and the contamination of whole regions in the exporting developing countries are also an issue in the public debate [*Schuster, 1993*]. Yet, it is almost impossible for environmentally conscious consumers to distinguish environmentally sound products from others. There is a growing market share for 'eco-textiles' (which claim to be produced with 'clean cotton', that is, cotton with a low content of harmful chemicals). Even large department stores and mail order houses venture into eco-textiles and find a rising demand for them. Parallel to the rising share of eco-textiles, there is a trend both in legislation and at the industry level to introduce stricter eco-requirements for textiles.

It is not yet clear whether the recent debate on health hazards of textiles and clothing and environmental problems caused by textile industries will lead to new legislation soon. The German textile industry is taking the lead by introducing its own eco-label for textiles which meet certain criteria of low chemical content and so on. In 1992 the Central Association of the German Textile Industry made a first attempt to introduce an eco-label for textiles which are environmentally compatible or have been examined for harmful substances, with the aim of making it easier for retailers and consumers to opt for eco-textiles. The 'MUT' is to be placed on intermediate textile products and will set norms for the production process. In contrast, the 'MST' will provide the consumer with information on clothing with a controlled low content of dangerous substances.[21] Since 1993, this eco-label is to be awarded by the Association for Environment- and Consumer-friendly Textiles, which has its registered office in Frankfurt.[22] The test criteria will be influenced both by ecological criteria, that is, criteria relating to the manufacturing and finishing process, and health criteria. Experts at a symposium on the ecology of the textile chain held in October 1991 argued in this context that the high process standards set by German legislation justified the application of these requirements to textiles produced abroad if their manufacturers applied for the eco-label [*Mecheels, 1992*].

The eco-label has been criticised in various quarters: consumer associations and environmental organisations claim it does not go far enough because it does not meet their demands for details of auxiliary agents used; clothing manufacturers and retailers object to it because they see it as a hidden protectionist measure, intended to promote the sale of (expensive) German textiles and clothing rather than to protect the environment [*Vorholz, 1992*]. In the meantime the European Largest Textile and Apparel Companies (ELTAC), an association of 30 European manufacturers, has designed an eco-label similar to the MST. The origin of clothing as well as ecological criteria play a part in this case, since safeguarding Europe as a manufacturing location is one of ELTAC's objectives. Full agreement with the association sponsoring the MST has yet to be reached.

If these eco-labels are introduced, their eventual success in the market will depend on their acceptance by the retail trade and the consumer. In this case two scenarios are conceivable: on the one hand, a strong high-quality segment for which the eco-label is a 'must', and which tends to be dominated by domestic or European products, may emerge in the German clothing market. The confusing number of eco-labels could, however, limit their success. On the other hand, this trend may be more broadly based, with the eco-label becoming a general criterion for access to the market. This is what is hoped for the European eco-label. The latter possibility is likely to occur where health protection motives override interest in fashion (baby and children's clothes, underwear), since surveys prove that many women shoppers consider fashion more important than health and the environment [*Grassl, 1992*]. This may change, however, if education and information on risks to health and the environment is stepped up.

There are as yet only few legal requirements for the eco-quality of textiles. Consumer protection is based on the Foodstuffs and Essential Commodities Act. Section 30 of this Act requires 'the manufacturer to ensure that the only finishing agents used are substances which, it can be assumed from the current state of scientific knowledge, will not render the product likely to be detrimental to health if it is used correctly'. At present, the following statutory requirements exist to protect the consumer:

- compulsory labelling of formaldehyde in excess of 1,500 mg/kg since 1986 (declaration requirement, which is set out in the Regulation on Dangerous Substances and dates back to the Chemicals Act);
- ban on the use of carcinogenic substances to reduce the flammability of fabrics;
- ban on the use of asbestos yarns for protective clothing (Regulation on Dangerous Substances; DIN 60650);
- ban on the use of PCP.[23]

Due to growing public awareness some activity to tighten up environmental laws and standards relating to the textile industry can be expected, including the prohibitions of certain chemicals. In 1992 the Federal Health Agency set up a Working Party on Textiles in which the industry is represented as well to consider health and environmental requirements. Since March 1992 a Committee of Inquiry of the Federal Parliament (named Protection of Man and Environment) has been considering aspects of environmentally compatible substance cycles, and has also investigated the effects on health and the environment of textile production, use, cleaning and waste disposal problems.[24]

India's Response[25]

There is a growing awareness in India of the seriousness with which eco-standards for products and the packaging regulation are being introduced in Germany and the EU. Thus, export-oriented industries see no alternative to adjusting to new government regulations and buyers' specifications, even if their scientific justification is frequently questioned. Indian exporters often complain that the evidence given by the German authorities on the alleged health or environmental risks of banned substances and processes or packaging materials is weak. There is a widespread feeling in the Indian business community that, since affluent consumers in rich countries are so preoccupied with what is regarded from an Indian perspective as minor risks compared to the hazards of everyday life in a developing country, they or their governments should bear at least a substantial share in the adjustment costs developing countries' export industries are facing.

Obviously, the awareness of the relevance of eco-standards is highest in those industries which are highly export-oriented and which have already experienced difficulties for their exports due to newly introduced eco-standards. India's leather industry in particular, from tanneries to garment manufacturers, is well aware of Germany's virtual ban of PCP in all leather goods. Although the new regulation had been announced in advance, some exporters have not taken the PCP ban seriously and have faced rejections of shipments. Of course, this must have been the most efficient lesson. Meanwhile, most tanneries have adopted alternative chemicals for the preservation of leather and leather goods. The Indian government has even introduced a regulation banning PCP for the domestic market as well.

The Indian government is highly interested in preventing a similar negative experience for other industries by actively promoting awareness campaigns on foreseeable new eco-requirements for other export industries, for example, the textile and clothing industries. There are specialised export promotion agencies for each sub-sector of the textile industry which should be able to collect and disseminate the relevant information on new standards and requirements on export markets. Indo-German and Indo-EU Chambers of Commerce are also providing information and seminars about new requirements. Experts on the technical aspects of how to adjust to new standards have been invited by an Indo-German export promotion project in order to present technical alternatives to the industries concerned.

Besides the specialised agencies for export information, public awareness of environmental risks of industries is on the rise in India, thanks to the revolution in information that links the remotest village to the rest of the world. Satellite television is regularly reporting on the state of the environment in developing countries and propagating remarkable solutions to similar problems developed in other countries. International conferences such as the UNCED in 1992 have also contributed to the awareness, building on the globalisation of environmental threats, and making common efforts of both developed and developing countries in the field of cleaner technologies and products ever more necessary.

India is one of the few developing countries with a long tradition of NGO activities in the area of environmental policies and action programmes. They are able to launch campaigns against the worst polluters in industry. Water pollution in particular is taken more and more seriously in a country where water is scarce in large areas, and where industry is competing with agriculture and households for clean water. In some areas the neglect of polluted effluents over decades has become a problem even for the polluting industries themselves. Both leather and textile industries are consuming relatively large quantities of clean water which are no longer available in some of the places where these industries are highly concentrated. Therefore, effluent treatment, which is compulsory under India's environmental legislation for every new plant, seems to be accepted by the industries themselves. They will have to rely more and more on recycled water for their own water-intensive production stages. In this area, India's leather industry and, with a time lag, the textile industry as well, might be well prepared for future eco-standards on process technology and effluent treatment which may become relevant for export marketing in the near future.

Reaction of Industry

Despite the increasing awareness of the new challenges to exports, many export companies stick to the 'wait and see' attitude. Some argue that there is not sufficient scientific evidence on the health and environmental risks of the substances and processes under scrutiny. Others see the new eco-standards as another protectionist manoeuvre of the developed countries, directed specifically against developing countries which are prevented from exploiting their comparative advantages of having less stringent environmental laws and regulations, and a less effective enforcement capacity of the authorities concerned. However, this argument does not withstand closer scrutiny, since the use of environmentally friendly products is not so expensive, at least in those cases where only the substitution of a less harmful or hazardous substance for a banned one is required, and where drastic technological changes in the production process are not necessary.

Many companies simply rely on their buyers in Europe, expecting them to provide not only the relevant information on new requirements, but also the means to comply with them. This attitude is deeply ingrained since most exporters are used to working according to detailed specifications and samples given by their customers abroad. The best exporters are able to meet whatever is required in terms of design, fashion, quality and so on, so they see no reason why they should not be able to meet whatever will be required in terms of eco-norms and eco-fashion, provided their buyers give them the necessary instructions and ingredients.

Only very few companies are following a proactive strategy in the sense of creating new eco-friendly products and collections and of marketing these products for the growing eco-market segment in Europe. There are several reasons why there are not more eco-pioneers in India and in other developing countries. First, the trend toward eco-products in textiles, clothing and leather products is of too recent origin, and is seen as not reliable enough to allow for large investments in new designs, new sourcing for raw materials and new production methods. Second, under the Indian economic system an eco-pioneer faces a number of obstacles, such as the non-availability of new eco-friendly ingredients many of which still have to be imported. Another obstacle is the aversion of economic policy-makers against large-scale companies and vertical integration that would provide for better control of the eco-quality of inputs. 'Clean cotton' (cultivated with little spraying of pesticides and insecticides) is available in India, but it is difficult for a garment manufacturer to assure the utilisation of clean cotton through the different steps of the production chain that are handled by different companies.

There is an encouraging new trend to be seen in many exporting industries in India: it has become fashionable to 'go for ISO 9000' (ISO = International Standards Organisation) which is the international standard for quality management. ISO 9000 is being introduced as the quality gauge for the SEM. An increasing number of Indian manufacturers oriented towards the European market therefore realise the advantages of following the strict prescriptions for quality management laid down in ISO 9000, and of using the certificate from an independent body as a recommendation for new European buyers. Since ISO 9000 requires a closer scrutiny of the suppliers' capacity and motivation for quality production, it should not be too difficult to take the next step towards a more careful assessment of the eco-quality of the suppliers' products, as well as their entire manufacturing process. Anyhow, in the not too distant future ISO 9000 or related quality standards will comprise eco-standards as well. And then Indian exporters will have to pay more attention to the eco-quality of the whole 'textile chain' (or 'leather chain') they represent *vis-à-vis* their customers abroad. Another encouraging trend can be seen in eco-collections being advertised for the domestic market. Since India's not so small middle class is highly receptive to the latest trends in rich countries eco-textiles and garments might soon become trendy in India as well. Then even those companies mainly oriented towards the domestic market which have not seen a need to go for eco-qualities will have to change.

Support for Export Industries' Adjustment to Eco-standards

The Indian government seems to realise that the green consumerism movement and the increasing concern for the environment of governments and industry in the developed world will create a new challenge for India's recent export drive. India has neglected the world markets for such a long time that it now has to go through a 'crash course' on the latest requirements of international marketing. One lesson is about the quality standards that have been continuously raised in the climate of global competition; this lesson is being absorbed by Indian export industries. The next lesson is about the possibilities available today of making manufacturing and manufactured products cleaner and more suitable to the natural environment. This has been realised by industry associations and a few large enterprises, but it will take some time for it to trickle down to the lower ranks of industry.

The government of India can support the adjustment to new eco-standards on export markets in several ways:

(1) It must remove existing obstacles against efficient manufacturing. This refers in particular to the facilitation of access to the necessary inputs, that is, access without bureaucratic delays and hassles to imported inputs if they are not available in India or not available in the required specifications and qualities. Backward integration should also be possible whenever an exporting company sees the necessity to assure a high (eco-)quality of inputs from the forward production stages by bringing these stages under its control.

(2) The government should take responsibility for the quality of exports in order to make the label 'made in India' a reliable quality label on international markets. This is not an easy task in a phase when the government has decided to adopt a rather non-interventionist attitude with regard to the affairs of private industry. Export controls are being dismantled to reduce the cumbersome administrative procedures that have prevented exports from flourishing in the past. The risk of non-intervention, however, is that there is too little control over the capacity of individual exporters to continuously meet the quality standards of export markets. One alternative to government controls is already being discussed: India's economic policy-makers should allow the formation of large export houses which would guarantee the quality of their export goods *vis-à-vis* foreign buyers and that would take the responsibility of introducing and enforcing the necessary quality standards *vis-à-vis* their domestic suppliers. The Japanese owe much of their early export success to their large export houses. Meanwhile, quality control of exports can also be assigned to specialised private firms that already operate in India as well as in other developing countries.

(3) The government could accelerate the process of adjustment by introducing an eco-label of its own that guarantees the same properties of the labelled products as those relevant in the export markets. This could facilitate exporting once foreign buyers have become confident that the Indian label is reliable, for testing procedures are the same as in their own countries. This confidence-building is the only way to prevent the whole export business from being jeopardised by too many eco-quality checks in the importing countries. Introducing an eco-label in India would also contribute to awareness-building among Indian consumers of the environmental properties of the consumer goods they buy. In the long run, consumers and not governments should control the quality of manufactured goods. Once the discrepancy between the quality standards demanded on the export markets and on the domestic market have been overcome, the consumers can play a key role in guaranteeing a steady export quality level. It is a well-established fact that high-quality exports can only thrive if quality is also demanded on the domestic markets

[*Porter, 1990*]. The lack of quality consciousness under the old regime of scarcity has been one of the major impediments for high quality exports from India. The new economic policy of dismantling government interference in industry and liberalising imports could soon lead to a fundamental change in consumer behaviour putting all industries under pressure to meet international quality and design standards.

(4) The government must set and enforce environmental standards *vis-à-vis* domestic as well as export industries. This is again illustrated by the Indian example. Following the German ban on PCP, India imposed a corresponding ban on PCP. In a similar way, stricter environmental standards could be set for the Indian textile industry to anticipate possible problems on the export markets.

It would be a short-sighted strategy to push exports at the expense of the environment, for there is always a risk that protectionist tendencies in importing countries will be fuelled by the argument that industries in developing countries are following a strategy of 'eco-dumping'. Stricter environmental legislation in developing countries and a better enforcement of these laws and regulations should not only be viewed as a costly, however necessary, concession to the interests of rich countries. The old idea that developing countries have to go 'through the "dark satanic mills" phase of industrial growth' has come under attack recently, even in World Bank publications.[26] With more realistic comparisons of the costs of pollution abatement in industry to the potential health risks and environmental damages of a careless industrial development strategy, the new concept is gaining ground that it is in their own interests if developing countries adopt a cleaner industrial development path than, maybe, the old industrialised countries followed in their early development stages.

V. WHAT LESSONS FOR DEVELOPMENT CO-OPERATION?

Whatever the GATT or its successor, the WTO, will say on trade conflicts with an environmental background, developing countries should not forget that OECD countries have not always kept to the GATT rules of the game when they felt the need to restrict competition from low cost sources. Therefore it makes sense to defuse the conflict by improving the capacity of developing countries to comply with the new eco-requirements that are valid on OECD markets.

OECD countries should not be restrained from implementing effective environmental controls on industry because of eventual negative effects on developing countries' exports. However, instead of restricting access to their markets through regulations or import barriers, they should offer technical and financial assistance for upgrading institutional and technological capacities in developing countries for a more effective monitoring of industries for their environmental behaviour. By encouraging developing countries to adopt the basic principles of environment protection such as the polluter pays principle or the precautionary principle [*Hunter et al., 1994: 25*], development co-operation will prevent trade conflicts, and contribute to a globalisation of the market economy that is not detrimental to the environment, but helps to solve some of the environmental problems associated with industrialisation in the Third World.

The risk that stricter environmental requirements – both product and process-related – cause trade conflicts between industrial and developing countries can be reduced by appropriate co-operation measures. As regards the conflict between the Germany and India on the appropriateness of the PCP ban on imported leather goods, an Indo-German export promotion project helped to a considerable extent to explain the consequences of the PCP ban for the Indian leather industry and to point to technological alternatives.

Trade and aid policies of OECD countries will have to take account of the new challenge of eco-standards for Third World exports. The debate on what the aid system can do in this respect has already started within the OECD.[27] The following approaches seem to be relevant:

– OECD countries should provide all relevant information on eco-standards and eco-labels to potentially affected exporting countries. The requirements must be transparent and information-cum-technical-assistance should be provided to developing countries' exporters to meet new requirements;
– in case of product standards or eco-labels for products of particular relevance for developing countries their interests should be taken into account, for example, through prior consultation. This would give the exporting countries more time for adjustment;
– Export promotion programmes of aid agencies must take account of the greening of markets in OECD countries. They should assist their clients in developing countries to identify new eco-products and develop them into commercially viable exports;
– the development of eco-friendly exports from developing countries could be stimulated by offering special trade concessions (for example, exemption from quantitative import restrictions, special green tariff preferences) for these products;
– eco-labels in OECD countries must be open for developing countries' exports provided they comply with the criteria for the label;
– co-operation in the field of environmental policy in developing countries should be expanded so that the differences of environmental protection are

gradually overcome, consequently helping to mitigate the conflict about alleged or actual eco-dumping of exporters from developing countries.

In a globalising economy there will be a need for more harmonisation of environmental (and social) standards in order to have fair competition between countries on different levels of development. Aid agencies therefore should take the threat of 'green protectionism' as a starting point to propagate co-operation with developing countries in all fields of environmental policies. They should convince their own governments that there is no need for protectionist measures against 'eco-dumping' if they help developing countries by means of technical and financial assistance to improve their capacity to meet OECD health and environmental regulations.

NOTES

1. See Shrybman [*1990*], Arden-Clarke [*1991*), Postel and Flavin [*1991*], French [*1993*], Ekins, Folke and Costanza [*1994*], Daly and Goodland [*1994*]. A more balanced view from an environmental standpoint presents Repetto [*1994*].
2. See Low [*1992a*], Anderson and Blackhurst [*1992*]. An excellent account of the main arguments in the papers of the latter is given by Palmeter [*1993*].
3. GATT [1992, *Vol. I, Ch. III*]: 'Trade and the environment'; see Thomas and Tereposky [*1993*]. For an up-to-date and detailed discription of the GATT position on eco-standards see Rege [*1994*].
4. It might be difficult, however, to win a case in GATT against a technical standard on the allegation that it creates an 'unnecessary obstacle to trade' because the GATT Technical Standards Code does not provide criteria for the distinction between justified and injurious technical standards. See Thomas and Tereposky [*1993: 38–9*].
5. Empirical findings, however, show that this has not taken place on a large scale. The costs of emission and effluent controls are normally only a small fraction of total costs, and environmental protection is only one among many factors a company takes into consideration when deciding about relocating a plant. See Lucas, Wheeler and Hettige [*1992*]; Low and Yeats [*1992*].
6. Low and Safadi [*1992, 40*]: 'It may be noted that there are some quite widely supported proposals before the Uruguay Round for extending the GATT Standards Code to cover PPMs. There are similar moves afoot to include PPMs in an agreement on sanitary and phytosanitary measures in the sphere of agriculture. The application of trade restrictions by one country to oblige another to adopt specified PPMs may be expected to gain wider acceptance over time, particularly when the case is argued on health or consumer protection grounds. If this trend is inevitable, emphasis should be given to the development of agreed standards.' A US economist who works for the Congress openly advocates the extension of the GATT Standards Code to production processes [*Foy, 1992*].
7. Canada sets process standards on imported meat and drugs. See Thomas and Tereposky [*1993: 41*].
8. See Tolba and El-Kholy [*1992: Ch. 21*]: perceptions and attitudes.
9. See Emnid opinion poll May 1991, in MARIA [*1992: Part 1*]. The green consumer movement is not confined to Germany. Books and articles on how to behave as an

eco-conscious consumer and how to react as a responsive entrepreneur abound. See Elkington and Hailes [*1988*], Davis [*1991*], Charter [*1992*], Elkington, Knight and Hailes [*1992*], and Knight [*1994*].

10. Wicke, Haasis, Schafhausen, Schulz [*1992: 672*]; Vergabehandbuch des Landes Berlin VOL (Guideline of the city state of Berlin for public purchasing), Allgemeine Anweisung über die Beschaffung umweltfreundlicher Produkte und Materialien vom 10.03.87 (general directive on the purchasing of environment friendly products and materials).

11. See Elkington and Hailes [*1988*], Davis [*1991*], Charter [*1992*], Robins and Trisoglio [*1992*].

12. For an actual account of the difficult choices the green consumer is facing, see Knight [*1994*].

13. See OECD [*1991*], Jha, Vossenaar and Zarrilli [*1993*].

14. Umweltbundesamt (Federal Environmental Agency), RAL (German Institute for Quality Assurance and Certification), [*1992: 3 and 16*].

15. See Task Force Environment and the Internal Market [*1990*].

16. This chapter borrows from Scholz and Wiemann [*1993*] and from Wiemann *et al.* [*1994*].

17. See *Öko-Test Magazin* [*12/1990: 16–23*], and Vital [*4/1992: 40–43*].

18. See Aktionsgemeinschaft Solidarische Welt (ASW) [*1990: 15*].

19. See Cetinkaya and Schenek [*1986*], Pfitzenmaier [*1990*] and *Öko-Test Magazin* [*5/1992*].

20. *Öko-Test Magazin* [*5/1992*], *Öko-Test Magazin* [*4/1989*], Rosenkranz and Castellò [*1989*].

21. The MST is based on the product standards prescribed in Öko-Tex Standard 100 and developed by German and Austrian textile research institutes.

22. The members of this association, which was founded in 1992 at the suggestion of the Central Association of the German Textile Industry, are manufacturers and trade associations.

23. See *Federal Law Gazette* of 22 December 1989. A limit value of 1000 mg/kg applies in the EU; see Official Journal L 85 (9 April 1991).

24. Deutscher Bundestag [*1993: 225–270*] (subchapter on textiles and clothing).

25. This subchapter is based on the results obtained by a study group which stayed in India from February to April 1993 within the framework of the GDI postgraduate training programme. The working group carried out research on the adjustment of Indian leather, textile and refrigeration industry to new international eco-standards: Wiemann *et al.* [*1994*]. The Indian case can be applied to other developing countries provided the appropriate modifications are made.

26. World Bank [*1992*]. Recent calculations show that the costs of pollution abatement might not be as high as is sometimes said by those who regard the greening of industries as a luxury which only rich countries can afford. According to the World Bank, in 1989 the annual costs of pollution abatement in all manufacturing industries of the United States do not exceed 0.5 per cent of total value of output [*World Bank: Table 6.2, 128*].

27. The DAC (Development Assistance Committee of the OECD) Working Party on Development Assistance and Environment is debating the role of aid agencies in preventing negative implications of environmental measures in OECD countries on developing countries' exports and in promoting exports of green products.

REFERENCES

Aktionsgemeinschaft Solidarische Welt (ed.) (1990): *Es stinkt zum Himmel...*, Materialsammlung zur Lederindustrie, Berlin.

Anderson, K. and R. Blackhurst (eds.) (1992): *The Greening of World Trade Issues*, New York, London, Toronto.

Arden-Clarke, C. (1991): *The General Agreement on Tariffs and Trade, Environmental Protection and Sustainable Development*, WWF Discussion Paper, Geneva.

Arden-Clarke, C. (1994): *Green Protectionism*, WWF Discussion Paper, Geneva.

Cetinkaya and Schenek (1986): 'Untersuchung verschiedener Rohbaumwollen auf Organopestizidrückstände', in: Faserinstitut Bremen (ed.), *Jahresbericht*, 1986.

Charnovitz, S. (1991): 'Exploring the Environmental Exceptions', GATT Article XX, *Journal of World Trade*, Vol. 25, No. 5, 37–55.

Charter, M. (ed., 1992): *Greener Marketing. A Responsible Approach to Business*, Sheffield.

Daly, H. and R. Goodland (1994): 'An Ecological-Economic Assessment of Deregulation of International Commerce under GATT', *Ecological Economics*, Vol. 9, pp. 73–92.

Davis, J. (1991): *Greening Business. Managing for Sustainable Development*, Oxford.

Deutscher Bundestag (1993): 'Enquete-Kommission "Schutz des Menschen und der Umwelt", Verantwortung für die Zukunft-Wege zum nachhaltigen Umgang mit Stoff-und Materialströmen', Bonn.

Dohlman, E. (1990): 'The Trade Effects of Environmental Regulations', *OECD Observer*, No. 162, pp. 28–32.

Ekins, P., Folke, C., and R. Costanza (1994): 'Trade, Environment and Development: The Issues in Perspective', *Ecological Economics*, Vol. 9, pp. 1–12.

Elkington, J. and J. Hailes (1988): *The Green Consumer Guide: High Street Shopping for a Better Environment*, London.

Elkington, J., Knight, P. and J. Hailes (1992): *The Green Business Guide. How to Take Up – and Profit From – the Environmental Challenge*, London.

Federal Law Gazette (Bundesgesetzblatt) of 22 December 1989.

Fleckenstein, E. (1991): 'Chemie und Ökologie in der Textilindustrie – Vor welchen Herausforderungen steht die Textilveredlung?', in Forschungsinstitut Hohenstein (ed.), *Ökologie in der textilen Kette*, Bönnigheim.

Foy, G. (1992): 'Towards Extension of the GATT Standards Code to Production Processes', *Journal of World Trade*, 26, pp. 121–31.

French, H. F. (1993): *Costly Tradeoffs. Reconciling Trade and the Environment*, Worldwatch Paper No. 113, Washington, DC.

Gagelmann, M. (1991): 'Gesundheitsgefahren durch PCP: Kein Ende der Belastung', *Globus*, 10,11.

GATT (1992): *International Trade 90–91*, Geneva.

Grassl, T. (1992): 'Zwischen Industrie und Verbraucher – Wie reagiert der Handel auf die Umweltdiskussion?', in Forschungsinstitut Hohenstein (ed.), *Ökologie in der textilen Kette*, Bönnigheim.

Heimann, S. (1991): 'Textilhilfsmittel und Umweltschutz – eine Übersicht'. *Melliand Textilberichte* 7.

Hunter, D., Sommer, J. and S. Vaughan (1994): *Concepts and Principles of International Environmental Law: An Introduction*, UNEP Environment and Trade Series No. 2, Geneva.

Jha, V., Vossenaar, R. and S. Zarrilli (1993): *Ecolabelling and International Trade*,

Jürgen Wiemann

UNCTAD Discussion Papers, Geneva.

Knight, P. (1994): 'How Green is my Trolley', *Financial Times*, 20–21 Aug. 1994.

Low, P. (ed., 1992a): *International Trade and the Environment*, World Bank Discussion Papers No. 159, Washington, DC.

Low, P. (1992b): 'Mini-symposium: Trade and the Environment', *World Economy*, Vol. 15, No. 1.

Low, P. and R. Safadi (1992): 'Trade Policy and Pollution', in Low (ed.) [*1992a:* 29–52].

Low, P. and A. Yeats (1992): 'Do "Dirty" Industries Migrate?', in Low, (ed.) [*1992a*].

Lucas, R.B., Wheeler, D. and H. Hettige (1992): 'Economic Development, Environmental Regulation and the International Migration of Toxic Industrial Pollution: 1960–88', in Low (ed.) [*1992a*].

MARIA (1992): *Marktanalyse. 11.5.3, Umweltbewußtsein/Umweltfreundliche Produkte*, parts 1, 2, Verlag Gruner und Jahr (ed.), Hamburg.

Mecheels, J. (1992): 'Wie läßt sich Kleidung ökologisch bewerten?', in Forschungsinstitut Hohenstein (ed.), *Ökologie in der textilen Kette*, Bönnigheim.

OECD (1991): *Environmental Labelling in OECD Countries*, Paris.

OECD (1992): *Joint Report on Trade and Environment*, June 1991, Paris.

OECD/DAC (1994): *Trade, Environment and Development Co-operation* (DCD/DA/ ENV(94) 2.

Öko-Test Magazin, 12/1990, 5/1992.

Palmeter, D. (1993): 'Environment and Trade: Much Ado About Little?', *Journal of World Trade*, Vol. 27, No. 3.

Petersmann, E.-U. (1991): 'Trade Policy, Environmental Policy and the GATT. Why Trade Rules and Environmental Rules Should be Mutually Consistent', *Aussenwirtschaft*, Vol. 46.

Pfitzenmaier, G. (1990): 'Dieser Test geht unter die Haut', *Natur*, 9.

Porter, M. (1990): *The Competitive Advantage of Nations*, New York.

Postel, S. and C. Flavin (1991): 'Reshaping the Gobal Economy', in L.R. Brown (ed.), *State of the World. A Worldwatch Institute Report on Progress Toward a Sustainable Society*, New York and London.

Rege, V. (1994): 'GATT Law and Environment-Related Issues Affecting the Trade of Developing Countries', *Journal of World Trade*, Vol. 28, No. 3.

Repetto, R. (1994): *Trade and Sustainable Development*, UNEP Environment and Trades Series No. 1, Geneva.

Robins, N. and A. Trisoglio (1992): 'Restructuring Industry for Sustainable Development', in J. Holmberg (ed.), *Policies for a Small Planet*, London.

Rosenkranz, B. and E. Castello (1989): *Leitfaden für gesunde Textilien*. Kritische Warenkunde und Rechtsratgeber, Hamburg.

Schmidheiny, S. (1992): *Changing Course, Business Council for Sustainable Development*, Cambridge, MA and London.

Schneider, P. (1993): 'The Cotton Brief', *New York Times*, 20 June, Section 9, pp. 1–11.

Scholz, I. and J. Wiemann (1993): *Ecological Requirements to be Satisfied by Consumer Goods – A New Challenge for Developing Countries' Exports to Germany*, German Development Institute, Berlin.

Schuster, G. (1993): 'Gefährlicher Stoff. Gift in Kleidern', *Stern*, Vol. 46, No. 18, pp. 95–110.

Shrybman, S. (1990): 'International Trade and the Environment: An Environmental Assessment of the General Agreement on Tariffs and Trade', *Ecologist*, Vol. 20, No.

1, pp. 30–34.

Sorsa, P. (1992): 'GATT and Environment', *World Economy*, Vol. 15, pp. 115–33.

Stevens, C. (1994): 'The Greening of Trade', *OECD Observer*, No. 187, pp. 32–4.

Subramaniam, A. (1992): 'Trade Measures for Environment: A Nearly Empty Box?', *World Economy*, Vol. 15, pp. 135–52.

Task Force Environment and the Internal Market (1990): *'1992'. The Environmental Dimension*, Bonn.

Thomas, C. and G.A. Tereposky (1993): 'The Evolving Relationship Between Trade and Environmental Regulation', *Journal of World Trade*, Vol. 27, pp. 23–45.

Tolba, M.K. and O.A. El-Kholy (eds.) (1992): *The World Environment 1972–1992. Two Decades of Challenge*, London, Nairobi (UNEP).

Umweltbundesamt (Federal Environmental Agency or RAL) (1992): *The Environmental Label Introduces Itself*, Berlin.

UNEP/IEO (1990): *Environmental Auditing*, Paris.

UNEP/IEO (1991): *Tanneries and the Environment. A Technical Guide to Reducing the Environmental Impact of Tannery Operations*, Paris.

United Nations (1992): *Agenda 21: Programme of Action for Sustainable Development*, New York.

Vorholz, F. (1992): 'Redlich oder raffiniert?', *Die Zeit*, 21 Aug. 1992

Wicke, L., Haasis, H.D., Schafhausen, F. and W. Schulz (1992): *Betriebliche Umweltökonomie. Eine praxisorientierte Einführung*, München.

Wiemann, J. (1992): *Environmentally Oriented Trade Policy: A New Area of Conflict Between North and South?*, German Development Institute, Berlin.

Wiemann, J., Bünning, T. , Danne, G. , Hagenmaier, C. , Kölling, F., Siller, R. and A. Wender (1994): *Ecological Product Standards and Requirements as a New Challenge for Developing Countries' Industries and Exports*, German Development Institute, Berlin.

World Bank (1992): *World Development Report 1992: 'Development and the Environment'*, Oxford.

7

Multilateral Trade and Technical Standards: Theoretical Approaches to Harmonisation

MARIAROSA LUNATI

I. INTRODUCTION

During the 1970s, when the recourse to non-tariff barriers started to become a worrying phenomenon in international trade, the use of national standards and regulations as (potential) obstacles to trade was soon identified. Irrespective of the real aims of their introduction, ranging from environment and consumers' protection to information on product quality, national technical standards may become protective tools against imported products.

Following international negotiations in GATT on the way to suppress technical barriers, a multilaterai Standards Code was adopted in 1980. It was an attempt between governments to develop international rules for the establishment and operations of standards and conformity assessment activities. During the Uruguay Round the Standards Code has been put under review in order to identify its omissions and problems, in particular with regard to the developing countries.

Among the main problems discussed, for example, was the extension of the Standards Code to Processes and Production Methods (PPMs), that was finally approved. Before this extension the Code regulated national conduct in setting industrial and agricultural product standards, but not the establishment of process standards, leaving countries free to set the process rules they choose. On the contrary, the revised version of the Code allows in principle trade restrictions by countries adversely affected by low environmental regulations. The 'trade and environment' debate, linked to PPMs, has led the environmentalists, the economists, the developing as well as the developed countries to argue on this point [Foy, 1992; Charnovitz, 1993].

It is our opinion that the current debate concerning environmental regulations and, more generally, technical standards has taken place independently of the development of theoretical contributions on the effects of technical harmonisation. To be honest, theoretical studies on this subject are very few, at least those belonging to the international economics field. We argue, in the present study, that there is a need for a more detailed analysis of harmonisation of technical regulations and standards on the theoretical ground. In most contexts, when considering how to suppress technical barriers to trade, the proposed solution involves procedures of harmonisation of technical regulations [*CEC, 1988*]. The carried idea is simple: if differences in national technical regulations create barriers to trade, harmonisation of national regulations eliminates obstacles by introducing a unique harmonised standard. Although the reasoning is appealing, two main aspects are left unsolved. On one side, the way harmonisation is realised is not specified; different harmonisation procedures can actually end in different results. On the other side, and even more important, there is the implicit hypothesis that technical harmonisation would equally benefit all the participating countries, what is again just a simplification. If the effects of the suppression of technical barriers to trade are quite obvious, the effects of implementing harmonisation are less evident, and strongly depend on the chosen procedure.

The chapter investigates theoretically what are the expected consequences and problems of implementing technical harmonisation, separating the harmonisation process occurring between homogeneous countries from that involving non-homogeneous countries. In section II regional and international policy on standardisation[1] and technical harmonisation will be briefly presented. The third section goes through the actual *state of the art*, starting from the most general analysis to cover two recent specific contributes [*Hansson, 1990; Lutz 1993*]. Section III also proposes a non-conventional analytical framework modelling the harmonisation process, which allows for a wider interpretation of the phenomenon compared to the one sorted out by the two cited theoretical contributes. Each of the presented studies provides some helpful insights into the evaluation of the effects of technical harmonisation. Moreover, they are complementary rather than alternative explanations. Section IV will end the chapter with some concluding notes.

II. INTERNATIONAL AND REGIONAL POLICY ON STANDARDISATION AND TECHNICAL HARMONISATION: COMMON FEATURES AND SPECIFICITIES

To oppose the increasing importance in the use of national technical regulations as barriers to trade, in the late 1970s and early 1980s specific measures were defined, both at the international and regional levels. Even if the two levels share common aspects in the defined policies, one fundamental distinction must be pointed out. Harmonisation of national technical regulations and standards represents the relevant procedure as far as regional areas are concerned; in particular, this applies to the European Union (EU). When the international context is considered, dispositions on standards never refer to technical harmonisation, enhancing instead programmes of international standardisation on an extended basis.

What do international and regional technical policies look like? The main objective pursued by these policies is to ensure that technical regulations and standards, including packaging, marking and labelling requirements, and procedures for assessment of conformity with technical regulations and standards do not create unnecessary obstacles to international trade.

The already mentioned Standards Code of the GATT, signed in 1980, is meant to encourage the use of international stardards and conformity assessment systems as a method to avoid the raise of technical barriers due to national differences. The Agreement on Technical Barriers to Trade firstly recognises the right of each country to adopt the measures necessary to assure the quality of exports, or for the protection of human, animal and plant life or health, and for other relevant reasons. However, national measures should not be applied in a way that would constitute a means of arbitrary discrimination between other countries and a tool for restrictions on international trade. There must indeed be proportionality between adopted regulations and the risks that non-fulfilment of legitimate objectives would create.

The parties to the Agreement are thus invited to use existing international standards as a basis for their technical regulations whenever possible. In addition, parties are required to inform the GATT secretariat and all the other parties when preparing a new technical regulation that may have a significant effect on trade; they have to explain the justification for that regulation in terms of legitimate objectives and allow other parties to present their comments and objections.

For what concerns harmonisation of technical regulations is not at issue in the Standards Code. Countries are asked to participate in the preparation of international standards, to give a contribution to the formation of a set of common standards; there are, however, no obligations involving international harmonisation of technical regulations. Conversely, the EU's policy with respect to technical regulations and standards is based on the principle of harmonisation. This is not surprising, if one accepts the idea that it is easier to find consensus among a small group of similar countries than within a wide multilateral context of heteregeneous countries.

The EU policy keeps aspects of similarity with the Standards Code international provisions. First of all, information procedures on new standards national projects are explicitly previewed to anticipate the emergence of technical barriers. A distinctive character is the role attributed to technical harmonisation. With the exception of selected domains where mutual recognition of national regulations on products is accepted between member countries, the suppression of technical barriers to trade passes through a process of technical harmonisation. Harmonised standards are agreed upon by member countries, and the use of those standards, combined with the obtention of conformity certificates mutually recognised, assures access to the internal market. The definition of the harmonisation process has been quite complicated in the EU and required no less than ten years to arrive at its actual formulation. This contrasts sharply with the simple intuition that finding a common denominator in terms of standards between homogeneous countries is an 'innocent' procedure. Moreover, one has to recognise that in the path leading from suppression of trade barriers to trade liberalisation technical harmonisation is not just a neutral instrument but contains in itself elements of ambiguity. In the next section we will explore the issue in more detail.

III. THEORETICAL APPROACHES TO HARMONISATION: THE EXPECTED EFFECTS

From Suppression of Technical Barriers to Trade Liberalisation: Something Missing

Apart from the recognised property of allowing the exploitation of scale economies in international good markets [*Drèze*, 1960] described. Standards are indeed considered only as far as different national regulations and certifications procedures are concerned, because of a potential diminution of trade flows. Different standards may imply increased costs of import whether to adapt the product to foreign regulations or to submit it to new testing procedures, making trade between countries somehow less convenient, if not impossible.

In international economics technical barriers to trade are typically assimilated to other cost-increasing barriers [*CEC, 1988*]. In a traditional framework of perfectly competitive markets and comparative advantages in trade, suppression of technical obstacles is shown to cut fictitious costs and leads to an improved situation in which net global welfare is expected to raise. For what it concerns consumers' welfare, the gains are sure, as far as products are available at a reduced price and in augmented quantities. Following Smith and Venables [*1986*], if imperfect competition and scale economies are introduced in the framework, elimination of technical barriers fostering trade liberalisation is expected to produce even more beneficial effects.

It is easy to recognise that the above analysis is not really specific to the effects of technical barriers, but it applies in general to any cost-increasing barrier. The analysis focuses on the effects of the suppression of technical obstacles, while the way the suppression is technically realised is not considered. If we assume the method to be technical harmonisation, the above interpretation leads to treating harmonisation as a costless process, which is quite unrealistic. Leaving such an assumption allows for a more detailed analysis.

Modelling Technical Harmonisation

Technical harmonisation is explicitly modelled in two studies, by Hansson [*1990*] and Lutz [*1993*]. Starting from different perspectives, both present interesting results. Hansson analyses the general equilibrium effects of international harmonisation efforts with regard to technical standards. His model describes a small open economy with three sectors of production, manufacturing, agriculture and public sector; only the first two sectors produce tradable goods, while the government sector produces for domestic consumption. Two types of technical harmonisation are considered: total harmonisation, when all products within the category of products covered by regulations have to meet the agreed standards to be marketed in whatever countries; optional harmonisation, when national standards still exist in each national markets and harmonised standards are to be met only to export in the whole market. Hansson investigates whether technical harmonisation between two asymmetric groups of countries should be total or optional and what should be chosen as the internationally agreed standards. One group is called 'rich' and the other 'poor'. Effects on global welfare are evaluated firstly; effects on prices and quantities are also considered, to see how various groups in the society will be affected by technical standards harmonisation.

From the analysis Hansson concludes that minimum standards harmonisation is welfare superior to the other types of standards harmonisation, for it is the method that permits liberalising trade without excluding the group of poorer countries from production and/or export. This conclusion, however, does not coincide with the public choice conclusion: optional maximum harmonisation is indeed more likely to be agreed on, even if it is shown to be welfare inferior. It is crucial, in drawing the above results, to note the role Hansson recognises of political pressure in the success of negotiations on standardisation. Optional maximum harmonisation is indeed the procedure that collects the most support by 'powerful' groups of interest, where 'powerful' stays for producers and workers in the richer set of countries.

It is also crucial to note the hypothesis Hansson draws on asymmetry in commercial partners' economic development. The results he obtains depend strictly on the assumed asymmetry between the two groups of countries, and the analysis is only significant when applied in such a context. The same asymmetry is considered by Lutz [*1993*], who studies the simultaneous determination of minimum standards quality by governments of two regions, a peripheric and poorer region with a core and richer region. In a partial equilibrium model of vertically differentiated products Lutz analyses the effects on global welfare determined by alternative harmonisation procedures.

Under specific assumptions on costs structure[2] and consumers' preferences (or consumers' income levels), a conventional results of vertically differentiated products models is that the introduction of (compulsory) minimum quality standards produces exit from market of some of the firms and some of the acquirers. In the context modelled by Lutz, the poorer region or the richer countries alternatively ends up with losses depending on the chosen harmonisation procedure.

As for Hansson's analysis, the model by Lutz is a good explanation of what can happen when heterogeneous countries decide to implement a technical harmonisation policy. However, none of them helps in understanding why harmonisation also creates contrasts when pursued by countries with homogeneous characteristics.

The Costs of Changing Standards: A Simple Analytical Framework

We present in this section a simple analytical framework to evaluate the effects of technical harmonisation when firms are supposed to be asymmetric with regard to market power. The relevant argument is again the fact that the way harmonisation of technical regulations is implemented may widely affect the distribution of gains and losses among the participating countries, and within countries among firms. Different from the attributes considered above, the analysis also applies to similar commercial partners not specific to contexts with asymmetric development.

The framework we consider is modelled on Rothschild's [1986] interpretation of the model of d'Aspremont et al. [1983]. After an essential presentation of the model, we look at the effects of a costly harmonisation of national technical regulations. Harmonisation is meant to improve product quality and safety, and is implemented by introducing new regulations that all firms wishing to participate in international trade have to satisfy, independently of their country of origin.

We consider one industry which comprises n firms, each producing a variety of a given differentiated product. All firms in the market are subject to identical cost conditions. The cost function for each firm is $C(q) = F + g(q)$. Marginal costs are $mc = g'(q) > 0$, with $g''(q) = m > 0$; and average costs: $AC = (F + g(q))/q$. The industry inverse demand function is $p = A - bQ$, with $A, b > 0$. $Q(p)$ is the total output of the n firms at price p. In order to make the analysis as simpler as possible, strong assumptions on consumers' demand in the tradition of Dixit and Stiglitz [1977] are introduced. All consumers are supposed to have identical tastes and incomes. At any given price each consumer buys some of every variety of the differentiated product in proportion to its share in total sales. This means that a change in the quantity supplied of any variety results in an equiproportional change in the demand for all other varieties.

All the n firms in the industry are initially price-takers, and each obtains $1/n$ of the total market, q_o, at the competitive price p_o. One firm is now supposed to emerge and become the dominant firm. The move of breaking away from the group is profit-increasing for the emerging firm if $p_d q_d - c(q_d) > p_0 - C(q_0)$, which means that the profits the firm can obtain as a dominant firm are strictly larger than the profits obtained as one of the n price taker firms [*d'Aspremont et al., 1983*]. By substituting: $p_d = \Delta p + p_o$ and $q_d = q_o - \Delta q$, the necessary condition for the emergence of a dominant firm is $p_o < \Delta p(q_o/\Delta q - 1)$ + mc which is satisfied for the initial configuration of price and quantity, where $p_o = $ mc [*Rothschild, 1986*]. Figure 1 shows the emergence of a dominant firm.

FIGURE I

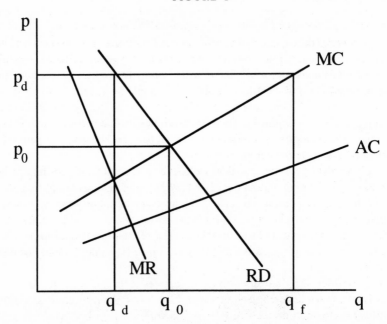

The firm that emerges as dominant faces a fringe made up of the (n-1) remaining firms, which act as price takers. The fringe determines a combined output $(n-1)S(p)$ by equating market price with the identical marginal costs. The dominant firm's demand curve is determined by subtracting the combined output of the fringe from market demand at all prices: $q_d(p) = Q(p) - (n-1)S(p)$. This curve is usually called the residual demand curve. The emerging firm, finally, equates marginal costs to the marginal revenues of the residual demand. Each firm in the fringe obtains larger profits than the dominant firm [*d'Aspremont et al., 1983*].

Up to now, no distinctions have been made between the firms' country of origin. We assume that each firm belongs to a different country, and we concentrate on the domestic market of the dominant firm. As a simplification we suppose that the dominant firm does not export, and we also do not take into account the markets which foreign firms may have in their own countries.

We suppose now that a process of technical harmonisation is agreed upon between the n countries, even if, in the initial equilibrium, differences of national regulations do not represent barriers to trade. The governments' decisions look at the improvement of product quality and at better protecting consumers' safety. New technical requirements are introduced for selling in the market under consideration (and also in other foreign countries' markets). The new regulations are supposed to raise production costs. In particular, marginal costs are supposed to raise, because of the necessity to redesign some of, or all, the products. Two distinct cases are analysed.

(a) We first suppose that the new regulations raise the costs of all the firms in the market in exactly the same way, the domestic firm as well as the foreign ones. In Figure 2 the effects of the introduction of the harmonised regulations are represented.

FIGURE 2

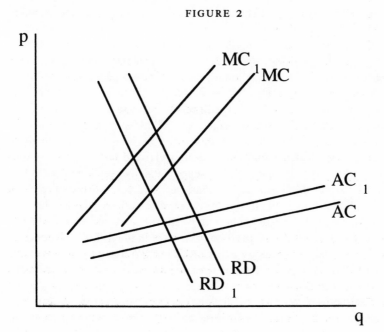

The marginal costs curve of a fringe firm has a leftward shift till MCl: at any given market price the output of each fringe firm is now reduced. As a total effect, there is a correspondent rightward shift of the residual demand curve of the dominant firm. The computation of the new residual demand takes into account the total output reduction of the fringe firms, which is given by (Δmcl/m)(n-l), the output reduction of each fringe firm multiplied by the number of firms in the fringe. If, at the original output of the dominant firm (q_d), the market price increases more than the increase in average costs, then the effect of the harmonised regulations is to increase the profits of the dominant firm. This amounts to requiring that $p_d\Delta p > \Delta AC$ [*Salop and Scheffman, 1983*]. It has to be noted that because of the negative slope of the market demand curve, it will be that $\Delta mc > \Delta p$. Combining $\Delta p > \Delta AC$ and $\Delta p < \Delta mc$ implies that $\Delta AC < \Delta mc$, which means that $\Delta F/q < 0$, that is, the increase in average fixed costs is negative. Thus for the dominant firm to have still positive profits after the governments' trade agreement, technical harmonisation is supposed to reduce average fixed costs while increasing variable costs.

In the considered case of identical initial cost conditions and identical costs consequences after harmonisation is implemented, if the condition $\Delta p > \Delta AC$ is verified for the dominant, it will also be for the fringe firms. Thus all the firms in the market enjoy higher profits as a consequence of the technical harmonisation agreement.

(b) Suppose now that the harmonised regulations affect firms' costs in different ways. In particular, assume firms are divided into two groups. For the dominant firm and for k among the n-l firms of the fringe the marginal costs of modifying the product are MC1, with a shift of total average costs up to AC1. For the remaining n-1-k fringe firms the increase in marginal costs is also MC1, but the rise in total average costs AC2 is quite large, because the increase of average fixed costs for this group of firms is supposed to be positive. The residual demand curve shifts rightward and a higher market price is fixed by the dominant firm. We suppose that the condition $\Delta p > \Delta AC1$ is verified for the dominant, at the initial q_d, and for k firms of the first group, while the remaining fringe firms are now suffering losses, because $\Delta AC2 > \Delta p$. Depending on the impact on production costs the firms in the two groups will end in a different position. The firms in group 2 will indeed exit the market, as it has been supposed that $\Delta AC2 > \Delta p$. A new equilibrium exists, in which a reduced number of firms is sharing the total output and, probably, some firms forego the entry.

If the harmonised technical regulations imply expensive new investments, for example, for certification activities, the adaptation to the new standards will be too costly and some firms will exit the market. Therefore, too, the effects among the fringe firms are no more equal, and harmonisation creates asymmetric benefits. Under what conditions will technical harmonisation be implemented? Conditions for a successful implementation of the harmonisation policy can be derived exactly;[3] the idea is that governments and firms can compute in advance if the increase in price following the increase in marginal costs is sufficient to assure higher profits to domestic producers. The implementation is considered successful when the firms of the countries fostering the harmonisation result as winners because they stay in the market and obtain higher profits.

We finally summarise the implications of a cost-increasing harmonisation with the following observations. When the harmonisation equally affects all firms by raising marginal costs to the same extent, each firm will enjoy higher profits, even if the dominant firm and the fringe benefit unequally from positive effects. In particular, the firm (or firms) enjoying a dominant position will gain market share at the expense of other firms: the higher the market power, the easier it is for firms to cover increases in costs due to costly harmonisation agreements, reflecting the effects of the well-known rising costs strategy of rivals [*Salop and Sheffman, 1983*]. Thus, in a situation of asymmetric market power, some firms will profit more than others from a technical harmonisation process that raises costs even if the cost conditions are identical.

If, starting from a situation of identical cost conditions, the harmonisation modifies the costs of each firm in a different way, then a multiplicity of equilibrium solutions are possible. When increases in costs are sufficiently high, one or more firms will exit the market, while the remaining will expand output. Governments can compute exactly the effects in their own country before supporting a costly harmonisation process. Countries with a higher degree of asymmetry in domestic firms' behaviour are expected to gain more from the costly harmonisation policy.

In addition to that, *each country is interested in promoting harmonised standards technical regulations which guarantee moderate increases in average costs, according to the available technology*. The amount of adjustment costs is not related to economic development degree, but depends on the distance between the adopted harmonised standards and the existing ones: changing standards is costly because of the existence of an installed base specific to each standard [*Farrel and Saloner, 1985; David, 1987*]. Adjustment costs are a crucial feature in understanding technical harmonisation, as it permits explaining a wide typology of situations, including reaching both an agreement between non-homogeneous countries and between similar countries.

So far, we have considered producers' gains and losses, independently of consumers' welfare. In the domestic market under consideration, total output decreases and price rises: the consumers' welfare is then negatively affected. Nevertheless, when considering the improved quality and safety of products due to the harmonised standards, it is possible that consumers are even more satisfied than before. Moreover, as far as variety is concerned, in the hypothesis of symmetric impact on firms' costs all the varieties are still sold in the market once the new regulations have been introduced.[4]

A final remark is needed about the chosen framework, that was meant to reflect two types of asymmetry: asymmetry between dominant and fringe firms, and asymmetry between 'ex-post' non-identical cost conditions firms. Furthermore, we have supposed that only one firm emerges as dominant; the results can be adapted to the case where k among the n identical firms form a cartel.

IV. CONCLUSIONS

At the beginning of the chapter we argued that when issues on technical barriers to trade are discussed, no special attention is devoted to theoretical contributions evaluating the effects of technical harmonisation. It was also recognised that these contributes are very few at present. In addition to that, the common knowledge on technical barriers is that they act exactly as cost-increasing obstacles to trade [*CEC, 1988*], what is, in fact, a partial truth.

We presented different theoretical approaches to technical harmonisation, starting with a generic analysis describing the effects of the suppression of technical barriers to trade. Models that strongly relay the hypothesis of asymmetric countries can only explain part of the problem, namely, the problems arising between developed and developing countries in the matter of technical regulations and standards. The results reflect the intuition that it is difficult to reach consensus on technical standards when a group of countries is probably not able to afford the major costs of adjustment, due to their technological disadvantage. To analyse and explain technical harmonisation between homogeneous countries one has to take into account a wider interpretation of the adjustment costs, recognising that these costs may arise independently of asymmetries in economic development.

NOTES

1. With standardisation is meant both the action of bringing things to an unique standard and the process by which standards are set up, through both legislative mandate (*technical regulations*) and voluntary agreement (*standards*). Certification is the act of controlling a given product accomplishes the required technical regulations.
2. Costs of increased quality fall on fixed costs but not on variable costs; see Shaked and Sutton [*1983; 1984*].
3. The conditions involve the slope m of marginal costs, the increases in marginal costs and in average costs, respectively Δmc and ΔAC, and the residual demand

curve; complete analytical proofs are given in Rothschild [*1986*].

4. Rothschild [*1986*] suggests considering other interesting features, for instance, how the degree of products substitutability and the number of competitors in the market affect the results.

REFERENCES

Baldwin, R.E. (1991): 'Measuring the Effects of Nontariff Trade-Distorting Policies', in J. de Melo and A. Sapir (a cura di) *Trade Theory and Economic Reform. Essays in honor of Bela Balassa*, Cambridge, MA.

CEC (1988): 'L'economia del 1992. Una valutazione degli effetti economici potenziali del completamento del mercato interno della Comunità europea', *Economia europea*, 35.

Charnovitz, S. (1993): 'Environmentalism Confronts GATT Rules', *Journal of World Trade*, Vol. 27.

d'Aspremont, C., Jacquemin, A., Gabszewicz, J.J. and J.A.Weymark (1983): 'On the Stability of Collusive Price Leadership', *Canadian Journal of Economics*, 16.

David, P.A. (1987): 'Some New Standards for the Economics of Standardization in the Information Age', in P. Dasgupta and P. Stoneman (eds, 1987) *Economic Policy and Technological Performance*, Cambridge: Cambridge University Press.

Dixit, A.K. and J.E. Stiglitz (1977): 'Monopolistic Competition and Optimum Product Diversity', *American Economic Review*, 67.

Drèze, J. (1960): 'Quelques réflexions sereines sur l'adaptation de l'industrie belge au Marché Commun', *Comptes Rendus des Travaux de la Société Royale d'Economie Politique de la Belgique*, 275, Décembre.

Farrell, J. and G. Saloner (1985b): 'Economic Issues on Standardization', Working Paper No.393, Department of Economics, Massachusetts Institute of Technology.

Foy, G. (1992): 'Toward Extention of the GATT Standards Code to Production Processes', *Journal of World Trade*, Vol. 26, No. 6.

Gabel, H.L. (ed., 1987): *Product Standardization and Competitive Strategy*, Amsterdam, Elsevier Science Publishers.

Gabszewicz, J.J. and J.F. Thisse (1979): 'Price Competition, Quality, and Income Disparities', *Journal of Economic Theory*, 20.

Gabszewicz, J.J., Shaked, A., Sutton, J. and J.F. Thisse (1981): 'International Trade in Differentiated Products', *International Economic Review*, 22.

Hansson, G. (1990): *Harmonization and International Trade*, London: Routledge.

Low, P. (ed., 1992): *International Trade and the Environment*, World Bank Discussion Papers, No. 159.

Lutz, S. (1993): 'Minimum Quality Standards and International Trade Policy', EADI, VIIth General Conference, Berlin, 15–18 September.

Nogues, J.J., Olechowski, A. and L.A.Winters (1986): 'The Extent of Non-Tariff Barriers to Industrial Countries' Imports', *World Bank Economic Review*, 1.

Rothschild, R. (1984): 'Market Price and the Stability of Cartels', *Economics Letters*, 15.

Rothschild, R. (1986): 'Raising Rivals' Costs: Regulation as a Competitive Strategy in Intra-Industry Trade', in D. Greenaway and P.K.M. Tharakan (eds.), (1986): *Imperfect Competition in International Trade*, Amsterdam: North Holland.

Salop, S. and D. Scheffman (1983): 'Raising Rivals' Costs', *American Economic*

Review, 73(2).

Shaked, A. and J. Sutton (1983): 'Natural Oligopolies', *Econometrica*, Vol. 51, 5, September.

Shaked, A. and J. Sutton (1984): 'Natural Oligopolies and International Trade', in H. Kierzkowski (ed.) (1984) *Monopolistic Competition and International Trade*, Oxford, Clarendon Press.

Smith, A. and A.J. Venables (1986): 'Trade and Industrial Policy under Imperfect Competition', *Economic Policy*, October.

Agreement on Technical Barriers to Trade, *Dunkel Text*, DFA (1991).

The Final Act of the Uruguay Round: A Summary, *GATT Focus*, No. 104, December 1993.

8

GATT and the Theory of Intellectual Property

SANDRO SIDERI

I. INTRODUCTION

Technology, or more specifically, the ability to utilise effectively new technologies and absorb them into the productive process, is increasingly crucial in determining comparative advantages, creating competitiveness, and promoting economic growth and development. Although most basic research, as well as a good deal of agricultural research, is freely available to developing countries, industrial technology must be acquired by hiring or by stealing from firms that have developed it. The price for this acquisition depends on the nature of the legal system protecting technology in the originating countries, and on the bargaining position of the parties concerned [*Stewart, 1990: 303*].

The chapter's second section defines intellectual property rights (IPR), and the third considers the new role of the GATT in fostering their protection. The fourth section reviews the theoretical basis for IPRs and their protection; in the fifth section the main conclusions are presented.

II. INTELLECTUAL PROPERTY AND THE NEED TO PROTECT IT

'The most important characteristic' of knowledge is the possibility of being possessed and enjoyed jointly – even simultaneously – by different individuals, a characteristic referred to as 'nonrival possession' [*Romer, 1990*] or 'perfect expansibility'. Yet the production and distribution of additions to the stocks of scientific and technological information – technology being knowledge employed in the production of goods and services for the satisfaction of human needs – absorbs resources. This implies the existence of some institutional arrangements for their allocation. One such arrangement is the construction of IPRs and the mechanisms for the protection of what amounts to a private monopoly that enables inventors 'to collect (differential) fees for the use of their work by others' [*David, 1993a: 219; 226*].

IPRs include industrial property and copyrights and neighbouring rights.[1] Industrial property deals principally with patents for inventions, trademarks and geographical indications for identifying names or symbols, industrial designs for designs and shapes (of which the topography or layout of semi-conductor chip products, also called integrated circuits, are the most notorious),[2] plant breeders' rights to new plant varieties, and trade secrets[3] for proprietary information. While 'patents cover ideas to the extent that the ideas can be embodied into tangible forms ... primarily to mass-produced articles of commerce', copyrights, and most of the other IPRs, are utilised for literary and artistic creations, 'not ideas as such, but only particular expression of ideas in a particular tangible written form' [*Stern, 1987: 198; 200*].

More recently, attempts have been made also to bring under copyright coverage some articles of commerce, such as computer software, while the misappropriation of commercial values, such as trade secrets and slavish copying, is protected also by the legislation relative to so-called 'unfair competition', which may also be covered under industrial property. Lately a re-evaluation of basic copyright policies has taken on greater urgency because (a) 'improved technologies for duplicating copyrighted media have lowered the costs of infringement'; and (b) 'the emergence of new products and technologies in computer programs, semiconductor devices, and electronic transmission of data and broadcast signals has blurred the basic distinction between patentability and eligibility for copyright' [*Maskus, 1993: 175*].

Both the substantive content of IPRs and their enforcement influence the conditions of trade, hence, most intellectual property (IP) issues are bound to be 'trade related'. In fact, inadequate IP protection is thought to cause three types of trade-related problems: (a) loss of export and foreign sales, royalties and value of investments of innovating firms in the markets where their IPRs are appropriated without compensation; plus losses of sales by the same firms; (b) unauthorised products sold in third markets; and (c) imports involving unauthorised use of goods, works or processes covered by domestic IP laws in the home market [*Weiss, 1990: 89*].

If these problems are treated as a trade, rather than IP, violation, 'the enforcement mechanisms of the GATT, rather than the apparently ineffectual ones of local courts could be used' [*Page et al., 1991: 47*]. Furthermore, differential national treatments of IPRs as, for instance, copyright infringement,[4] may effectively constitute non-tariff barriers (NTB) to knowledge-intensive products [*Braga, 1989: 244*].

III. GATT'S ROLE

All the above considerations have been used to justify the role of GATT in IP matters, a role that should not necessarily exclude other institutions that have already been dealing with some of them. Besides, one of the main instruments used to transfer technology internationally and to force some harmonisation of IP protection has been foreign direct investment (FDI). Since firms increasingly engage in FDI to protect their IPRs through the internalisation of the market, this has also increased the awareness of differences in regulatory regimes across countries and the need to harmonise them. Hence, the linkage between the so-called Trade Related Intellectual Property Measures (TRIPs)[5] and the Trade Related Investment Measures (TRIMs) – both issues to be included on the agenda of GATT's Uruguay Round for the first time.

It must be stressed that (a) 'the ongoing debates about proposals for global harmonisation of intellectual property protection are in large measure about the desirability of achieving such uniformity at a strong, rather than a weak standard of property rights enforcement' [*David, 1993: 3*]; (b) the establishment of minimum standards for IP protection is a rather complex task and even GATT has not been 'a standard-setting institution', having 'relied instead on national treatment and the MFN principle', when it is clear that 'national treatment achieves nothing in the absence of standards' [*Benko, 1988: 223*], that is, without the specification of minimum conditions against which a firm's or country's behaviour can be measured; and (c) achieving such a harmonisation at world-wide level implies resolving eventual conflicts with regional schemes of IP protection, as well as co-operating with already existing international institutions responsible in this area.

The drive toward harmonisation of stronger standards of IP protection derives both from the ongoing process of globalisation and the direction taken by technological innovation. The attempt to replace the principle of national treatment, meant to promote domestic industry by the importation of technology, with an internationally mandated protection of IPRs, reflects the interests of Developed Countries' (DCs) own national industries to secure the world-wide exploitation of their innovations.[6]

The diffusion and assimilation of new technologies are affecting strongly the patterns of competition, growth and trade shaping the world economy, since (a) the role of knowledge as a productive input has sharply risen; (b) imitation has become relatively easier and more widespread as the number and competence of potential imitators increases; and (c) product cycles have become shorter, with firms coming to consider it important to search for new ways of protecting their IP, including resorting to so-called alliances to share technology [*Mody, 1990: 212*][7].

The area of conflict concerns mostly situations characterised by 'high copiability' that 'can almost tautologically be defined as the lack of need for technology transfer' when, however, 'the co-operation of the creator is unnecessary in developing the product as indigenous producers can imitate it cheaply' [*Subramanian, 1990: 517*]. Not only have technologies for duplicating become more advanced, and the reproduction of IP made easier and cheaper, but a product of the new technologies, such as a computer programme or an integrated circuit design, or even a biogenetically altered organism,[8] tends to *'bear its know-how on its face*, a condition that renders it as vulnerable to rapid appropriation by second comers as any published literary or artistic work' [*Reichman, 1989: 136–7*].

It must be emphasised, however, that 'the failure of the (international) patent system to provide effective protection for inventions and innovations in electronics', as well as in other areas most affected by the new technologies, has also caused their more rapid imitation and diffusion both nationally and internationally [*Soete, 1985: 417*].

Since most of today's more valuable innovations 'flow from incremental improvements in applied industrial know-how', they also remain embodied in products that are widely distributed all over the world [*Reichman, 1989: 136*]. The difficulty of maintaining secret both this know-how and the new technologies, and the ease with which they may be appropriated by those who have not shared in the enormous investment in R&D, is demonstrated by estimates for the mid-1980s showing that counterfeit products made up more than six per cent of total world trade [*Slaughter, 1990: 418*].

The loss of competitiveness experienced by several DCs – that is, the shift in comparative advantage in a wide range of manufactures, including not just low-tech products but also high-tech sectors such as consumer electronics and semi-conductors – has convinced them that inadequate or inefficient protection of IP is depriving them of a competitive advantage in the high technology sectors [*Kostecki, 1991: 271*]. Besides, the stiffer international competition tends to reduce profit margins, hence making 'illegal copying of technologies a more serious problem than it was before when there was little interest in Third World markets and when copying companies were less export oriented' [*Wijk and Junne, 1992: 95*], while the growth of trade deficits in the US and other DCs has made such a practice less acceptable by innovating countries [*Hartridge and Subramanian, 1989: 895–6*].[9] As DCs are losing their comparative advantage in some traditional sectors, they are shifting resources into activities which present greater comparative advantages, namely those that are creativity-, research-, and knowledge-intensive, all of them IP-intensive. Thus there is the need for stricter IP protection and the temptation to use trade policy as a tool to deal with a range of issues, such as those related to IP protection, beyond the traditional scope of trade negotiations.

The effectiveness of trade leverage, that is, conditioning trade concessions on the provision of IP protection without being accused of unilateralism and becoming exposed to retaliation is, however, 'in fact quite limited if its use cannot somehow be justified under GATT rules'. Yet, GATT contains only limited references to IPRs [*Gadbaw, 1989: 230*], addressing only states, with the result that private citizens are not entitled directly to invoke rights or obligations by referring to GATT rules. This contrasts with the main IP conventions that are largely self-executing, that is, they contain either formulations appropriate for becoming national law or such language that has been transferred into domestically applicable national law, thus allowing individual claimants also to invoke the conventions' rules [*Fikentscher, 1989: 109–10*]. A GATT–IP system does therefore place private IPRs 'at the hand of national economic policy makers' with the likely result that the exploitation of IP 'will have to follow the imperatives of the policy they make'. Moreover, by subjecting standards of national IP protection to a negotiating process, it relies on 'a quid pro quo mechanism whereby private intellectual property rights are traded against commercial advantages' [*Ullrich, 1989: 136–7; 139*].

The differences present in the various national systems for IP protection have caused bitter disputes [*Beath, 1990: 424*] because interdependence and international integration requires the improvement of technical compatibilities. Hence the call for international standardisation, that is, an essentially voluntary method of achieving compliance with a prescribed set of specifications that, by virtue of various interests, including consumer pressure, will assume the characteristics of an international public good [*Kindleberger, 1986*]. The process is characterised by the emergence of a circular relationship in which globalisation pushes for uniformity that in turn will enhance globalisation. Meanwhile, technology is rapidly eroding the basic notion of national sovereignty in many areas of economic affairs.

Furthermore, because the number of 'routes' available for obtaining the same product has increased, causing the so-called 'pharmaceutical syndrome', and because firms do not really know what is easily copiable and what is not, different productive sectors find themselves allied in requesting more IP protection. Moreover, the rapid rate of technological innovation has also affected international competitiveness and has rendered more markets important. The resulting need to extend IP protection is in contrast with an earlier tendency towards a steadily declining role of patents [*McCulloch, 1981: 117*] (and, for a different view [*Mansfield, 1986: 178–9*]).

Finally, it must also be remembered that the drive towards harmonisation was already implicit in the Third World's attempt to establish the New International Economic Order during the 1970s, and particularly in the proposal for a 'Code of Conduct on the Transfer of Technology'. Although the UNCTAD Code was based on the principle of preferential treatment for developing countries, having pressed earlier for an international regulation of the technology issue has made it the more difficult to resist the prospective introduction of TRIPs into the Uruguay Round and the harmonisation that the DCs demand.

The issue of infringement of IP rules does not concern only the straightforward matter of piracy[10] and theft, but also the more relevant 'patent protection of technological inputs critical for industrialisation, food security (for example, fertilisers) or health of poor populations which have to pay more for patent-protected goods'. While developing countries have shown from the beginning a willingness to negotiate a multilateral framework of rules on the counterfeit trade, they have objected to embarking on difficult discussions 'on the nature of intellectual property protection itself ...' and 'to get involved in any attempt to improve standards of protection' [*Kostecki, 1991: 271–2*]. Instead, from the outset the DCs in the TRIPs negotiations have pushed beyond the issue of counterfeiting in the pursuit of a comprehensive, global GATT agreement on all internationally important aspects of IP protection, including basic principles, substantive standards of protected rights, and rules on national enforcement [*Reinbothe and Howard, 1991: 158*].

Clearly, however, the introduction of TRIPs into the GATT system and the harmonisation of IP protection may amount to 'setting the multilateral framework for the conditions of international competition into the next century' [*Subramanian, 1990: 509–10*]. The resulting changes will affect most business practices since the main aims of this multilateral framework are (a) 'to alter significantly the balance of negotiating power in favour of the transnational enterprises compared to that of the governments of host countries, both developed and developing'; and (b) 'to limit the economic sphere for government' [*Vaitsos, 1990: 82*], namely, its ability to intervene and regulate two crucial and highly interlinked sectors such as FDI and technology transfer. There is the need to change following from 'the inescapable conclusion ... that technology requires that many traditionally national policies be rethought' and that 'in some cases, strictly national rules lose much of their meaning', while 'in others, at least the thrust of the rules requires change' [*Blumenthal, 1988: 540*].

IV. THE THEORY OF INTELLECTUAL PROPERTY

Present resources are needed to create technology which will then generate a stream of future benefits. Once created, the use of technology by others will not preclude that an innovator will continue to use it, but it will definitely reduce the latter's private returns (see Magee's 'appropriability theory' below).

If, then, the main difficulty in dealing with IP protection derives from 'the dual role of knowledge as a private good in production and a public good in consumption', it also follows that the patent system represents 'an unsatisfactory compromise' [*Johnson, 1976: 420–21*].[11]

The fact that behind the whole patent system there is the 'lack of theoretical principle' [*Plant, 1934: 51*] and of 'logic ... so that it survives only because there seems to be nothing better' [*Jewkes, 1958: 252–3*] has been recognised before. Hence the protection offered by the patent system rests on 'a basic economic inconsistency', that is 'not only to tolerate but to encourage individual limited islands of monopoly' within free-enterprise economies [*Machlup, 1958: iii*]. A recent survey of the topic concludes that 'the theory of intellectual property protection is fragmented and provides no robust answer to the question of the appropriate or optimal level of protection under various sets of real-world circumstances. In particular, its relevance to developing country concerns must be considered marginal' [*Braga, 1990: 32*].

Therefore, any IP system is no more than a rationalisation for government intervention in a situation of market failure [*Arrow, 1962: 164–5*]. This is due to the fact that from the supply side technology presents the hallmark of public good and, moreover, a durable and 'strong' one due to its economies of scale [*Kindleberger, 1983: 377*]. It is this very nature that causes the public or social return on innovation to be greater than the private return, hence, the tendency for private investment to remain short of the socially optimal amount needed for science and technology generation.[12]

Given that the main properties of a public good are non-rival possession, low marginal cost of reproduction, and substantial fixed costs[13] of original production, perfect market conditions fail properly to allocate resources to its production, since they create no financial incentive for innovation except for cost-reducing inventions, although once an innovation is developed it would be almost freely available. The 'appropriability problem' of Arrow is due to the intangible nature of the good that makes its benefits not necessarily and perfectly appropriable.[14] This incomplete appropriability, that is, divergence between the marginal social product of each input used and its market compensation, is a relevant feature of knowledge. Treating it 'as a nonrival good makes it possible to talk sensibly about knowledge spillovers, that is, incomplete excludability' [*Romer, 1990: S96 and S75*].[15] An eventual successful appropriation, on the other hand, causes an underutilisation of the investment in research, so that there is a tendency to underinvest in Research and Development (R&D) both under competition and monopoly [*Arrow, 1962: 175 and 172; Nelson, 1959: 161–2; Dasgupta and Stiglitz, 1980: 267*]. In other words, the larger the gap between the social and the private rates of return from innovative activities, the more likely that underinvestment will mar these activities.

Since it is 'most unlikely that the market mechanism can be relied upon to produce knowledge in appropriate amounts' [*Dasgupta and Stoneman, 1987: 1*], the creation of a private monopoly is one of three alternative ways for coping with this market failure, the other two being either a subsidy or public involvement in R&D both to be financed by means of general taxation. Yet, none of these three alternatives, for short also called 'property', 'patronage' and 'procurement',[16] 'provides a complete and perfect solution to the problem that they all address' [*David, 1993a, 226–27; Nordhaus, 1969: 88–90*].

By 'internalizing the external economies of knowledge ... the patent system increases incentives for invention ... but ... only at the expense of higher prices, lower output, and the inefficiencies usually associated with monopoly' [*Nordhaus, 1969: 88–9*]. The other main limitation of the property solution is that it undoubtedly reduces availability of knowledge, since the temporary monopoly granted by the patent law[17] is but a compromise between the need to provide incentives to firms for promoting invention and innovation, and the desire to diffuse the benefits of technological progress among the consumers, benefits that 'are increased if competitors can imitate and improve on the innovation to ensure its availability on favorable terms' [*Levin et al., 1987: 783*]. In fact, the more protected the IP, the more the fee for its use can be raised. Therefore, this fee, that is, the price of the industrial technology one wishes to buy, 'is dependent on the nature of the legal system protecting technology in the originating countries, the monopoly or oligopoly position of the technology sellers, and the bargaining position of the technology buyers' [*Stewart, 1990: 303*].

Apart from the problem of resources wasted in parallel efforts and 'research races' in order to be the first to obtain the patent – although in the latter case 'pressure of competition will ensure that only a few firms engage in R&D activity; in extreme cases at most one firm' [*Dasgupta and Stiglitz, 1980: 289*][18] – R&D may also concentrate on research fields assumed to yield higher profits, while leaving under-researched other areas that, from the societal point of view, are more important. Naturally, whatever society's viewpoint is taken is also relevant to establish whether or not the allocation of resources under the IPRs' regime is efficient or not.

It has also been argued that the only way to ensure that firms undertake every research project that is efficient is to let the firms collect as profit all the social value they create. In this way 'households still benefit, but in their capacity as shareholders rather than as consumers' [*Scotchmer, 1991: 31*]. The problem then arises at the international level because shareholders may belong to one country and consumers to another. Since IP protection leads to the transfer of income from consumers in the protected markets to the inventors or producers, mostly in the DCs, harmonisation tends to cause a redistribution of welfare away from Third World countries and in favour of the most industrialised ones. At any rate, 'if protection of intellectual property does indeed enhance *global* efficiency, then the North ought to be willing and able to compensate the South for any losses that it would incur in the course of providing such protection' [*Chin and Grossman, 1990: 106*].

To the extra profits accruing to patent owners, often foreigners, one must add other effects to fully assess the impact of increased IP protection. The most important of these effects and, also, the most dynamic ones, consists in strengthening (a) the patent owners' technological accumulation that these extra profits may serve to finance; and (b) the incentives for increased R&D

and innovation, although this latter effect is neither widely accepted[19] nor does it imply in any way that the resulting innovations will be of more relevance to developing countries. Another often forgotten effect is the cost of establishing and staffing administrative mechanisms to monitor and enforce IP regulations.[20]

It seems therefore that, on the whole, 'the expected dynamic benefits from stronger and more harmonised IP regimes would fall largely on the industrial countries' [*Maskus, 1990: 407*]. It has been shown that by viewing infringement as equivalent to a reduction of patent life, the harmonisation of IPR systems – such as that which is under discussion in the Uruguay Round – would lead to increasing the effective patent life and 'would bring about some global welfare gain. Admittedly the costs of imperfect competition increase but their effect on welfare is more than offset by the saving in fixed costs that arise from the delay in imitative entry.' If, instead, the 'dominant firm/competitive fringe' approach is used, it 'shows that infringement will occur' which 'limits the potential to exploit the monopolistic elements of the patent'. To increase their market share, innovators are then motivated to carry out more R&D, hence providing a welfare basis for the NICs' argument against enhancing IP protection [*Beath, 1990: 423–4*].

Furthermore, there remains the tendency of strong IP protection causing socially inefficient monopoly pricing and deficient incentives to develop second generation products. If a strong IP protection 'need not be an enemy of diffusion', it can also be argued that a weak protection 'need not be inimical to economic growth' [*Ordover, 1991: 44*]. Besides, 'even if technology competition were fierce, the resulting industrial structure would be oligopolistic' anyway [*Dasgupta, 1988: 1*].

Historically, the very idea of a patent system has been opposed ardently, causing very heated controversies in most countries. If its birth coincided with the expansion of the granting of various types of privileges of monopoly (a practice born in fourteenth-century Italy that later spread to Northern Europe and finally to England), it came under attack during the second and third quarters of the last century. It achieved universal acceptance only after the economic crisis of 1873 when 'protectionists won out over the free traders' [*Machlup and Penrose, 1950: 6*] and when the 'increasing interdependence of nations' became 'for many the chief argument in favour of the international protection' [*Penrose, 1951: 89*]. More than 40 years ago, Penrose warned that 'no amount of talk about the "economic unity of the world" can hide the fact that some countries with little export trade in industrial goods and few, if any, inventions for sale, have nothing to gain from granting patents on inventions worked [exploited] and patented abroad' [*Penrose, 1951: 116–17*]. Actually developing countries nationals hold in their own countries no more than about one per cent of the world stock of patents [*UNCTAD, 1975: 38*].

Although this is still valid for many developing countries, many others have moved away from such a predicament, and for them harmonisation and stricter IP protection remains an open question. Yet, the Paris Convention 'does not address the problems that exist for a country that is a large importer or purchaser of technology, but is not a large exporter of technology' [*Evenson, 1990: 354*] and there still 'appears to be little reason for small countries to adopt a patent system' [*Lyons, 1987: 199*]. The alternative is to allow developing countries a free-riding position. This position has re-emerged recently in the literature based on the consideration that because DCs' innovations are not conceived or developed for developing country markets, the world's supply of such innovations would not be affected by developing countries' adopting them without paying for them.

It seems necessary, however, to review more accurately the various arguments on which the case for extending stricter IP protection to developing countries has been based. In brief, the arguments are that such protection encourages FDI and fosters technological progress, although it may hamper diffusion of innovations; that southern consumers may in some circumstances benefit; that it fosters the innovative capacities within developing countries; and that a system of IP protection and licensing creates an environment for the transfer of tacit knowledge that is not visible in the product or codified in its patent.

(i) The first argument is based on the positive link that seems to exist between stricter IP protection in a country and the inflow of FDI and technology. FDI is considered to be essential for creating high-technology sectors. This view is supported by studies made of specific sectors, summarised by the United Nations Centre of Transnational Corporations [*UNCTC 1990: 4*], but while some authors feel confident enough to conclude that this is generally the case [*Siebeck, 1990: 92*], others consider the evidence inadequate to permit a definitive analysis [*Braga, 1990: 83; Maskus, 1993: 167*]. The UNCTC warns that the interrelation between IP protection and the promotion of investments 'is much more complex' and no simple causal link can be established between the two. Actually, it appears that IPRs are usually not considered an important determinant of investment decisions by firms' executives; levels of protection in DCs have varied over time with no discernible relation to FDI flows [*UNCTC, 1990: 5*].

Turkey abolished patents in the pharmaceutical sector in 1961, yet the absence of protection has not influenced negatively the inflow of FDI, nor has it stimulated the development of a domestic technological infrastructure and innovation capabilities, or reduced anti-competitive practices, such as transfer-pricing, usually associated with patent protection [*Kirim, 1985*]. Brazil abolished patent protection on pharmaceuticals, foodstuffs, agricultural chemicals and some metal alloys in 1969. Once again there is little evidence on the impact of Brazil's IPR system on FDI flows and on the transfer of technology [*Frischtak, 1990: 78–80*]. Pharmaceuticals were the least protected sub-sector, yet international firms' share of total sales in this sector was the second highest of all industrial sectors, at 71 per cent, in the period 1970–85. FDI flows in pharmaceuticals grew from $113 million in 1971 to $971 million by 1984, while the market share of Brazilian companies decreased from 33 per cent in 1967 to 15 per cent in 1988 [*Grynszpan, 1990: 107*]. It may be that the Transnational Corporations (TNCs) increased their presence in these sectors to pre-empt the development of pirate industries.

(ii) The second argument for stronger IP protection in developing countries emerges from questioning the supposed trade-off between promoting technological progress and technology diffusion, or transfer. If innovation and diffusion are seen as parts of one process, short-term gains from faster diffusion of existing knowledge under a lax system will in the longer term be offset by the slower rate of innovation in the originating countries. Thus the developing countries themselves stand to profit from technological accumulation in the DCs. However, the argument that stronger IP protection in developing countries favours innovation in the DCs is challenged by the consideration that 'unimpeded diffusion of existing technology is immediately beneficial not only for consumers but also for those who would improve that technology. Because technological advance is often an interactive, cumulative process, strong protection of individual achievements may slow down the general advance' [*Levin et al., 1987: 788*]. Even if strong IP protection by developing countries enhances a faster rate of innovation in the North, some of the global gains thus generated may accrue to developing countries only where they are large consumers of the goods produced (see argument (iii) below). There is then a counter-argument that impending imitation from the South raises the North's incentive to innovate because firms in the North earn greater profits during their period of monopoly production. Thus continual, but not immediate, diffusion of new discoveries spurs innovators to search for the next generation development that will restore their monopolies. As the South's imitation causes production to contract in the North, displaced workers are absorbed into R&D activities, leading to accelerated technological innovation [*Grossman and Helpman, 1990: 90*].

Also related to the development/diffusion dichotomy is the argument that if strong protection of IPRs serves to promote technological progress rather than diffusion, developing countries' limited capacity to innovate forces them to seek weak or minimal IP protection. If the acquisition and diffusion of technological knowledge is also promoted by standardisation, its introduction and, even more, switching to other standards, that is, other countries's standards, is a costly process. This explains why each country has a strong interest in having its own standards accepted by others in order to retain its positive externalities.

The suggestion of fostering innovation by government financed R&D, thus avoiding IP protection, has been rejected on the assumption that it may actually delay diffusion [*David, 1993a: 237–8*]. Yet, this proposition can be criticised also because often (a) foreign R&D is beyond the scope of policy in the technology-adopting country; (b) domestic R&D may be directed to developing new products for exports; and (c) the mechanism by which certain kinds of innovations are diffused to small and medium-sized enterprises in developing countries may differ from that assumed by David, except in the case of radical innovations in DCs [*Teubal, 1993: 254*].

To conclude, the problem of the trade-off at the international level is in some sense similar to that arising at the domestic level, the solution of which is advocated in terms of stronger IP protection. Yet, the trade-off referred to here cannot continue to be resolved by those that are presently doing it, namely, the TNCs and the governments of the DCs, which clearly in no way can be assumed to represent world interests. There are, therefore, two aspects one can distinguish in this argument. The moral one, namely, who decides to introduce more protection in order to obtain more innovation and in whose interest; and the practical aspect that makes it impossible to be sure that an increase of IP protection may produce more innovation.

(iii) It has also been argued that the South, that is, its consumers, may bene-fit from protecting Northern IPRs, hence eliminating the conflict of interests between the two regions. Theoretically, and within a partial equilibrium model of duopolistic competition between a Northern and a Southern firm, such a possibility seems, however, valid only in cases where Southern consumers 'absorb much of the world's output of the good subject to cost reduction or when the cost savings to be reaped from innovation are quite dramatic'. In other words, the South should accept protecting IPRs only when the effec-tiveness of R&D in reducing production costs, that is, the market structure pre-vailing with protection, is high enough to make the South gain much on the consumption side from the research efforts of the Northern firm. In all other cases developing countries' social welfare 'will be higher when it eschews protection of foreign intellectual property than when it succumbs to pressure from the North'. Since, instead, the North 'always benefits from having the patents of its firm respected outside of its borders' – even in the extreme case that 'the Northern firm capture *none* of the surplus from any licensing agree-ment that materializes between itself and its Southern rival' – the interests of these two regions with respect to the system of IPRs do conflict. Since, how-ever, the protection of IPRs – thus the potential licensing of patents – enhances global efficiency, at least for substantial innovations, 'then the North ought to be willing and able to compensate the South for any losses that it would incur in the course of providing such protection'. Furthermore, the conflict becomes one 'between the benefits of widespread diffusion of technology and the increased competition that such diffusion entails, and the costs of dampened incentives to generate technological breakthroughs' [*Chin and Grossman, 1990: 97; 103–6*].

In this connection the argument has been made even for unequal treatment to foreigners in patent enforcement procedures by countries possessing some domestic capacity for innovating. Based on a simple application of the new strategic trade theory, the call for discrimination to promote indigenous R&D effort 'hinges on the fact that monopoly profits accruing to foreign nationals do not enhance national welfare'. That discrimination can enhance the country's welfare seems possible in at least two cases: (a) when the 'small country' assumption holds in respect of foreign technologies but not for domestically created ones, so that there are no dynamic gains from granting protection to to foreign nationals because then the dynamic gains of a protection limited to domestic nationals tend to ouweigh the static losses if a minimum R&D capability exists in the country; and (b) even when 'the "small country" assumption is relaxed so that cost reductions in the domestic market cannot be secured in the absence of intellectual property protection to foreign nationals' because 'for a wide variety of situations discrimination can be welfare enhancing even though the R and D generated domestically is *inferior* to that generated abroad'. The higher welfare generated by the poorer technology is related to 'the nature of the monopoly profit-consumer surplus trade-off', which amounts to a kind of infant industry argument for promoting or protecting the creation of R&D in developing countries [*Subramanian, 1990a: 549; 1991: 946*].

Related, but different, is the call for low protection without discrimination, that is, without unequal treatment of foreigners and nationals, a policy considered more appropriate for small developing countries for which the gains from a high level of IP protection may appear to be negligible. In fact, since information is not a free good, developing countries should not endanger future information imports by refusing to pay for it but, instead, push the costs as low as allowed by 'the importance of developing countries markets in calculations by technology creators of the profit maximizing levels of future technology to be supplied to the world' [*Magee, 1977: 335*].

(iv) The general theoretical arguments advanced for the patent system itself may also be argued to apply to the case of the developing countries' own R&D capacities. However, the developing countries, at the less privileged end of a dynamic North–South system, and facing the threat of the imposition of an international patent system, are in a quite different situation to that faced by the DCs when they were establishing their national patent systems and R&D capabilities. Whether in present circumstance, stricter IP protection would enhance R&D in developing countries remains a moot point. After all, DCs themselves have only recently adopted improvements and extensions of their industrial property system that they now expect from the developing countries. Indeed, before the revision of national patent laws following the entry into force of the Munich Patent Convention of 1968, the levels of protection prevailing in Europe were relatively low [*Ullrich, 1989: 132 fn.10*].

There is general agreement that developing countries underinvest in R&D, but the available literature is inconclusive on whether higher returns and investments take place in those developing countries which more strictly protect IP [*Siebeck, 1990: 2*]. At any rate most authorities, according to Braga [*1990: 80*], agree that such protection is 'neither necessary nor sufficient for strong technological activity.' Moreover, to adopt stronger IP protection 'on the OECD model might be globally optimal, but it would not be optimal for individual developing countries' because it would probably hinder domestic adaptive R&D and eliminate the options to copy and reverse engineer [*Evenson, 1990: 353*]. This is so at least for pirating countries. According to the same Evenson, strengthening IPRs seems needed more by the less developed countries because they require 'stronger incentives for domestic adaptive invention to develop the capacity and the industrial relevance of their current R&D' and because, since 'most of their technology purchase arrangements are inter-linked, complex contracts calling for technical assistance, capital, etc.', any lack of protection of the potential seller's IPRs is bound to raise rather than lower the cost of such a package [*Evenson, 1990: 354*]. Not only does this view conflict with that expressed by many, including Deardorf [*1990: 505–6*], but (a) it is irrelevant in most developing countries where R&D activities require much stronger incentives than merely stricter IP protection, and (b) it ignores the fact that by far the majority of patents in developing countries are held by foreigners, most of which are in the hands of corporations, and almost all of them unused. The fact that these patents are not used arises from the strategic considerations of foreign enterprises, and not from any domestic conditions in the developing countries [*UNCTAD, 1975: 52*].

On the whole, the evidence appears to support the overall conclusion reached some time ago by Vaitsos, that the registration of patents in developing countries bears practically 'no direct causal relationship whatsoever with inventive activity, domestic or foreign' [*Vaitsos, 1972: 90*]. Moreover, for large countries particularly, a process of industrialisation that does not rely too much on imports of technology may result in a diverse and deep technological capability [*Lall, 1985: 70–1*].

(v) More recently, the argument for strict IP protection by developing countries has been based on the not too new recognition that 'most industrial R&D generates two distinct types of output. The first type consists of product-specific information that enables a firm to manufacture a particular new good (or an old good by a new and cheaper process)'. This 'codified' component, in the form of blueprints, drawings, specifications and design, amounts to the transformation of experience and information into symbolic form. The second output comprises more general technical information, that may facilitate the undertaking of subsequent innovations.

While the returns to the product-specific information will be appropriated by the innovator most of the time with the help of patents and secrets, the additions to general knowledge are more difficult to appropriate [*Grossman and Helpman, 1992: 335*]. Although slow and costly to transmit, as it often requires face-to-face communication [*Teece, 1981: 83*], without this uncodi-fied or tacit knowledge potential, users will not be able necessarily to make use of the codified information, that is, 'production processes will not deliver out-put of the expected quality at the anticipated rate' [*David, 1993a: 240*]. As firms tend to codify whatever can be protected as IP, while everything else is kept secret, IPRs pertain primarily to the codified aspects of technology [*Arora, 1991: 1–4*]. It is maintained, therefore, the more protected the codified information, that is, the stricter the enforcement of IPRs, the easier the trans-fer of tacit knowledge.

Furthermore, tacit and codified components of technology are comple-mentary, and form part of a continuum of which patents and trade secrets are only some elements. Because IPRs concern only one of these elements, namely, patents, their 'conceptualisation is inadequate' either to explain or facilitate the process of technology transfer. Given that the scope of patent protection will affect the incentives to transfer tacit know-how, Arora main-tains that arm's length contracting, that is strongly affected by IPR regimes, can achieve successfully the transfer of technological know-how, although he recognises that in weak IPR regimes 'complementary investment plays an important role in the transfer' [*Arora, 1991: 3 and 5*].

Since 'tacit know-how is more valuable when used in conjunction with the codified components of the technology, *inter alia*, because both are strongly influenced by the specific conditions under which the licensor operates the technology, and learns about it' [*Arora, 1991: 36*] when 'the tacit knowledge components are vital and remain unavailable domestically' [*David, 1993a: 243*] and when the knowledge has a high tacit component, clearly the transfer of technology 'cannot be separated from the transfer of personnel, which is typically difficult if the contractual relationship is arms-length and non-exclusive' [*Jorde and Teece, 1990: 80*]. Actually, technology transfers to the South differ from North–North transfers because the tacit know-how component is much more important, so that the potential competition posed by the licensee is less, and because new and untried technology rarely enters the exchange [*Arora, 1991: 7–9*].

The conclusion that has been drawn from this argument is that the amount of tacit know-how provided increases in line with the degree of protection afforded to the codified element of the technology to be transferred, with the degree of complementarity between these two elements [*Arora, 1991: 36–7*] and with the 'technological distance' between the firms involved. It is therefore maintained that when IP protection is weak, very likely licensors tend to supply lower levels of technological know-how by restructuring the flow of tacit knowledge. This analysis is advanced as a reason for developing countries adopting stricter IP protection in order to facilitate the design of 'contracts for the successful implementation of technologies by bundling the provision of assistance (conveying tacit knowledge) together with licensing of the use of codified information such as patents and copyrights' [*David, 1993a, 242–3*].

David and Arora have also pointed out that, although stricter protection of IPRs may hamper the process of discovery and invention, it may be instrumental in bringing about the successful transfer and commercial application of new scientific and technological knowledge [*David, 1993: 19*] because effective licensing under an IPR regime must be complemented by assistance contracts for conveying tacit knowledge. David then claims that weaker IP protection 'involves accepting the tradeoff of slower and less widespread diffusion of technological innovation to the developing countries in exchange for a more rapid pace of knowledge accumulation that may eventually become available to all' [*David, 1993a: 242–243*].

The argument based on tacit knowledge, however, does not seem to take fully into account that at any rate not much complementary know-how can be transferred to countries possessing little technological capability (see Westphal and Evenson [*1993*] and Lall [*1990*]). The difficulty extends even to North–South transfers taking place within TNCs [*Teece, 1976*]. Where, instead, some technological capability does exist, the need for tacit knowledge becomes less pressing, or it can be obtained from domestic sources. Furthermore, if the role of tacit knowledge is proportional to the complexity of the process or the product design, its relevance for the simpler and less sophisticated technologies most needed by developing countries is bound to be minor. It seems, therefore, that the tacit knowledge argument might be relevant only for the most advanced developing countries, mainly for a few newly-industrialised countries (NICs). However, since these already posses technological capabilities, they are better equipped either to provide themselves with most of the tacit knowledge necessary for operating new technologies or to receive it through FDI or other assistance arrangements with foreign suppliers of codified technological information. In other words, their 'learning to borrow' is already rather well developed.

In fact, the tacit, uncodified character of much innovative activity would be a reason to argue that 'the problem with the property rights regime may lie less with the lack of patent protection than with the lack of a robust legislative instrument for trade secrets protection that is effectively enforced' [*Frischtak, 1990: 61*]. Trade secrets are considered particularly vital during the weeks and months from the moment of innovation or discovery until the day a patent application can be prepared and filed. Informal surveys of executives engaged in technology transfer licensing suggest that trade secrets represent very roughly two-thirds of the technology transferred [*Sherwood, 1990: 130*].

Furthermore, the more complex the process or the product design and the more technologically distant the firms or the countries involved, the more serious are the transfer problems posed by tacit knowledge. Since this is often the case where developing countries are concerned, their potential advantage as latecomers seems largely exaggerated. Yet, together with the need for 'learning to borrow' [*David, 1993a: 240–41*], developing countries must be reminded that not only IPRs are required to make technology work. Further, since the more successful a firm at absorbing technology the higher the chance of becoming an innovator and a dangerous competitor, the stronger is the incentive for the foreign firm providing the technology to withhold some uncodified information. Thus, strengthening and armonising IPR protection becomes less relevant and the only important issue is the control of piracy, control of which can be performed at DC points of entry.

It seems correct, therefore, to conclude with Maskus that it is 'difficult to envision any clear interests of the poorest countries' in the stronger IP protection which the Uruguay Round is attempting to set up [*Maskus, 1990: 407*]. There remains, however, the conflict between the technological innovators and the imitators, that is, those that copy or 'invent around',[21] a conflict that is made more evident by both the growing control retained by TNCs on new technologies and the large role they play in international trade and technology, and the overall process of globalisation of the world economy. As early as the end of the 1970s Magee maintained that TNCs favour the production of technologies that are more complex and sophisticated so as to make their transmission through markets less efficient, that is, more difficult, than within firms.

The difficulty of appropriating the returns of simple inventions, together with the efficiency of transfering high technology world-wide inside firms rather than through the market, explain the tendency of TNCs and private markets to seriously undersupply the technologies most needed by developing countries, namely, simple product technologies and production technologies which intensively utilise unskilled labour [*Magee, 1977: 335; 1981: 124*].

Very relevant is the consideration that 'the model of knowledge as a public good with a transfer cost near zero is largely irrelevant for North–South technology tansfer. For these transactions the major costs of making the transfer lie in creating required local know-how and infrastructure. The ineffectiveness of compulsory licensing as a remedy for the non-working of Southern patents suggests that even making patented technology freely available to Southern users would have little immediate impact on its local application by Southern firms [*McCulloch, 1981: 118–9*].[34] The discussion of the free-riding option tends to overlook two facts: the different technological needs and tastes in the South; and the South's potential to undertake innovation for these needs. It follows that not only may 'Southern patents ... have a role to play in promoting the development of technologies appropriate to the South', but 'increased patent protection in the South need not always be good for the North'. Just as the increase in innovative activity in the North, due to patent protection, may be at the cost of some products being particularly suited to Southern requirements, increased patent protection in the South raises the range of innovations but also shifts it away from the North's preferences. Although 'it is not clear a priori whether the South ought to have a lower or higher level of protection than the North', it appears that the South's greatest incentive to free ride is for products presenting little taste differences between the two regions (computer software or economics textbooks), while it should grant strong IP protection to other products, such as some pharmaceuticals or agricultural innovations [*Diwan and Rodrik, 1991: 28–9, 37, 46–7*].

Another important consideration in this balance of benefits is that the effects of progress work asymmetrically. Technical progress in the North, even where it widens the technological gap between the two areas, always benefits the South, whereas a narrowing of the gap, that is, a 'catch-up', by a developing country may not benefit the North, and may possibly adversely affect it. Since progress in the North tends to be biased towards goods not produced by the South, while progress in the South competes with the North's exports, the closing of the gap reduces the North's gains from trade. Hence, the real and relative income of the technological leader becomes a function of maintaining the lead, an objective that may be obtained also through technological protectionism [*Krugman, 1985: 36, 45–47*].

Krugman has demonstrated also that while developing countries always gain from faster *process* innovation in the North but may lose from faster *product* innovation, the North gains in both cases. With technology transfer, the North always loses if product technologies are more rapidly transferred, but may not do so if process technologies are transferred. Developing countries always gain; thus, progress in process technology may lead to less inherent North–South conflict. TNCs' apparent bias toward transferring product technologies may be detrimental to the welfare of Northern labour, since it is the North's special ability to produce certain goods that constitutes the only source of inequality in wages. Consequently, the transfer of technology to developing countries shifts demand towards the goods they produce, capital starts moving there and the relative income of developing country labour rises [*Krugman, 1979: 255; 264*].

Extending Krugman's early model, Dollar shows that the North's ability to introduce and temporarily monopolise new technology enables its workers to earn a premium over the wages paid to their counterparts in the South. This difference in labour costs constitutes the main incentive for the diffusion of the technology to the South. An increase in the labour force in the South causes wages in the North to rise by increasing demand for Northern products, hence improving its terms of trade. In the long run, however, the improvement of the North's terms of trade leads to the more rapid diffusion of technology and a capital flow towards the South, leading in turn to a fall of Northern real wages. The growing downward pressure exercised over time on Northern wages by the increased supply of labour in the South is due to the combined effect both of a reduction in Northern labour's marginal physical productivity and a decline in the latter's terms of trade. Consequently the South experiences a real increase in wages. The same effects are caused by a more rapid diffusion of technology to the South. Indeed, the North's specialisation in exporting capital-intensive and importing labour-intensive goods is due less to initial differences in factor endowments than to the North's ability to keep introducing new products.

Finally, since 'over time the technology and capital that nations have available will be as much the result as the cause of trade ... some government control of the process of capital and technology transfer may be desirable in order to prevent further erosion of the world's relatively open trade in goods' [*Dollar, 1986: 178, 185, 188–9*]. If the innovation process is perceived not as 'a number of stages which proceed sequentially ... in a linear and predictable fashion' (the traditional serial model) but rather as 'an incremental and cumulative activity' – and irreversible [*David, 1993a: 218*] – resting on 'the existence of tight linkages and feedback mechanisms which must operate quickly and efficiently, including links between firms, within firms, and sometimes between firms and other organisations like universities' (the simultaneous model), then it is the organisation of innovation, rather than just the organisation of R&D, which must change [*Jorde and Teece, 1990: 77–8*]. Since, in the simultaneous model 'lateral and horizontal linkages as well as vertical ones' become essential to obtain the necessary capabilities, it has been argued that anti-trust laws may seriously hinder the innovation process, particularly in middle-sized firms [*Jorde and Teece, 1990: 76–9*]. Therefore, complex bilateral and multilateral contracts, internal organisation, or various hybrid structures are often required to shore up obvious market failures [*Jorde and Teece, 1990: 80*] and to deal with the imperfections characteristic of the market for know-how. This is more so the closer one moves to real, cutting-edge capabilities that are mostly 'generated by precompetitive, collaborative research and development' as in microelectronics, biotechnology and new materials [*Teubal, 1993: 253*].

In the simultaneous model of innovation, firms, in seeking 'to bring technology to the market and to hold competitors at bay', rely less on the price mechanism or the administrative processes within the firm and more on inter-firm agreements, particularly strategic alliances (the commitment of two or more firms to a common goal) that include consortia and joint ventures. When the national anti-trust legislation is hostile to joint R&D activities, as is the case in the US, it also tends to inhibit technological innovations and international competitiveness [*Jorde and Teece, 1990: 84–86*]. Therefore, if 'innovative firms confront significant challenges in capturing value from new technology ... they must quickly position themselves advantageously in the appropriate complementarity assets and technologies' [*Jorde and Teece, 1990: 94*]. This positioning must extend to the international level, hence the stronger IP protection requested by most DCs.

V. CONCLUSION

The present evolution of the technological process may present some advantages for developing countries, such as (a) cheaper access to more traditional technology, due to the acceleration of technological developments and the shortening of product life cycles; (b) the proliferation of public as well as private sources for technology transfer, although this advantage is counteracted by the diminished political incentive to transfer technology to the Third World since the end of cold war; and (c) a broader spectrum of chances for co-operation, an advantage that may apply mainly to the more advanced countries in the Third World [*Wijk and Junne, 1992: 9–12*].

Yet, if the concept of technology is extended to include the organisation and management of production systems, from research to design, production, distribution and marketing, then what is the importance of norms and standards, and even IP protection as currently understood, and their harmonisation for the acquisition of technology by developing countries? The crucial element for an effective acquisition of technology becomes, firstly, to build up an adequate human capital base and, secondly, to explore more accurately the conditions for the utilisation of the means of obtaining foreign technology other than those generally employed, namely, the purchase of new equipment, FDI and technology licensing. Other recognised means of obtaining foreign technology are the use of non-proprietary technology, acquisition of knowledge from returning skilled nationals, R&D, reverse engineering, copying, foreign publications, trade fairs, data bases, foreign experts, informal linkages with nationals abroad, local education and training [*Dahlman, 1993: 313*].

The difficulty of demonstrating that, in general, developing countries have no need for stricter IP protection derives from the notion that only those countries with a significant concentration of imperfectly competitive inventive enterprises have 'an incentive to maintain a high degree of patent protection as well as to press for longer patent protection elsewhere'. When, instead, 'competition prevails in the invention markets, any individual country would benefit from *abolishing patent rights* for run-of-the-mill process inventions' [*Berkowitz and Kotowitz, 1982: 12; 16*]. Since developing countries do not fall into the first category, stricter protection may be recommended only to NICs and some more advanced developing countries in the rather unlikely case that it is necessary in order to prevent them starting to appropriate technologies from each other [*Chin and Grossman, 1990: 105*].

The correct conclusion is therefore that 'there is neither a theoretical basis nor an institutional capability for forging a worldwide consensus on appropriate levels and mechanisms of protection ... (that anyway) are already becoming counterproductive in some areas' [*Mody, 1990: 204*]. Even if it is somehow possible to justify the attempt to improve the protection of the innovator's rights with the aim of stimulating research and rewarding investment, the danger remains that internationally uniform IP laws, particularly those relative to patent, may also stifle the creativity of other innovators and freeze technological advantages, hence negatively affecting the rate of economic growth.

NOTES

1. Strictly speaking intellectual property covers copyright for literary and artistic works and related rights, while DCs use the term IP in an all-embracing manner in order to include all types of industrial property rights. Furthermore, trademarks 'fall more appropriately under the economics of product differentiation and, despite their categorization as intellectual property, they have an economic rationale which differs significantly from that of patents and copyrights' [*Benko, 1988: 218*].
2. 'Because industrial design partakes of both art and industry, it sits astride the Berne and Paris Conventions' [*Reichman, 1989: 8*] hence integrated circuits have become the object of a particular 'Treaty for the Protection of Intellectual Property in Respect of Integrated Circuits' (IPIC) adopted at Washington on May 1989.
3. The concept of trade secrets, also referred to as know-how, manufacturing data or technical assistance, is probably one of the most important and least understood forms of IPRs. Trade secret protection supplements the patent system, but while the first may extend to business information not related to technology, the second is limited to technological improvements of products or processes. Consequently, while the patent protection is absolute, that of trade secrets 'only protects against disclosure by parties who derive the information from the original developer'

[*Keating, 1991: 61*]. Furthermore, although patent aims at discouraging duplications of efforts, trade secrets may very well encourage them. For trade law, this much 'neglected orphan in economic analysis', also see Friedman *et al.* [*1991: 61–65*].

4. A survey of executives in the American motion picture and television, publishing and advertising industries conducted in 1984 found that copyright infringement to be the most frequently mentioned barrier to trade [*Benko, 1988: 221*].

5. Officially this Negotiating Group is called 'Trade Related Aspects of Intellectual Property Rights, including Trade in Counterfeit Goods'.

6. In fact, because 'a few of the most important new technologies do not fit clearly into any of the existing categories of intellectual property ... their eligibility for legal protection is consequently uncertain ... [and] it is questionable whether any of the traditional intellectual property laws would in fact be adequate or appropriate' [*Benko, 1988: 228*] and also Gadbaw [*1989: 227 fn.10*]. The 'extraordinary rapid technological change in the 1970s and 1980s ... has thrust upon us new and as yet unresolved problems of governance in the national and international spheres'. While the technology 'evolves much more rapidly than the body politic can absorb', this 'revolutionary change is occurring in a much more interdependent world' [*Blumenthal, 1988: 531–2*].

7. Based on a problem of market failure, i.e. the absence of complete appropriability of returns – see later Magee's theory – co-operative agreements in R&D represent 'an alternative to either pure market transactions or integration' into a single firm, but they also tend to cause 'a harmful reduction of competition'. Until now, however, they have not been very frequent [*Jacquemin, 1988: 552–3*]. However, the 'increasing complexity and multi-disciplinarity of resources required for innovation. and of the stock of knowledge itself tend to make technological innovations the outcome of interactions and cooperation among fundamentally autonomous organizations commanding complementarity resources. As a result ... the locus of innovation could well be a 'network' of various types of organizations', as it seems that is happening particularly in biotechnology where 'the large firms are no longer the sole locus of innovative activity', which instead 'should be thought of as a 'network' of inter-organizational relations' [*Arora and Gambardella, 1990: 362; 374*].

8. Biotechnological inventions can easily be duplicated as these inventions are embodied in self-replicating living material [*DGIS, 1991: 14*].

9. Particularly in the US, the pressure for tighter IP protection has emerged from the 'twin perception that the erosion of the competitive position of the U.S. technology leadership in certain sectors, in particular in pharmaceuticals, chemicals, computer software and semiconductors, is due to copying in foreign countries and to unfair practices of certain countries, including inadequate protection of intellectual property' [*Weiss, 1990: 89*].

10. It has been suggested replacing the word piracy with the more appropriate 'world 'corsoirs' because most pirates in Third World countries have all the legal mandates and abide by local laws to do what they do' [*Braga, 1989: 313*]. Besides, the countries presently insisting on higher IP standards 'were the pirates of not even a century ago, and began to find a value in enhanced intellectual property protection only as their technological capabilities developed and their economic structures changed' [*Naresh, 1989: 358*].

11. It is also argued that 'science, as a social organization, views knowledge as a *public consumption good*, while technology regards it as a *private capital good*'. The patent system is then presented as 'both interesting and problematic because

it represents a conjunction of the distinctive and antithetical mores of science and technology in regard to the treatment of new information. Looking backward it seeks to reward additions to knowledge that are disclosed, and does so on the basis of priority. But to finance the award it looks ahead to a contrived limitation of access to the new knowledge' [*Dasgupta, 1987: 10; 12*].

12. For an interesting analysis of the distinction between science and technology, see Dasgupta and David [*1987*].

13. fixed costs are by definition a source of scale economies in production, while the presence of learning possibilities connected to the process of using a piece of knowledge – learning-by-doing, learning-by-using, leaning-to-learn – implies 'not only an intertemporal *externality*, it implies – if powerful enough – dynamic scale economies in production activities' [*Dasgupta and Stoneman, 1987: 3–4*]. Since fixed costs act as a barrier to entry and limit competition in R&D, this also tends to reduce wasteful duplication of R&D spending. In respect of the increase in the number of firms, there is a tradeoff between two types of efficiency: namely static efficiency, which pushes price closer to marginal cost, and dynamic efficiency, which limits the actual amount of cost reduction, while raising the total level of R&D spending in the industry, at the same time as each firm spends less [*Dasgupta and Stiglitz, 1980: 279–81*].

14. Empirical studies such as Taylor and Silberston [*1973*] have amply shown that patents rarely confer perfect appropriability.

15. Romer explains that each research investment generates not only a patentable blueprint, but also a non-appropriable contribution to the stock of general-knowledge capital [*Romer, 1990*].

16. By Dasgupta earlier identified as 'Lindahl market mechanism', 'Samuelsonian contrivance', and 'Pigovian public finance', respectively [*Dasgupta, 1988: 3*].

17. '... a patent system is instituted when mechanisms for producing information efficiently are not available under the price system' [*Nordhaus, 1969: 70*].

18. That 'the market can sustain excessive duplication ... is a special kind of market failure', although 'the prescription of an externality tax is incompatible with incentives'. Furthermore, 'even if technological competition were very fierce, the resulting industrial structure would be oligopolistic' [*Dasgupta, 1988: 10 and 1*]. Moreover, with free entry into the patent race, it is likely that there will be only one actual entrant who will spend so much on R&D that most potential profits are exhausted [*Dasgupta and Stiglitz, 1980: 285*].

19. 'Theoretical economics is genuinely divided on this point' and the notion that 'the ex ante inducement to R&D that ex post protection is meant to provide is largely an article of faith' [*Subramanian, 1990: 514*] since market conditions and competitive rivalry often constitute the main determinant of innovation, rendering monopoly protection unnecessary [*Maskus, 1993: 170*]. In fact, accumulated evidence shows that while patents are certainly important for some inventions and industries, such as pharmaceutical, fine chemicals, petroleum and machinery, they are much less or not relevant at all to the remaining sectors [*Mansfield: 1986: 174–5*]. Empirical evidence collected by Mansfield indicates that information about new products and processes becomes available to a firm's competitors fairly rapidly, on average within about 12 to 18 months [Mansfield, 1985: 219]. Even if it seems that 'this evidence is outdated ... [and] it is likely that patents have taken on increasing importance as R&D-stimulative devices as technological competition has become stronger and more globalized ... in truth ... the important empirical question of whether greater protection of IPRs would call forth substan-

tially more inventive activity ... [remains] unresolved' [*Maskus, 1993: 171–2*].

20. And the more the regulations the longer the time to obtain a patent and consequently the shorter the length of its effective protection. This phenomenon is very evident in the case of drugs, particularly in the US, considering the average time it takes from the moment when research on a new chemical compound starts until the moment the new drug is allowed onto the market – from 13.6 years to 9.5 years between 1966 and 1979 according to a study by M. Eisman and W. Wardell quoted by Nogues [*1990: 100*].

21. Since 'patents rarely confer perfect appropriability ... many patents can be "invented around"'. Besides, 'the effectiveness of patents is highly nonuniform ... most effective, absolutely and relatively, in industries with chemical-based technologies'. Whereas, product patents are seen 'as moderately effective in a few industries producing relatively uncomplicated mechanical equipment and devices' and much less so in most other industries, patents on new products appear more effective than process patents in most industries, particularly in the drug industry [*Levin, 1986: 199–200*]. Furthermore, patents 'are not the only nor necessarily the primary barriers that prevent general access to what would otherwise be pure public goods. Lead time accrues naturally to the innovator, even in the absence of any deliberate effort to enhance its protective effect. Secrecy, learning advantages, and sales and service efforts can provide additional protection, though they require the innovator's deliberate effort' [*Levin et al., 1987: 816*].

REFERENCES

Arora, A. (1991): 'Transferring Tacit Knowledge in Technology Transfer: How Can Intellectual Property Rights Legislation Help the Industrialising Countries?', Department of Economics, Stanford University, May.

Arora, A. and Gambardella (1990): 'Complementarity and External Linkages: The Strategies of the Large firms in Biotecnology', *The Journal of Industrial Economics*, Vol. 38, No. 4, June.

Arrow, K. (1962): 'Economic Welfare and the Allocation of Resources for Invention', in N. Rosenberg (ed.) (1971), *The Economics of Technological Change*, Harmondsworth: Penguin Books.

Beath, J. (1990): 'Innovation, Intellectual Property Rights and the Uruguay Round', *The World Economy*, Vol. 13, No. 3, Sept.

Benko, R.P. (1988): 'Intellectual Property Rights and the Uruguay Round', *The World Economy*, Vol. 11, No. 2, June.

Berkowitz M.K. and Y. Kotowitz (1982): 'Patent Policy in an Open Economy', *Canadian Journal of Economics*, Vol. 15, No. 1, Feb.

Blumenthal, W.M. (1988): 'The World Economy and Technological Change', *Foreign Affairs*, Vol. 66, No. 3.

Braga, C.A.P. (1989): 'The Economic of Intellectual Property Rights and the GATT: A View From the South', followed by his 'Remarks', *Vanderbilt Journal of Transnational Law*, 22.

Braga, C.A.P. (1990): 'Guidance from Economic Theory' and 'The Developing Country Case For and Against Intellectual Property Protection', in W.E. Siebeck *et al.*, *Strengthening Protection of Intellectual Property in Developing Countries. A Survey of the Literature*, World Bank Discussion Papers 112, Washington, DC: World Bank.

Chin, J. and G. Grossman (1990): 'Intellectual Property Rights and North-South Trade', in R.W. Jones and A.O. Krueger (eds), *The Political Economy of International Trade*, Oxford: Basil Blackwell.

Dahlman, C. (1993): 'Comment', *Proceedings of the World Bank Annual Conference on Development Economics 1992*, World Bank, Washington, DC, March.

Dasgupta, P. (1987): 'The Economic Theory of Technology Policy: An Introduction', in P. Dasgupta and P. Stoneman, *Economic Policy and Technological Performance*, Cambridge: Cambridge University Press.

Dasgupta, P. (1988): 'The Welfare Economics of Knowledge Production', *Oxford Review of Economic Policy*, Vol. 4, No. 4.

Dasgupta, P. and P.A. David (1987): 'Information Disclosure and the Economics of Science and Technology', in G.R. Feiwel (ed.), *Arrow and the Ascent of Modern Economic Theory*, London: Macmillan.

Dasgupta, P. and J. Stiglitz (1980): 'Industrial Structure and the Nature of Innovative Activity', *Economic Journal*, 90, p. 358.

Dasgupta, P. and P. Stoneman (1987): 'Introduction', in P. Dasgupta and P. Stoneman, *Economic Policy and Technological Performance*, Cambridge: Cambridge University Press.

David, P. (1993): 'The Evolution of Intellectual Property Institutions', paper to be published in A. Aganbegyan, O. Bogomolov and M. Kaser (eds), *System Transformation: Eastern and Western Assessments*, London: Macmillan.

David, P. (1993a): 'Knowledge, Property, and the System Dynamics of Technological Change', *Proceedings of the World Bank Annual Conference on Development Economics 1992*, World Bank, Washington, DC, March.

Deardorff, A.V. (1990): 'Should Patent Protection Be Extended to All Developing Countries?', *The World Economy*, Vol. 13, No. 4, Dec.

DGIS (1991): 'The Impact of Intellectual Property Protection in Biotechnology and Plant Breeding on Developing Countries', Ministry of Foreign Affairs, The Hague.

Diwan, I. and D. Rodrik (1991): 'Patents, Appropriate Technology, and North–South Trade', *Journal of International Economics*, 30.

Dollar, D. (1986): 'Technological Innovation, Capital Mobility, and the Product Cycle in North-South Trade', *The American Economic Review*, Vol. 76, No. 1, March.

Evenson, R.E. (1990): 'Intellectual Property Rights, R&D, Inventions, Technology Purchase, and Piracy in Economic Development: An International Comparative study', in R.E. Evenson and G. Ranis (eds), *Science and Technology. Lessons for Development Policy*, Boulder, CO: Westview Press.

Fikentscher, W. (1989): 'GATT Principles and Intellectual Property Protection', in F-K. Beier and G. Schricker (eds): *GATT or WIPO? New Ways in the International Protection of Intellectual Property*, Weinheim: VCH Verlagsgesellshaft.

Friedman, D.D., Landes, W.M. and R.A. Posner (1991): 'Some Economics of Trade Secret Law', *Journal of Economic Perspectives*, Vol. 5, No. 1, Winter.

Frischtak, C.R. (1990): 'The Protection of Intellectual Property Rights and Industrial Technology Development in Brazil', in F.W. Rushing and C.G. Brown (eds.), *Intellectual Property Rights in Science, Technology, and Economic Performance*, Boulder, CO: Westview Press.

Gadbaw, R.M. (1989): 'Intellectual Property and International Trade: Merger or Marriage of Convenience?', *Vanderbilt Journal of Transnational Law*, Vol. 22, No. 2.

Grossman, G.M. and E. Helpman (1990): 'Trade, Innovation, and Growth', *American Economic Review, Papers and Proceedings*, Vol. 80, No. 2, May.

Grynszpan, F. (1990): 'Case Studies in Brazilian Intellectual Property Rights', in R.M. Gadbaw and T.J. Richards (eds.), *Intellectual Property Rights. Global Consensus, Global Conflict?*, Boulder, CO: Westview Press.

Hartridge, D. and A. Subramanian (1989): 'Intellectual Property Rights, The Issues in GATT', *Vanderbilt Journal of Transnational Law*, 22.

Jacquemin A. (1988): 'Cooperative Agreements in R$D and European Antitrust Policy', *European Economic Review*, Vol. 32, No. 2/3, March.

Jewkes, J., D. Sawers and R. Stillerman (1958): *The Sources of Invention*, London: Macmillan.

Johnson, H.G. (1976): 'Aspects of Patents and Licenses as Stimuli to Innovation', *Weltwirtschaftliches Archiv*, Bd. 112.

Jorde, T.M. and D.J. Teece (1990): 'Innovation and Cooperation: Implications for Competition and Antitrust', *Journal of Economic Perspectives*, Vol. 4, No. 3, Summer.

Keating, W.J. (1991): 'The European Community – 1992 and Beyond: The Implications of a Single Europe on Intellectual Property', *Dickinson Journal of International Law*, 9, Winter.

Kindleberger, C.P. (1983): 'Standards as Public, Collective and Private Goods', *Kyklos*, Vol. 36, No. 3.

Kindleberger, C.P. (1986): 'International Public Goods without International Government', *The American Economic Review*, Vol. 76, No. 1.

Kirim, A.S. (1985): 'Reconsidering Patents and the Economic Development: A Case Study of the Turkish Pharmaceutical Industry', *World Development*, Vol. 13, No. 2.

Kostecki, M.M. (1991): 'Sharing Intellectual Property Between the Rich and the Poor', *European Intellectual Property Review*, 8.

Krugman, P. (1979): 'A Model of Innovation, Technology Transfer, and the World Distribution of Income', *Journal of Political Economy*, Vol. 87, No. 2, April.

Krugman, P. (1985): 'A 'Technology Gap' Model of International Trade', in K. Jungenfelt and D. Hague (eds.), *Structural Adjustment in Developed Open Economies*, London: Macmillan.

Lall, S. (1985): 'Trade in Technology by a Slowly Industrializing Country: India', in N. Rosenberg and C. Frischtak (eds), *International Technology Transfer: Concepts, Measures, and Comparisons*, New York: Praeger.

Lall, S. (1990): *Building Industrial Competititveness in Developing Countries*, Paris: OECD.

Levin, R.C. (1986):'A New Look at the Patent System', *American Economic Review, Papers and Proceedings*, Vol. 76, No. 2, May.

Levin, R.C., Klevorick, A.K. Nelson, R.R. and S.G. Winter (1987):'Appropriating the Returns from Industrial Research and Development', *Brookings Papers on Economic Activity*, 3.

Lyons, B. (1987): 'International Trade and Technology Policy', in P. Dasgupta and P. Stoneman, *Economic Policy and Technological Performance*, Cambridge: Cambridge University Press.

Machlup, F. (1958): *An Economic Review of the Patent System*, Study No. 15 of the 'Subcommittee on Patents, Trademarks, and Copyrights' of the 'Committee on the Judiciary', United States Senate, 85th Congress, Second Session, Government Printing Office, Washington, DC.

Machlup, F. and E. Penrose (1950): 'The Patent Controversy in the Nineteenth Century', *The Journal of Economic History*, Vol. 10, No. 1, May.

Magee, S.P. (1977): 'Information and the Multinational Corporation: An Appropriability Theory of Direct Foreign Investment', in J. Bhagwati (ed.), *The New International Economic Order: The North–South Debate*, Cambridge, MA: MIT Press.

Magee, S.P. (1981): 'The Appropriability Theory of the Multinational Corporation' , *Annals, AAPSS*, 458, Nov.

Mansfield, E. (1985): 'How Rapidly Does New Industrial Technology Leak out?', *The Journal of Industrial Economics*, Vol. 34, No. 2, Dec.

Mansfield, E. (1981): 'The Appropriability Theory of the Multinational Corporation' , *Annals, AAPSS*, 458, Nov.

Mansfield, E. (1986): 'Patents and Innovations: An Empirical Study', *Management Science*, Vol. 32, No. 2, Feb.

Maskus, K. (1990): 'Normative Concerns in the International Protection of Intellectual Property Rights', *The World Economy*, Vol. 13, No. 3, Sept.

Maskus, K. (1993): 'Trade-Related Intellectual Property Rights', *European Community*, 52.

McCulloch, R. (1981): 'Technology Transfer to Developing Countries: Implications of International Regulation', *Annals, AAPSS*, 458, Nov.

Mody, A. (1990): 'New International Envoronment for Intellectual Property Rights', in F.W. Rushing and C.G. Brown (eds. *Intellectual Property Rights in Science, Technology, and Economic Performance*, Boulder, CO: Westview Press.

Naresh, S. (1989: 'Remarks of Professor Suman Naresh', *Vanderbilt Journal of Transnational Law*, 22.

Nelson, R. (1959): 'The Simple Economics of Basic Scientific Research', in N. Rosenberg (ed.) (1971), *The Economics of Technological Change*, Harmondsworth: Penguin.

Nogues, J. (1990): 'Patents and Pharmaceutical Drugs: Understanding the Pressures on Developing Countries', *Journal of World Trade*, Vol. 24, No. 6, Dec.

Nordhaus, W.D. (1969): *Invention, Growth, and Welfare. A Theoretical Treatment of Technological Change*, Cambridge, MA: MIT Press.

Ordover, J.A. (1991): 'A Patent System for Both Diffusion and Exclusion', *Journal of Economic Perspectives*, Vol. 5, No. 1, Winter.

Page, S. with M. Davenport and A. Hewitt (1991): *The GATT Uruguay Round: Effects on Developing Countries*, London: Overseas Development Institute.

Penrose, E.T. (1951): *The Economics of the International Patent System*, Baltimore, MD: Johns Hopkins Press.

Plant, A. (1934): 'The Economic Theory Concerning Patents for Inventions', *Economica*, 1.

Reichman, J.H. (1989): 'Design Protection and the New Technologies: The United States Experience in a Transnational Perspective', *University of Baltimore Law Review*, Vol. 19, No. 1/2.

Reinbothe J. and A. Howard (1991): 'The State of Play in the Negotiations on Trips (GATT/Uruguay Round)', *European Intellectual Property Review*, 5.

Romer, P. (1990): 'Endogenous Technological Change', *Journal of Political Economy*, 98. 5, Part 2, Oct.

Scotchmer, S. (1991): 'Standing on the Shoulders of Giants: Cumulative Research and the Patent Law', *Journal of Economic Perspectives*, Vol. 5, No. 1, Winter.

Sherwood, R.M. (1990): 'A Microeconomic View of Intellectual Property Protection in Brazilian Development', in R.M. Gadbaw and T.J. Richards (eds.), *Intellectual Property Rights. Global Consensus, Global Conflict?*, Boulder, CO: Westview Press.

Siebeck, W.E. (1990): 'Introduction' and 'Conclusions and Recommendations', in

W.E. Siebeck *et al.*, *Strengthening Protection of Intellectual Property in Developing Countries. A Survey of the Literature*, World Bank Discussion Papers 112, Washington, DC: World Bank.

Slaughter, J. (1990): 'TRIPs: The GATT Intellectual Property Negotiations Approach their Conclusion', *European Intellectual Property Review*, 11.

Soete, L. (1985): 'International Diffusion of Technology, Industrial Development and Technological Leapfrogging', *World Development*, Vol. 13, No. 3.

Stern, R.M. (1987): 'Intellectual Property', in J.M. Finger and A. Olechowski (eds.), *The Uruguay Round. A Handbook of the Multilateral Trade Negotiations*, Washington, DC: World Bank.

Stewart, F. (1990): 'Technology Transfer for Development', in R.E. Evenson and G. Ranis (eds.), *Science and Technology. Lessons for Development Policy*, Boulder, CO: Westview Press.

Subramanian, A. (1990): 'TRIPs and the Paradigm of the GATT: A Tropical, Temperate View', *The World Economy*, Vol. 13, No. 4, Dec.

Subramanian, A. (1990a): 'Discrimination in International Economics of Intellectual Property Right Protection', *Economic and Political Weekly*, 17 March.

Taylor, C.T. and Z.A. Silberston (1973): *The Economic Impact of Patent System: A Study of the British Experience*, Cambridge: Cambridge University Press.

Teece, D.J. (1986): *The Multinational corporation and the Resource Cost of International Technology Transfer*, Cambridge, MA: Ballinger.

Teece, D.J. (1981): 'The Market for Know-How and the Efficient International Transfer of Technology', *Annals, AAPSS*, 458, Nov.

Teubal, M. (1993): 'Comment', *Proceedings of the World Bank Annual Conference on Development Economics 1992*, Washington, DC: World Bank, March.

Ullrich, H. (1989): 'GATT: Industrial Property Protection, Fair Trade and Development', in F-K. Beier and G. Schricker (eds.), *GATT or WIPO? New Ways in the International Protection of Intellectual Property*, Weinheim: VCH Verlagsgesellschaft.

UNCTAD (1975): *The Role of the Patent System in the Transfer of Technology to Developing Countries*, New York: United Nations.

UNCTC (1990): 'Transnational Corporations and Technology Transfer: Effects and Policy Issues', ST/CTC/86, New York: United Nations.

Vaitsos, C. (1972): 'Patents Revisited: Their Function in Developing Countries', *Journal of Development Studies*, Vol. 9, No. 1, Oct.

Vaitsos, C. (1990): 'Radical Technological Change and the New 'Order' in the World Economy', in *Technology, Trade Policy and the Uruguay Round*, UNCTAD/ITP/23, New York: United Nations..

Westphal L.E. and R.E. Evenson (1993): 'Technological Change and Technology Strategy', draft paper to be published in T.N. Srinivasan and J. Behrman (eds.), *Handbook of Development Economics*, Vol. 3, Amsterdam: North-Holland. (Presented at The first INTECH Conference, Maastricht, 21–23 June 1993, the paper is here quoted with the permission of the Director of INTECH, Professor C. Cooper.)

Weiss, F. (1990): 'TRIPs in Search of An Itinerary: Trade-Related Intellectual Property Rights and the Uruguay Round Negotiations', in G. Sacerdoti (ed.), *Liberalization of Services and Intellectual Property in the Uruguay Round of GATT*, Fribourg: University Press of Fribourg.

van Wijk, J. and G. Junne (1992): 'Intellectual Property of Advanced Technology. Changes in the Global Technology System: Implications and Options for Developing Countries', INTECH, Maastricht, Oct.

9

Disarmament and International Trade: A General Equilibrium Approach

BRUNO VAN ROMPUY

I. INTRODUCTION

Since the end of the cold war there exists considerable scope for reducing military expenditures. It is said that the peace dividend opens a range of opportunities for both rich and poor nations. For rich nations, it is a chance to direct more resources to their own social problems and to poorer countries. For the developing countries and Eastern European countries it is an opportunity to invest more in the health of their people, their infrastructure and industries [*UNDP, 1992: 84–7*]. This study aims at analysing the impacts of a reduction in military spending on different regions and sectors. In particular it aims to investigate which sectors benefit and which sectors lose the most when rearranging this type of government expenditure. To analyse these effects we use a computable general equilibrium model (CGE) which is inspired by the Michigan model of world production, trade and employment.[1] We elaborate this large linearised model by using a general two-stage dynamic formulation that allows us to redistribute real capital between industries.

The presented model is able to investigate the impacts of a multilateral reduction in military spending on 14 sectors in 14 countries. To perform this simulation we assume that the initial military expenditures of a country are all concentrated in domestic industries. As with Haveman *et al.* [*Haveman, 1991: 15*], we argue that this reflects the preference given to domestic manufactures when military contracts are signed. A second assumption states that the reduction in military spending will be appropriately redistributed across non-defence final demand. In section II we briefly describe the structure of the model. In this section we will also examine the expected impacts of reductions in military expenditures in terms of a simple theoretical model that captures some of the interactions of the CGE model. Section III presents and discusses the data and the simulation results. Conclusions and topics for further research are given in section IV.

II. A COMPUTABLE GENERAL EQUILIBRIUM MODEL

The Structure of the Model

To explain how the comparative static part of the model works, we use the pictorial overview of the model as given in Deardorff and Stern [*Deardorff, 1990: 9–12*]. This method of presentation will also be used to explain the two-step dynamic formulation that we use to convert the static model into a dynamic model. The model itself is composed of two parts: a country system and a world system. The country system is shown in Figure 1. For each country there are separate blocks of equations which take the form shown in the figure. Horizontally the figure is divided into separate industries. Since it is assumed that these industries have an identical structure, only one industry is shown in Figure 1.

At the top of the figure the exchange rate, the consumer expenditure and the money wage variables are listed. These variables pertain to the country as a whole and not to specific industries. Vertically the figure separates world system variables, country-specific endogenous variables and exogenous variables. Four exogenous variables are shown in the figure: the country's tariff in each industry, its money wage and capital stock and two parameters which incorporate policy experiments. For illustrative purposes other exogenous variables are not depicted in figure 1. In what follows we assume that the tariffs and the money wage are not affected. In this study, only the capital stock and the policy parameters will be of importance.

The demand and supply interactions of consumers and producers of goods are presented in the centre of Figure 1. The exchange rate and the world price for each industry are shown at the left of the figure. These variables are determined in the world system. This world system contains a single set of equations for the world as a whole. The country system provides the export-supply and import-demand functions that depend on world prices and exchange rates. By calculating the trade balance of a country and equating it to the exogenous given net capital flow of that country, the model is able to calculate the exchange rate for that particular country. World prices are determined by equating the sum of all countries' export supplies with the sum of all countries' import demands. Once world prices and exchange rates are determined, these variables are entered back into the country blocks to obtain values for other relevant country-specific variables.

The model presented so far is purely static and has no explicit time dimension. In the short run it is assumed that capital cannot move from one sector to another. In the long run however, sectoral supply curves may shift because of technical progress and because of capital accumulation. In what follows we consider only the latter and assume that the allocation of investment by sector

162

FIGURE I
COUNTRY SYSTEM

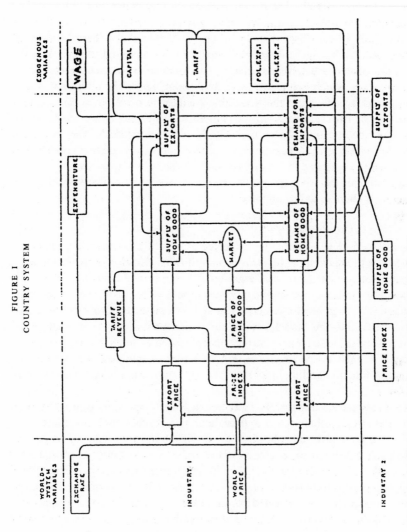

Note: This figure is taken and adapted from Deardorff and Stern [*Deardorff, 1990: 10*].

of destination in any given period is determined by the prices, production costs and profit rates of the previous period.[2]

What we really do is to specify what is known in the literature as a two-stage dynamic model.[3] The overall dynamic model is partitioned into a static within-period equilibrium model and a separate between-period model. The former was already discussed above. The latter model provides the necessary intertemporal linkages. It mainly helps to determine and allocate nominal investment over the different sectors. This enables us to calculate new actual capital stock which will lead to a sectoral supply shift. The allocation issue is addressed by allocating the investable funds in proportion to each sector's share in aggregate profits. In our simple dynamic model we use the more realistic specification of Dervis *et al.* [*Dervis, 1982: 176–7*]. They adjust the sectoral share in aggregate profits as a function of the relative profit rate of each sector compared to the average rate for the economy as a whole. Sectors with a higher-than-average profit rate get a larger share of investable funds than their share in aggregate profits.

Reductions in Military Expenditures

In this section we examine the expected effects of a cut in defence expenditures. As in Haveman *et al.* [*Haveman, 1991: 17–29*; *Haveman, 1992*] this is done with the aid of (partial equilibrium) supply and demand diagrams. It should be clear that this simple representation does not capture all of the interactions of the general equilibrium model. A cut in defence expenditures is introduced into the model through the parameters which incorporate policy experiments. These parameters are conceptualised as shifts in final demand for output in each of the industries. Figure 1 reveals that both the home-sector demand function and the import demand function are affected by these variables.

Because we assume that the reduction in military spending is proportionally absorbed by the other sectors of final demand, a defence cut in an industry will give rise to several effects. First, there will be an inter-industry shift. This means that demand in industries where defence expenditure is concentrated will fall, while demand in industries to which that expenditure is shifted will rise. Secondly, intra-industry shifts represent shifts from defence spending (which we assume was devoted exclusively to home-produced goods), to other demand that is diverted to imports. Finally, in the long run there will also be supply-side effects due to changes in actual capital stocks of industries. In what follows we look at the partial equilibrium effects of a reduction in military expenditure in an industry where total demand increases due to a defence cut.

The top panels of Figures 2 and 3 show the markets for home-produced goods in an industry in which a cut in defence spending raises total demand. In this market, supply and demand depend on the home prices, but also on various prices of imports. These prices matter for demand because of consumer substitution, and are also important for supply because of the use of imports as inputs in the production of home-produced goods. In the figure this dependence is only shown for the price of the imported good in the same industry.

The bottom panels show the markets for export and import for the same industry. For convenience, prices and quantities of exports and imports are drawn on the same axis.[4] The world price is multiplied by the exchange rate to obtain the export price. It is straightforward that the supply of exports depends upon this price. Again, due to use of home goods as inputs, supply does also depend upon the price in the home market. The import price equals the export price augmented by an *ad valorem* tariff. Hence, the demand for imports is a function of this import price, as well as of the price in the home market, again because of the possibility of substituting the imported good for home market goods.

In what follows we first consider the short-run effects of a cut in defence spending. We therefore concentrate on the two panels of Figure 2. In both panels a cut in defence spending shifts the demand curves to the right. The prices of exports and imports do not change as long as the world price and the exchange rate remain invariable. The top panel of Figure 2 shows a price increase in the home market due to the demand shift. As a consequence, demand for imports shifts further to the right, while the supply of exports shifts to the left.

From the figures it becomes clear that a cut in defence spending in an industry where demand increases, results in a rise in output in the home market, a fall in exports and a rise in imports. Haveman *et al.* [*Haveman, 1992*; *Haveman, 1992*] point out that the results may change somewhat if there are changes in prices of exports and imports. When we assume that the country is large enough in the world market, its increased demand for imports will raise world prices. In addition there will be a depreciation of the currency due to the worsening of the trade balance of the country. Both this depreciation and the increase in world prices will raise the prices of exports and imports. It should be clear that these changes will tend to offset the effects on exports and imports depicted in Figures 2 and 3. In the home market, the increase in import price will lead to further upward shifts in the demand and supply curves. This induces prices to rise further while it is not clear in which direction the quantity in the home market will evolve. In turn, due to the new price in the home market, supply and demand for traded goods will shift further. All these secondary (short-run) shifts are not shown in the diagrams, but are captured by the static part of the model.

Due to all these effects, the economy of a country generates additional savings. It is assumed that the total nominal investment is determined by total savings. In turn total nominal investment will determine the actual amount of

FIGURE 2
SHORT-RUN EFFECTS OF A DEFENSE CUT IN A SECTOR WHERE DEMAND
INCREASES

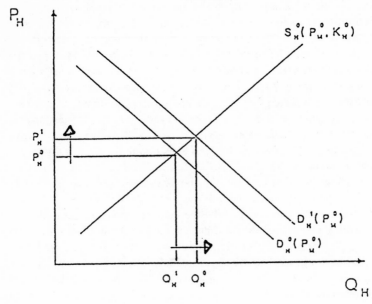

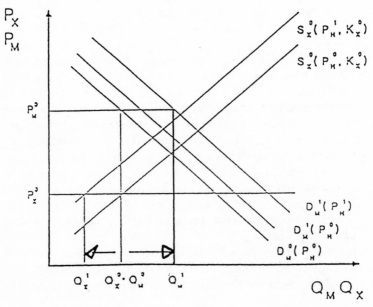

FIGURE 3
LONG-RUN EFFECTS OF A DEFENCE CUT IN A SECTOR WHERE DEMAND
INCREASES

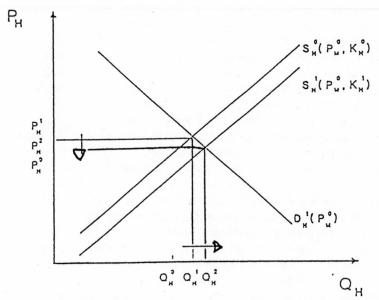

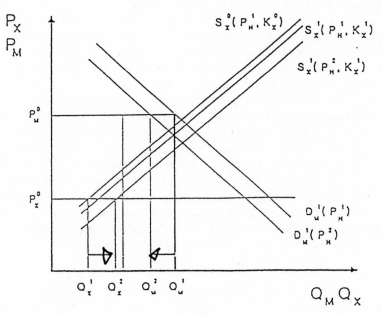

capital goods in each sector. An increase in total savings will unambiguously lead to an increase in real capital in sectors with a higher-than-average profit rate. Supply curves in the home as well as in the export market will face a rightward shift due to this increase in real capital. These two shifts are depicted in the two panels of Figure 3. In the home market as well as in the export market these shifts will certainly raise output. Again, an additional shift in supply and demand curves occur due to the fall in the home market price. Demand for imports shifts to the left, while the supply of exports shifts further to the right. From the bottom panels of Figures 2 and 3 it should be clear that the long-run effects are opposed to those described for the short run. This also applies to all the secondary shifts which are not shown in the figure.

A similar set of diagrams may be used to analyse the short and long-run effects in an industry where military expenditures are reduced severely and only a small amount of new final demand is created in that same industry. In this case total demand is reduced and as a consequence the demand curve in the home-sector shifts to the left, while the demand curve for imports will shift to the right. In the home market the output and price will fall. The latter shifts both supply of exports and the demand for imports down. Hence, in the short run, exports rise and imports fall.[5] Due to the rise in real capital the supply curves in the home market as well as in the export goods market shift to the right. Therefore, the price in the home market will drop further, while the produced output will increase. Due to the fall in price in the home-sector, the supply of exports and the demand for imports shift even further down. This increases the short-run effects in the export and import market.

Recall that the country as a whole tends to face a depreciation of the currency due to the worsening of the trade balance. If we also assume that the country is large enough in the world market to affect world prices, both world price changes and depreciation will raise the prices of exports and imports. In that case short and long-run impacts will increase further.

In summary, the partial equilibrium diagrams suggest that in sectors where demand expands, domestic prices and outputs will rise, while the opposite for sectors holds where demand contracts. In the long run prices will fall in both cases while domestic outputs will increase even further. When disregarding secondary effects, imports rise and exports fall in sectors where demand expands, while (again) the opposite is likely to occur where demand decreases. Still not accounting for secondary effects, a real capital increase will reduce the initial effects on imports and exports in an industry where demand increased. However, in an industry where demand contracted, the long-run adjustment will increase the initial effects on imports and exports.

III. ANALYSIS OF THE EFFECTS OF A 30 PER CENT CUT IN MILITARY SPENDING

The Data

The model includes ten tradable and four non-tradable industries in 14 countries. These countries are the United States (1976), Belgium and Luxembourg (1975), Finland (1982), Germany (1975), Norway (1980), Portugal (1981), Spain (1980), Sweden (1975), United Kingdom (1975), Argentina (1984), Brazil (1980), Chile (1986), Japan (1985) and South Korea (1988). The year of the input–output coverage is indicated within parentheses following the country-name. All data are adjusted so that our analysis starts in 1985. It is also assumed that all countries face flexible exchange regimes.

The industries used in the model are listed in Table 1, together with the two exogenous policy experiment variables for the United States. Recall that we described the two exogenous change (policy experiment) variables in a previous section. They both represent particular kinds of shifts in demand. The first is an inter-industry shift variable which simulates a reallocation of final demand across industries. The second shift variable is an intra-industry shift variable which captures a shift of demand within an industry from home-produced goods to imports [*Haveman, 1991: 7*]. When the procentual shifts listed in Table 1 occur for three succesive periods, the United States will face a 30 per cent reduction in its defence spending.

TABLE I

NET SECTORAL CHANGES IN TOTAL US DEMAND DUE TO A 30 PER CENT
CUT IN MILITARY EXPENDITURES

Sector	Inter and intra industry shift (percentages)	
Tradables	Inter	Intra
Agr., forestry, fishing	0.902	0.019
Food, beverages, tobacco	0.878	0.033
Textiles, apparel, leather	0.646	0.108
Wood products and furniture	0.721	0.076
Paper, printing	0.770	0.036
Chemicals products	0.228	0.067
Non-metallic mineral prod.	0.652	0.054
Ferrous and non-ferrous	-2.875	0.023
Fabricated metal products	-1.041	0.058
Other manufacturing	-0.027	0.177
Nontradables		
Mining and quarrying	0.549	
Electr., gas, st., water	0.700	
Construction	-0.431	
Services	0.243	

Note: These calculations are only correct for the US and if it is assumed that all resources flow back to the civilian sectors.

For the calculations of these sectoral changes in total demand we use information from the 1985 input–output table of the United States. The sectors which have large shares in federal defence purchases will be affected more by the cut in defence spending compared to sectors which face low defence purchases. As in Haveman [*Haveman, 1991: 16*] the total amount of saved resources due to the defence cut is then redistributed across other final demand in proportion to each sector's share in total 'other' demand. It is clear that a part of the redistributed money flows back to the civilian part of the sectors and to other sectors shown in the table (inter-industry shift). Another part will be shifted from the entirely home-produced military goods to imports (intra-industry shift).

Note that it is not necessary that all resources flow back to the civilian sectors. In what follows we therfore consider the case where only a part of the total peace dividend in each country is redistributed over the civilian sectors. Finally, all coefficients, elasticities and tariff levels needed in the model are based upon Deardorff *et al.* [*Deardorff, 1990: 40–41*]. For a detailed description of these data we refer the reader to their publication.

Simulation Results

Because the model is very large and involves a wide variety of non-linear functional forms, it is from a computational point of view quite intractable. Therefore we use the approach pioneered by Johansen [*1960*]. Linearisation of the model results in a system of linear equations in which the variables are percentage changes. As a consequence the proportional changes of the two calculated exogenous shifts may immediately be entered into the system and in turn the system will generate for each of the sectors a wide range of endogenous variables expressed as percentage changes. In what follows we discuss the simulation results for three selected variables: production, exports, imports and employment.

From the partial equilibrium diagrams we know that a shock in the system will induce new shocks which reinforce or reduce the initial effects upon the endogenous variables. Taking also into account the changes in exchange rates, the long-run effects and all the secondary effects between sectors, it becomes impossible to predict the final impacts for all variables using the simple partial equilibrium diagrams of section II. Therefore the general equilibrium model becomes a handy tool to calculate all mentioned effects and interactions that occur in our simulation.

In what follows we will discuss the results only superficially. Due to space limitation we present regional effects of the simulation. This, of course, also limits the possibility of discussing the results in detail.[6] Table 2 presents the short and long-run net effects on home production and on labour demand of a three-period 30 per cent reduction in military expenditure. Table 3 shows us the effects on exports and imports for the same simulation. As was already pointed out, the reduction in military spending yields for each country in the model.[7] We assume also that each country will face only a redistribution of 15 per cent of the total peace dividend available for that country. In both tables, ferrous, non-ferrous and fabricated metal products are severely influenced by the reallocation of resources. From Table 1 we knew that the initial demand shifts for these sectors (in the United States) were considerable. Almost all other sectors producing tradable goods are positively affected in the United States and Asia (Japan and South Korea). For European countries this becomes only true in the long run. In the short run Europe and Latin American countries face small negative growths in most sectors. This is probably caused by the redistribution ratio of 15 per cent. This relative low percentage is not able to compensate for the fall in sectoral military expenditures. The European labour market does not respond accordingly to the production because only four out of eight countries (Belgium-Luxembourg, Finland, Federal Republic of Germany and Norway) could here be taken into account.

Special attention is drawn to the sector chemicals, rubber and plastics. It seems that in Europe, Latin America and Asia this sector will get an incredible boost in the home as well as in the export market. The opposite applies to the United States. In the long run, the production for the home market falls, the growth of exports weakens while it increases for imports. The production of non-tradables faces a mildly negatively influence in all regions. Only Europe seems able to change this in the long run. The construction sector is affected the most by the simulation excercise. The labour market responds accordingly.

The tables in this section indicate that some sectors and regions may suffer severely from a 30 per cent reduction in military expenditures. However, there are also a number of technical reasons why these proportional changes may be considerably large. Because of the linearisation of the model, it will only generate accurate approximations of endogenous variables when the changes of the exogenous variables are small. Also, data limitations give rise to problems that are not easy to solve. Our main concern for further research will be to tackle these data problems.

IV. CONCLUSIONS

In the literature it is expected that a multilateral reduction in military expenditures has positive effects on the economy. However, when we discriminate between short-run and long-run effects and work on a disaggregated level, this picture changes. Certain sectors and countries bear a more-than-proportional burden due to the world-wide defence cut. This results in a smaller demand for labour in these sectors and countries. In the long run, some of these negative effects are reduced.

TABLE 2

A. SHORT-RUN NET CHANGES IN HOME PRODUCTION AND LABOUR DEMAND (percentages)

		Home Production				Labour	
		U.S.	Europe	Lat. Am.	Asia	U.S.	Europe
Tradables							
010	Agr.,Forestry,Fishing	0.44	-0.83	-0.26	1.10	0.54	4.61
031	Food,Bev.,Tobacco	0.25	-0.88	-0.29	0.77	0.38	1.13
032	Clothing	0.62	-0.45	0.00	2.75	1.16	3.40
033	Wood Prod.,Furniture	0.15	2.37	0.69	1.92	1.58	2.56
034	Paper, Printing	0.12	-1.01	-0.34	0.72	0.22	1.55
035	Chemicals,Rubber,Plast	0.09	4.55	5.45	3.57	0.62	4.20
036	Non-Metallic Mineral P	-0.29	-2.27	-0.94	0.32	-0.32	0.44
037	Ferrous And Non-Ferr.	-2.16	-7.03	-5.16	-3.55	-2.69	-3.59
038	Fabricated Metal Prod.	-1.15	-2.62	-2.12	-1.44	-1.50	-0.62
039	Other Manufacturing	-0.43	-2.77	-1.46	0.09	-0.21	0.66
Nontradables							
020	Mining & Quarrying	-0.30	-1.43	-2.14	-0.66	-0.39	0.20
040	Electr., Gas ,St., Wat	-0.10	-0.90	-0.35	-0.24	-0.16	0.46
050	Construction	-0.73	-1.32	-1.01	-0.87	-0.81	-0.37
6.9	Services	-0.39	-1.10	-0.70	-0.64	-0.45	0.09

Note: Due to inconsistency and/or availability not all data could be calculated.

TABLE 2 (CONT.)
B. LONG-RUN NET CHANGES IN HOME PRODUCTION AND LABOUR DEMAND (percentages)

	Home Production			Labour	
	U.S.	Europe	Asia	U.S.	Europe
Tradables					
010 Agr.,Forestry,Fishing	0.17	1.83	2.34	0.48	4.97
031 Food,Bev.,Tobacco	0.09	2.94	1.79	0.25	2.24
032 Clothing	0.59	0.42	4.93	-0.03	3.34
033 Wood Prod.,Furniture	-0.70	4.49	0.09	3.81	2.59
034 Paper, Printing	0.05	-1.61	0.28	0.42	2.02
035 Chemicals,Rubber,Plast	-3.25	5.66	5.69	-4.97	7.13
036 Non-Metallic Mineral P	-0.12	-2.35	-0.06	-0.44	0.46
037 Ferrous And Non-Ferr.	-2.14	22.85	-7.34	-2.37	-5.02
038 Fabricated Metal Prod.	-2.93	-4.21	-4.50	-2.59	-0.74
039 Other Manufacturing	-2.16	3.19	-2.81	2.03	0.93
Nontradables					
020 Mining & Quarrying	-0.82	0.77	-0.79	-1.31	-0.02
040 Electr., Gas ,St. ,Wat	-0.14	1.05	-0.28	-0.18	0.76
050 Construction	-2.59	-0.50	-2.20	-3.36	-2.29
6.9 Services	-1.33	0.02	-1.38	-1.12	-1.88

Note: Due to inconsistency and/or availability not all data could be calculated.

TABLE 3

A. SHORT-RUN NET EFFECTS ON EXPORTS AND IMPORTS (percentages)

		U.S.		Europe		Lat. Am.		Asia	
		Export	Import	Export	Import	Export	Import	Export	Import
010	Agr.,Forestry,Fishing	0.84	1.09	-0.48	-0.69	-0.59	-0.41	0.81	2.06
031	Food,Bev.,Tobacco	0.71	0.83	-1.34	-1.10	-0.94	-0.74	2.07	1.41
032	Clothing	3.29	2.32	-0.90	-1.18	-0.96	-1.17	4.37	2.54
033	Wood Prod.,Furniture	9.71	3.78	1.89	-0.40	0.69	0.25	6.73	3.64
034	Paper, Printing	3.19	1.30	-1.15	-0.93	-0.86	-0.63	2.14	1.07
035	Chemicals,Rubber,Plast	9.09	5.88	4.41	0.12	1.62	-4.91	7.24	3.78
036	Non-Metallic Mineral P	0.20	-0.03	-2.21	-1.87	-1.59	-1.70	0.10	0.12
037	Ferrous And Non-Ferr.	-11.84	-4.44	-9.33	-5.27	-4.83	-4.69	-8.81	-3.90
038	Fabricated Metal Prod.	-3.45	-0.94	-4.01	-2.60	-2.08	-2.23	-1.64	-1.07
039	Other Manufacturing	0.27	0.15	-3.65	-1.88	-2.29	-1.60	0.49	0.56

B. LONG-RUN NET EFFECTS ON EXPORTS AND IMPORTS (percentage)

		U.S.		Europe		Asia	
		Export	Import	Export	Import	Export	Import
010	Agr.,Forestry,Fishing	1.86	3.33	2.35	5.13	3.75	6.88
031	Food,Bev.,Tobacco	1.47	2.10	2.05	6.09	4.53	5.13
032	Clothing	-10.32	-3.80	1.88	11.54	5.39	-0.61
033	Wood Prod.,Furniture	47.21	-5.48	4.36	6.12	5.10	-5.31
034	Paper, Printing	1.57	-2.42	0.56	4.89	2.16	0.13
035	Chemicals,Rubber,Plast	7.63	11.95	5.79	5.30	7.58	-5.36
036	Non-Metallic Mineral P	-1.34	-3.61	-1.07	1.70	0.38	-0.13
037	Ferrous And Non-Ferr.	-1.22	22.52	2.54	11.44	2.67	26.77
038	Fabricated Metal Prod.	-6.68	-7.60	-5.33	-4.57	-3.95	-6.56
039	Other Manufacturing	32.10	-5.21	-3.43	-5.27	-0.25	-0.40

Note: Due to inconsistency and/or availability not all data could be calculated.

174

It seems that Europe and Latin American countries are negatively affected in the short run, while the United States, Japan and South Korea face positive rates of growth for most of the endogenous variables (production, export, import, employment). However, in the long run Europe is also able to make the conversion. While the Asian countries keep performing strongly in the long run, the performance of the United States falls back. The sectors of ferrous, non-ferrous and fabricated metal products as well as all non-tradable goods are negatively influenced by the defence cut.

Although some of the negative effects are reduced in the long run, conversion without government assistance will be problematic for the above mentioned sectors and regions. To analyse which measures have to be adopted to guarantee a smooth transition, further research and simulations are necessary. In this manner, the presented model might become a policy tool which facilitates the conversion of the military sector and which might even help in finding a sustainable development path.

NOTES

1. Special thanks to R.M. Stern (The University of Michigan) who gave his permission to use the Michigan model for our study.
2. Note that in this paper capital accumulation is not regulated by an intertemporal equilibrium system with perfect foresight of capital markets as a crucial part of that system. Instead we use the exogenous parameters and the past history of the economy to make the model dynamic. In this way, investment may still be governed by expectations about the future, but we assume that these expectations are formed on the basis of past experience. For a further discussion of this topic, see K. Dervis, *et al.* [*Dervis, 1982: 171–3*].
3. See, for example, Dervis, K. *et al.* [*Dervis, 1982: 173–5*] for a discussion of this approach. In I. Adelman and S. Robinson [*Adelman, 1978*] we find a formalisation of such a dynamic model.
4. In the model exports and imports are viewed as identical products in the world market. However, within a country imports of an industry are viewed as distinct from exports.
5. We assume that the effect in the home price has a larger effect on the import demand curve than the initial increase upon this demand curve.
6. It should be clear however that these regional results are based upon more detailed country results. For a more accurate discription of country results we direct the reader to a previous study of the author [*Van Rompuy, 1993*]
7. Due to inconsistency and/or data availability not all data could be calculated.

REFERENCES

Adelman, I. and S. Robinson (1978): *Income Distribution Policy in Developing Countries. A Case Study of Korea*, Stanford, CA: Stanford University Press.
Deardorff, A.V., Stern, R.M., and Ch.F. Baum (1976): 'A Simulation Model of

World Trade and Production', unpublished study, Ann Arbor, MI: Department of Economics, University of Michigan.

Deardorff, A.V. and R.M. Stern (1990): *Computational Analysis of Global Trading Arrangements*, Ann Arbor, MI: University of Michigan Press.

Dervis, K., De Melo, J., and S. Robinson (1982): *General Equilibrium Models for Development Policy*, Cambridge, MA: Cambridge University Press.

Dixon, P.B., Parmenter, B.R., Powell, A.A. and P.J. Wilcoxen (1992): *Notes and Problems in Applied General Equilibrium Economics*, Amsterdam: North-Holland.

Haveman, J.D., Deardorff, A.V. and R.M. Stern (1991): 'Some Economic Effects of Unilateral and Multilateral Reductions in Military Expenditures in the Major Industrialized and Developing Countries', unpublished seminar discussion paper No.270, Ann Arbor, MI: Department of Economics, University of Michigan.

Haveman, J.D., Deardorff, A.V. and R.M. Stern (1992): 'Sectoral Effects of Reductions in NATO Military Expenditures in the Major Industrialized and Developing Countries', unpublished study, Ann Arbor, MI: University of Michigan Press.

IMF (1991): *International Financial Statistics, Yearbook 1991*, Washington, DC: International Monetary Fund.

Johansen, L. (1960): *A Multisectoral Study of Economic Growth*, Amsterdam: North-Holland.

OECD (1993): *Industrial Structure Statistics 1991*, Paris: Organisation for Economic Co-operation and Development.

US Department of Commerce, Bureau of Economic Analysis (1991): 'Benchmark Input–Output Accounts for the U.S. Economy, 1982', *Survey of Current Business*, July 1991, pp. 30–71.

US Department of Commerce, Bureau of Economic Analysis (1991): 'Annual Input–Output Accounts of the U.S. Economy, 1986', *Survey of Current Business*, February 1991, pp. 35–50.

U.N. (1991): *International Trade Statistics Yearbook, 1986. Volume I: Trade by Country*, New York: United Nations.

Van Rompuy, B. (1993): 'Disarmament and Sustainable Development: A General Equilibrium Model for the World Economy', unpublished study, Louvain: Centre for Economic Studies, Catholic University of Louvain.

10

The Restrictiveness of the MFA: Evidence on Eastern European Exports to the EU

ALBERTO BRUGNOLI AND LAURA RESMINI

I. INTRODUCTION[1]

The textile sector has traditionally been an important vehicle for industrialisation and a major source of export earnings for developing countries, but it has always been limited by industrialised country protectionism. The Multi-Fibre Arrangement (MFA) is among the most important non-tariff barriers facing developing countries today. Although it is administered under the auspices of the General Agreement on Tariffs and Trade (GATT), it has been defined as 'one of the most comprehensive and discriminatory deformations of the international trading system' [*Herzan and Holmes, 1990: 191*].

Much has been said and written about the costs and the negative effects generated by the MFA. Most literature has concentrated on importing countries, but recently some authors have tried to investigate the economic effects of the MFA on developing and Eastern Europe countries. In both cases the evidence is far from being unequivocal. There is, in fact, disagreement as to the degree and trends in the restrictiveness of the MFA. Western Europe, the eastern bloc's main market in the industrialised world, has recently taken significant steps to improve trading arrangements with those countries which are newly embarking on a market economy. Association Agreements (the so-called 'Europe Agreements') have been signed with Poland, Hungary, the Czech and Slovak Republics, Bulgaria and Romania, while co-operation agreements have come into force with Albania, the three Baltic Republics and with the CIS. Previously facing more trade barriers than other developing countries, East European countries now benefit from more trade concessions than Latin America, Mediterranean region countries and even most non-EU industrialised states. Despite that, trade is still protected in sectors such as textiles and clothing, agriculture and steel.

This chapter examines the dominant features of the MFA and its impact on Eastern Europe's exports in the EU market. We wonder whether this protection is effective or not and to what extent it is able to slow down the restructuring process in East Europe. We concentrate on the five countries that have signed Association Agreements with the EU (hereafter EE5).[2] As far as data are concerned, quota levels (in quantities) were extracted from the EU Official Journal and since the EU publishes quota levels in advance, we consider the period 1988 to 1997. EU import data under MFA categories were made available by the EU and cover the period 1988–92. The choice of such a short time period is primarily based on the fact that in 1988 the EU adopted a new classification for product categories, the so-called 'Combined Nomenclature'.

Sections II and III give some background on the MFA and the Association Agreements negotiated between the EU and the EE5. Section IV briefly reviews the relevant literature on the impact of the MFA on EE5 trade in textiles and clothing. Section V analyses historical and future MFA quota growth for the EE5. In sections VI and VII we look at the recent EE5 export trends both for the direct trade and the Outward Processing Traffic (OPT) and we compute several restrictiveness indexes, some of which are commonly used in literature on MFA[3]. A concluding section sums up our findings.

The successful conclusion of the Uruguay Round is likely to produce a little revolution in the textile and clothing sector. Under the GATT deal reached om 15 December 1993, most of the tariffs and quotas on textiles and clothing will gradually be eliminated after 1995 and completely abandoned in 2005.

II. THE MFA: OBJECTIVES AND KEY CONCEPTS

The MFA consists of a series of bilateral quota restrictions negotiated between developed and developing countries. It was first signed in 1974 and re-negotiated three times, until 1991. Since then, it has been renewed on a yearly base until the end of 1994.[4] The main objective of the MFA is to 'achieve the expansion of trade, the reduction of barriers to such trade and the progressive liberalisation of world trade in textile products, while at the same time ensuring the orderly and equitable development of this trade and avoidance of disruptive effects in individual markets and line of productions in both importing and exporting countries' (art.1).

The key concept of the MFA is that of 'market disruption'. Importing countries can implement restricted measures in order to avoid serious damage, or threat of damage, to domestic producers. Market disruption occurs when there is a sharp and substantial increase, or imminent increase, of imports from particular sources and when exporting countries price their products substantially below the prevailing price in importing countries.

The MFA also contains some clauses to protect exporting countries, at least on a formal basis. New quotas must not be less than the actual trade levels during the previous year. For the existing quotas, the annual growth rate must not be less than six per cent. Moreover, some flexibility is allowed in the quota administration. If more than one product is subject to quota restrictions, a particular quota can be exceeded by seven per cent provided that another quota is reduced by the same amounts (swing provision); if quota restrictions are established for more than one year, up to ten per cent of the unused portion of a quota can be postponed to the following year (carry over provision), while up to five per cent of the following year's quota can be used in advance (carry forward provision), as long as the combined use of carry over and carry forward does not exceed ten per cent.[5] Flexibility provisions have an important role, because they give exporters the opportunity to offset partially the restrictiveness of the system and to respond to changes in the foreign market demand. However, we should not forget that the recourse to flexibility provision means that the exporting country has reached the ceiling of the quota. Therefore, in this case, quota restrictions limit the developing country's possibility to export.

It is clear that the MFA is contrary to the spirit of the GATT, since it derogates from the principles of the avoidance of quota restrictions and that of non-discrimination. Quota restrictions are bilaterally negotiated and their severity depends on elements such as the 'friendliness' of the relations between importer and exporter countries, the pressure of national producers on the government of the importing country, the expectation concerning the export potential of a supplier and so on. Moreover, there are important differences among the individual agreements as regards the number of restricted categories. Major exporters face up to 40 restrictions, while the smallest ones no more than two. Finally, restrictions are generally applied towards imports of textiles and clothing coming from developing countries and not from developed ones. The reason for this evident discrimination, deriving from a restrictive interpretation of the concept of market disruption, is that trade is in any case free among developed countries, while developing countries often restrict imports. However, this is not entirely true, for many less developed countries do not apply any restriction on textiles and clothing imports [*Raffaelli, 1990: 264*].

As an importer, the EU is one of the contracting parties of the MFA. In the context of the MFA IV, the EU has negotiated quota restrictions on imports coming from 20 exporting countries [*GATT, 1993: 208*]. Czechoslovakia, Poland, Hungary and Romania participated as exporters in MFA IV, while Bulgaria, not being a GATT member, is subject to a MFA-type agreement.[6] However, EE5 will benefit by a shortest phasing-out period. According to the 'Europe Agreements' the dismantling of the MFA quotas will last only five years, half the period agreed on in the Uruguay Round. While these changes are surely important, their impact on trade flows may not be drastic. As we show in the chapter, some quotas have already significantly changed and the MFA itself is much less restrictive than it was intended.

III. THE 'EUROPE AGREEMENTS'

Historically East European countries have not been favourably treated in their trade relations with the EC. However, the EC's attitude changed when these countries began their reforms towards democracy and the market economy, and one can reasonably expect a further reinforcing of the present trade relations, which undoubtedly will affect textiles and clothing sector, as well. The EU has been in the process of establishing special relations with the East European countries since 1989. In March 1990, the EU concluded additional protocols to textile agreements with Hungary and Poland. For 1990 and 1991, they provided for quota increases of 13 per cent and 23 per cent respectively and separate quota restrictions on OPT trade. In December 1991, Hungary, Poland and Czechoslovakia signed an Association Agreement (the so-called 'Europe Agreement') with the EC, while Bulgaria and Romania signed it in 1993. They aimed at establishing 'free trade areas, in the sense of Article XXIV of the General Agreement, over a maximum period of ten years'.[7]

Because the Association Agreements require ratification by all national parliaments, Interim Agreements were signed to enable trade provisions of the Association Agreements to come into force on 1 March 1992 as far as Poland, Hungary and Czechoslovakia were concerned. The Interim Agreement between the EU and Romania came into force on 1 April 1993, while the Interim Agreement between the EU and Bulgaria started on 1 July 1993. According to the parties, these agreements contain all GATT relevant trade provisions of the new Agreements. The Europe Agreements are considerably wider in coverage than the EC's previous association agreements, as, for example, those with Turkey, Malta and Cyprus. A clause in the Preamble holds that the final objective of the five signatory countries is to become members of the EU and that 'this association [...] will help to achieve this objective'.

As regards textiles and clothing, Protocol n. 1 of the Interim Agreements lays down specific rules. EU tariffs on these products will be eliminated over a six-year period. The elimination of quantitative restrictions instead has been linked to the outcome of the Uruguay Round. The EU will eliminate such measures in half the phasing-out period agreed on with the other countries in the GATT talks. Assuming that the Agreements begin to operate on 1 January 1995, it follows that trade in textiles and clothing between EE5 and the EU will be completely liberalised on 1 January 2000.

IV. AN OVERVIEW OF THE RECENT LITERATURE

Many studies have been carried out with different methodologies in order to assess the static and dynamic effects of the MFA. Among these, the effects on welfare have been widely discussed since they are generally assumed to be quite relevant. An estimation of the welfare costs borne by US, EU and Canada due to MFA III was calculated by Trela and Whalley [*1990*] with a computable general equilibrium model. They considered seven restricted and seven unrestricted specific textile and apparel product categories and residual GDP as the 'composite other good', and computed the annual global gains from elimination of quotas and tariffs on textile and apparel trade. They found gains of about US$15.3 billion per annum for the developed countries (US$12.3 for US, US$0.8 for Canada and US$2.2 for EC) and of about US$0.605 billion for the EE5. None of these was ranked among the developing countries which gained even more. But the costs calculated might overestimate the real ones since a significant assumption underlying the computation is that all bilateral quotas were fully binding in the year in question (that is, 1986).[8] This is a strong hypothesis, even if Trela and Whalley emphasised three reasons in order to support the thesis that data which seem to indicate non-binding quotas need to be looked at in a very careful way since they may in fact reflect binding restrictions. First, the capacity constraints of some firms and their unwillingness to reassign their quota allocation for fear of losing it in future years. Second, the fact that quotas in the EU were often allocated among the members on the basis of historical market shares, implying that quotas may be binding in some regions and not in some others. Third, sub-aggregate quotas may not seem to be binding while in fact they are at an aggregate level.

In contrast, Raffaelli [*1990*] suggests that if a quota is utilised at a level of 80 or 85 per cent, it can be assumed that the developing country, in the absence of a quota, would have exported more than its full level. Thus he implicitly assumes that if a developing country uses less than 80 or 85 per cent of a quota, its exports should not vary in the event of a cancellation of the quota, and therefore the welfare effects predicted in the Trela and Whalley model would not take place.

To compare the effects of MFA on the EE5 countries and on other suppliers, Erzan and Holmes [*1992*][9] relied mainly on the number of product categories facing quotas and binding quotas in the EU and the US over the period 1985–89 and on the same five main indicators of Erzan, Goto and Holmes [*1990*].[10] From the data which they reported three main considerations emerge:

(a) not considering the intra-EU trade, EU import from EE5 constituted, on average, only 5.8 per cent of the EC's total imports on textiles and clothing, and the percentage was decreasing from 1985 (6.24 per cent) to 1989 (5.30 per cent). Therefore, the coverage of the EC's MFA on EE5, specified by the number of product categories facing quotas and binding quotas, seemed to be particularly tightening;

(b) the decreasing performance over time of imports subject to quotas as a percentage of total imports (in every group) tended to suggest a general relaxation of restraints on textile imports;

(c) the averages over time of binding quotas as a percentage of total imports suggested that the EE5 countries were more restricted than the average supplier (42.5 per cent 35.96) and almost as restricted as the East Asian countries (45.27).

Based on these results, they concluded that 'the trade-restraining impact of the MFA on the EE5 countries was not very different from that on other MFA suppliers' [*Erzan and Holmes, 1992: 28*]. To predict the eventual performance of EE5 countries in the case of a relaxation of the MFA quotas, the authors analysed the factor intensity and degree of specialisation of EE5's textile and clothing exports in comparison with other MFA suppliers and found that:

(a) despite the more capital-abundant endowment of East Asian exporters, the capital intensity of EE5 country exports to the EU is greater, with the exception of Czechoslovakia;

(b) EE5 countries' exports are much less concentrated over few products compared to all major suppliers.[11]

Therefore, they conclude that 'if the MFA were abolished or relaxed *vis-à-vis* EE5, their exports of relatively labour-intensive products would expand more than proportionately and their degree of specialisation would increase' [*Erzan and Holmes, 1992: 28*]. More or less the same thesis is supported by Hamilton [*1990*] who stressed that Eastern European countries supply prices are probably much lower than those of producers now supplying the Western European market.[12]

Recently, Rollo and Smith [*1993*] investigated the foundations and the economic effects of the EU[13] trade policy towards the EE5 countries in all the five sectors for which considerable protection is still in place (that is, ores and metals; chemicals; textiles, clothing, leather, footwear; agriculture; food processing.[14] Their findings were based mainly on 1989 data and they concluded that:

> the scale of the adjustments required by liberalized trade with Eastern Europe seems quite manageable, even making no allowance for the growing market in Eastern Europe for Western European products. [...] To the extent that the Community's reliance on contingent protection acts as a deterrent to the development of new export industries there will be long-term losses from not liberalizing the current sensitive sectors. [...] the reliance on contingent protection means that any product is

potentially sensitive. Whenever some group of EU producers is damaged by competition from the East, the threat or often the substance of contingent protection is triggered. [...] sensitive products are not defined by criteria which refer to particular structural adjustment problems within the EC. Rather the emphasis on contingent protection reflects a mixture of competitive threat and regulatory capture [*Rollo and Smith, 1993: 16–17*].

Also Messerlin [*1993*], looking at the growth in the MFA quotas granted to the Czech and Slovak Republics, Hungary and Poland (CE4) in 1990–91 and 1992, stressed that the utilisation rates of the CE4 do not change greatly between 1989 and 1990, implying that the increase in EU quotas has been quickly followed by an alignment in the CE4 export capacities. This result seems to suggest, first, that CE4 exports are not a matter of production capacity but of restriction and that they could rapidly increase if totally liberalised. Secondly, since most of the growth in the quotas refers to the EU OPT regime, the real beneficiaries are the EU textile and apparel producers and not the CE4 ones. Two main conclusions are pointed out: first, the Association Agreements signed in December 1991 by the three countries are 'an exercise for containing free trade in the short run in sector crucial for the CE4 countries, hence introducing high risks of reversibility of trade policy in the long run', and second, 'the CE4 have to take a major initiative to salvage their recent efforts, namely, to create their own free trade zone or common market, by joining the EFTA or by adopting the Treaty of Rome between themselves' [*Messerlin, 1993: 90*].

V. THE EVOLUTION OF QUOTAS

The main instruments of the MFA are bilaterally negotiated quotas, usually administered by exporting countries. The EU has adopted a comprehensive system of restrictions covering the whole range of textile products made out of cotton, wool and manmade fibres and most clothing items.[15] Table 1 shows the evolution of the EU restrictions affecting the EE5.[16] The EU has progressively reduced the number of categories facing restraints. The five countries together faced 52 quotas in 1988; the figure has dropped to 26 in 1994 and it might fall further after 1995 when the MFA phasing-out process will begin.

The process of trade liberalisation started in the 1990s, but it followed different paths, according to the history of each country and its progressive integration with Western Europe. The first countries to benefit from MFA liberalisation were Czechoslovakia, Poland and Hungary. The number of categories facing restrictions dropped dramatically in 1992: about one-third of the restrictions existing at the beginning of the period were abolished for Poland and Hungary, while Czechoslovakia saw a reduction of about 40 per cent. Despite this great liberalisation, Czechoslovakia and Romania bear the tightest coverage of the MFA, facing respectively 25 and 29 (not considering regional quotas) out of 38 restrictions. The liberalisation process affected imports coming from Bulgaria and Romania only from 1994, when Europe Agreements came into force. In 1993 only regional quotas were liberalised, since they were incompatible with the Single European market.

The phasing out of most of the restrictions affecting trade in textiles and clothing between the EU and the EE5 coincided with the introduction of new quotas on OPT trade. Although it has played an important role since the 1980s, trade flows under this regime only increased rapidly these last years (see Figures 13–18). Western European textile and clothing producers were the first to understand the big opportunities offered by decentralising some production stages in Central and Eastern Europe countries because of the low cost of manpower and of the incentives granted by the EU itself. economic difficulties due to the long duration of the world recession led the EU to introducing new restrictions on OPT towards the EE5,[17] in order to avoid a surge of unemployment in its textile and clothing sector. Table 2 shows the number of categories subject to restrictions in the OPT regime. The number of restrictions *per se* do not show anything but the extension of the coverage of the MFA. What really matters is the quota growth rate.[18]

TABLE I

NUMBER OF CATEGORIES FACING QUOTAS DIRECT TRADE (1988–97)

	1988	1989	1990	1991	1992	1993	1994-97
Bulgaria	15	15	15	15	15	12	8
regional	3	3	3	3	3	–	–
binding	–	–	1	1	4	–	–
Czechoslovakia	43	43	43	41	25	24	24
regional	5	5	5	3	–	–	–
binding	4	4	4	7	1	–	–
Hungary	30	30	30	30	20	18	18
regional	2	2	2	2	–	–	–
binding	1	1	1	–	–	–	–
Poland	33	33	33	33	20	18	18
regional	7	7	7	6	–	–	–
binding	3	2	5	2	–	–	–
Romania	36	36	36	36	35	28	16
regional	7	7	7	7	6	–	–
binding	–	–	1	–	–	–	–
EE5 (*)	52	52	52	52	38	35	26
binding	7	6	9	8	5	–	–

(*) A quota is counted if it applies at least to one out of five countries. Regional limits are not included.

TABLE 2

NUMBER OF CATEGORIES FACING QUOTAS OUTWARD PROCESSING TRAFFIC
(1991–97)

	1991	1992	1993	1994-97
Bulgaria	10	8	9	6
regional	–	–	–	–
binding –	2	–	–	
Czechoslovakia	19	12	12	12
regional	–	–	–	–
binding	4	1	–	–
Hungary	16	11	11	11
regional	1	–	–	–
binding	3	2	–	–
Poland	18	10	10	10
regional	5	–	–	–
binding	–	–	–	–
Romania	20	23	16	11
regional	6	6	–	–
binding	–	3	–	–
EE5 (*)	23	17	17	14
binding	6	5	–	–

(*) A quota is counted if it applies at least to one out of five countries. Regional limits are not included.

The guideline in the MFA is a six per cent annual growth rate. However, our computations indicate that the average growth of quotas has been quite different, not only among countries but also across the years. We can distinguish three different time periods: the late 1980s (1988–90), the early 1990s (1990–93) and the middle 1990s (1993–97).[19] The first period consists of the final scheduled years of the MFA (see note 4). The average quota growth rates have been less than six per cent for all countries except Czechoslovakia, which, however, shows a large variation across product categories (see Table 3).[20] The years 1991–93 coincide with the beginning of the great transformation of the EE5. The EC's efforts to foster East European countries' restructuring process and transition towards the market economy has had an incredible increase in the quota growth rates as a consequence. As an example, we are reminded of the effects of the G–24 PHARE programme, a wide programme aimed at giving financial support to long-run projects in the field of privatisation, public companies and of the promotion of small and medium-sized firms. As far as the textile sector is concerned, participation in the PHARE programme enabled, first, Hungary and Poland, then Czechoslovakia, Bulgaria and Romania to enjoy incredible increases in quotas, impossible to continue in the future because of their extraordinary nature.[21] Finally, after a period in which the EU more than doubled EE5 import quotas, for 1993–97 the scheduled average growth rates returned to less than the benchmark rate of six per cent. This is not true for OPT restrictions, whose scheduled average growth rate is about seven per cent (see Table 4).

Synthetically, from the analysis of the pattern of quotas, it does not seem that the MFA is becoming much less restrictive for the EE5. This consideration is also supported by analysis of the liberalised quotas. A detailed investigation shows that the EU first liberalised the regional quotas and then the superfluous restraints, which meant those using less than ten per cent. Most quotas enlarged during the early 1990s will not be liberalised until 1997 at least. Filled quotas have not been liberalised, but only enlarged to allow the EE5 to increase their exports into the EU to the levels of other MFA producers.[22]

TABLE 3

AVERAGE QUOTA GROWTH RATES: DIRECT TRADE

	Aver.	St.Dv.	Min.	Max.
Bulgaria				
1988–90	2.9	1.1	1.4	4.1
1990–93	33.3	11.9	12.2	51.5
1993–97	3.9	1.4	1.9	6.0
Czechoslovakia				
1988–90	8.2	8.4	1.0	30.7
1990–93	41.7	27.5	6.3	107.0
1993–97	4.8	1.2	2.0	6.0
Hungary				
1988–90	3.8	1.4	1.0	5.9
1990–93	37.2	19.8	10.9	87.1
1993–97	4.9	1.3	1.9	6.0
Poland				
1988–90	3.8	1.3	1.5	6.0
1990–93	41.7	16.9	14.7	90.1
1993–97	4.8	1.3	2.0	6.0
Romania				
1988–90	3.9	1.6	1.0	6.0
1990–93	13.8	6.6	5.9	28.5
1993–97	4.7	1.4	1.9	6.0
EE5				
1988–90	5.1	2.8	1.3	19.0
1990–93	22.4	11.0	6.1	52.3
1993–97	5.04	1.2	2.0	6.0

FIGURES I–3
TRENDS ON DIRECT TRADE IN TEXTILES AND CLOTHING
(categories from 50 to 63-unit: tonnes)

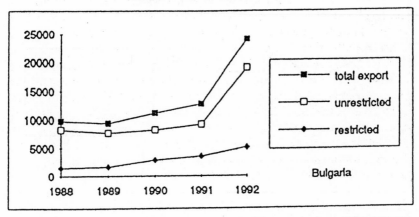

Bulgaria

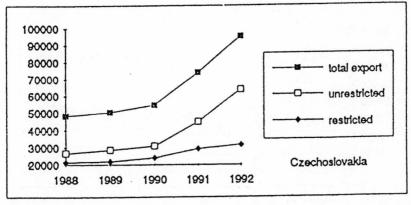

Czechoslovakia

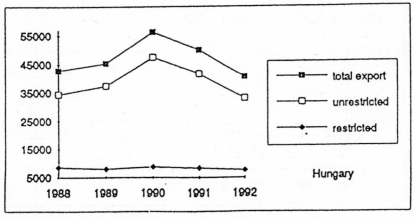

Hungary

FIGURES 4–6
TRENDS IN DIRECT TRADE IN TEXTILES AND CLOTHING (cont.)

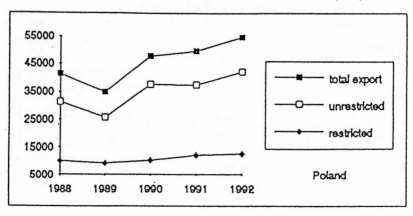

Poland

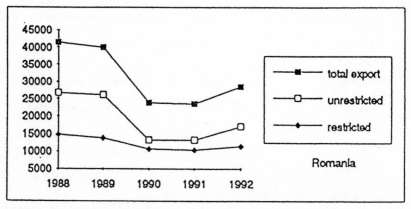

Romania

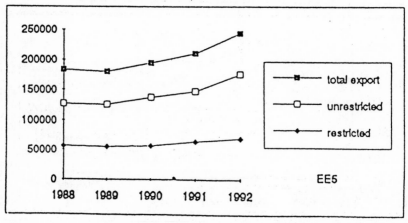

EE5

FIGURES 7–9
DIRECT TRADE IN TEXTILES AND CLOTHING: GROWTH RATES
(categories from 50 to 6-unit: percentages)

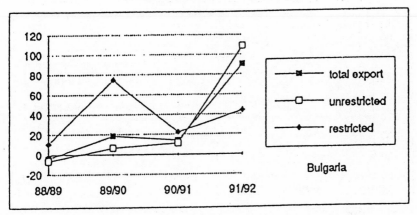

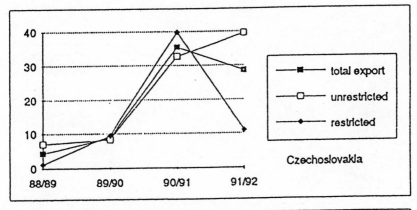

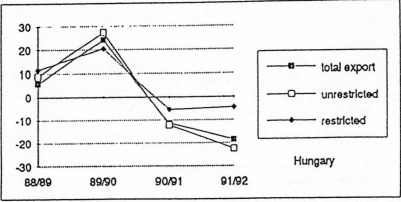

FIGURES 10–12
DIRECT TRADE IN TEXTILES AND CLOTHING: GROWTH RATES
(categories from 50 to 63-unit: percentages) (cont.)

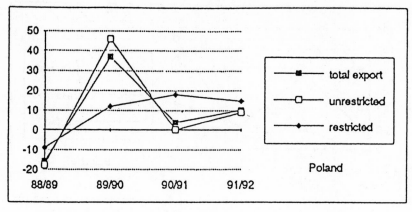

Poland

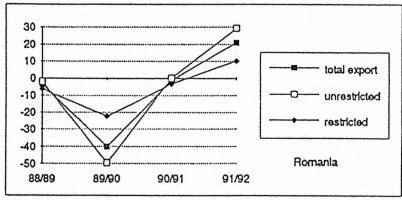

Romania

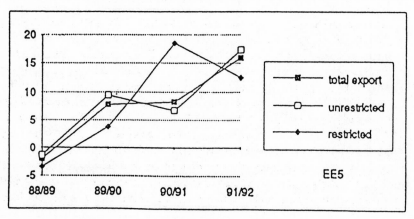

EE5

TABLE 4
AVERAGE QUOTA GROWTH RATES: OPT

	Aver.	St.Dv.	Min.	Max.
Bulgaria				
1988–90	–	–	–	–
1990–93	109.0	98.2	22.5	322.1
1993–97	7.0	1.2	5.3	9.0
Czechoslovakia				
1988–90	–	–	–	–
1990–93	120.2	57.5	54.9	229.1
1993–97	6.9	1.3	4.5	9.0
Hungary				
1988–90	–	–	–	–
1990–93	53.8	20.5	22.8	78.4
1993–97	7.7	1.5	4.5	9.0
Poland				
1988–90	–	–	–	–
1990–93	57.3	17.4	33.4	85.1
1993–97	8.0	1.5	5.3	9.0
Romania				
1988–90	–	–	–	–
1990–93	88.9	67.3	6.3	265.2
1993–97	7.6	1.6	4.5	9.0
EE5				
1988–90	–	–	–	–
1990–93	65.0	28.0	6.3	117.6
1993–97	7.8	1.3	4.8	9.0

VI. THE MFA IMPACT ON DIRECT TRADE

A separate analysis of restricted and unrestricted EE5 textile and clothing exports to the EU enables a judgement of the real restrictiveness of the EU trade policy in the sector.[23] From 1988 to 1989, EE5 exports dropped by about two per cent, while they grew incessantly during the subsequent period (see Figure 6). The pattern of trade for restricted categories does not differ dramatically from that of unrestricted ones although the former always shows lower percentage increases (or higher decreases) than the latter, except in 1990/91 when many quotas were significantly enlarged and a few were fully liberalised (see Figure 12).[24] In the last years, considering the level of exports, Czechoslovakia has undoubtedly experienced the most surprising percentage growth, primarily, but not exclusively due to the performance of unrestricted products (see Figures 2 and 8). Bulgaria has also recently known very high export growth rates which suggests it could play a more important role in the near future (see Figures 1 and 7). Romania and Hungary went through a negative period but, while the first seems to have reversed this trend, the second is still widely suffering from competition of other producers (see Figures 3, 5, 9 and 11).

From these data, two main considerations may be inferred. First, the fact that EE5 total exports grew at an increasing rate suggests that more and more resources were channelled into the sector. Consequently, from this point of view, we do not support the thesis that EU trade policy is negatively affecting the resources flow into the sector to a significant extent. Secondly, the different patterns of exports between restricted and unrestricted categories show that restricted trade was contained to some extent by the existence of quotas. This suggests that there could have been a certain distortion of resources towards unrestricted categories within the sector, but we cannot say anything definite on this purpose.[25]

To understand better the real effect of MFA, we have computed several indexes, some of which are commonly used in the literature. Specifically, we base our considerations on six indicators:[26]

(a) nB/nQ, i.e. the ratio between the number of product categories facing binding quotas (defined as quotas utilised more than 85 per cent) in the EU and the number of product categories facing quotas;

(b) Q/T, i.e. the ratio between the imports subject to quotas and the total imports of textiles and clothing;

(c) B/T, i.e. the ratio between the imports subject to binding quotas and the total imports;

(d) B/Q, i.e. the ratio between the imports subject to binding quotas and those subject to quotas;

(e) AQUR, i.e. the average quota utilisation rate, computed as the simple mean of the average quota utilisation rates for each category;

(f) AQUR*, i.e. a weighted average utilisation rate, computed as the ratio between the total volume of imports subject to quotas and the total levels of quotas.[27]

All the previous ratios except the first are calculated using quantities. This introduces a difference with respect to the Erzan and Goto [*1992*] analysis that is based on values in current dollars. Since quota levels are defined in quantities (tonnes and/or pieces), we preferred comparing imports and quotas in quantities since volumes are not subject to fluctuation as prices and they may be more safely used to judge the bindingness of a quota.

From the analysis of these indicators a well-defined picture emerges for the EE5 (see Table 5). In the period in question (1988–92), EE5 AQUR and AQUR* have never been greater than 39 per cent and 41 per cent respectively.

Their pattern over time has decreased continuously, reaching values around 30 per cent in 1992. The greatest drop occurred between 1991 to 1992 when they respectively experienced a decrease of 3.1 and 4.8 percentage points. Looking at the indicators for the single countries (see Table 5), it emerges that AQUR and AQUR* for Czechoslovakia (0.555 and 0.603) were on average much greater than the EE5 indicators, even if they were constantly decreasing since 1988 (with the exception of 1991). In contrast is the situation for Romania: not only were AQUR and AQUR* on average much lower than the aggregate for the EE5, but they were almost at every instance the lowest within the five countries. Only Bulgaria experienced increasing AQUR and AQUR* up to the high values of 1992 (0.758 and 0.509).

EE5 Q/T was quite stable over time even if it showed a certain decrease in 1992. In this case, too, the greatest value was in 1988 but not very high (0.306). Again, Czechoslovakia showed the highest ratios (0.409 on average) but this time it was Hungary that showed the lowest indicators (0.177 on average). EE5 B/Q was generally low. However, in 1992 it fell to 0.076, the lowest value ever experienced. Hungary showed binding quotas only from 1988 to 1990 and Romania only in 1990. Their B/Q average was very low, 0.013 and 0.016 respectively. In Bulgaria, binding quotas were found only after 1989 but B/Q for 1990 and 1992 were the highest among the five countries. As usual, Czechoslovakia had the greatest average values both for B/Q (0.294) and nB/nQ (0.108). EE5 B/T was on average around five per cent, but the values were scattered across the countries and the years, ranging from zero per cent to 19 per cent for Czechoslovakia in 1991.

TABLE 5
INDICATORS OF RESTRICTIVENESS: DIRECT TRADE

	nB/nQ	Q/T	B/T	B/Q	AQUR*	AQUR
Bulgaria						
1988	0.000	0.154	0.000	0.000	0.225	0.224
1989	0.000	0.177	0.000	0.000	0.241	0.208
1990	0.083	0.263	0.132	0.501	0.410	0.369
1991	0.083	0.231	0.027	0.117	0.335	0.401
1992	0.333	0.193	0.068	0.353	0.509	0.758
1988–1992	0.100	0.204	0.045	0.194	0.344	0.392
Czechoslovakia						
1988	0.105	0.449	0.177	0.394	0.642	0.565
1989	0.105	0.434	0.158	0.364	0.625	0.543
1990	0.105	0.437	0.054	0.123	0.607	0.566
1991	0.184	0.330	0.190	0.480	0.659	0.637
1992	0.040	0.396	0.037	0.111	0.484	0.465
1988–1992	0.108	0.409	0.123	0.294	0.603	0.555

TABLE 5
INDICATORS OF RESTRICTIVENESS: DIRECT TRADE (cont.)

	nB/nQ	Q/T	B/T	B/Q	AQUR*	AQUR
Hungary						
1988	0.036	0.202	0.004	0.021	0.359	0.362
1989	0.036	0.178	0.004	0.022	0.321	0.337
1990	0.036	0.156	0.003	0.022	0.337	0.347
1991	0.000	0.166	0.000	0.000	0.261	0.253
1992	0.000	0.182	0.000	0.000	0.236	0.242
1988–1992	0.022	0.177	0.002	0.013	0.303	0.308
Poland						
1988	0.115	0.243	0.035	0.144	0.469	0.491
1989	0.006	0.262	0.020	0.077	0.435	0.429
1990	0.192	0.214	0.062	0.281	0.470	0.487
1991	0.074	0.262	0.022	0.083	0.357	0.376
1992	0.000	0.231	0.000	0.000	0.289	0.275
1988–1992	0.092	0.242	0.028	0.117	0.409	0.412
Romania						
1988	0.000	0.346	0.000	0.000	0.268	0.301
1989	0.000	0.334	0.000	0.000	0.239	0.263
1990	0.034	0.437	0.035	0.080	0.180	0.223
1991	0.000	0.434	0.000	0.000	0.164	0.192
1992	0.000	0.410	0.000	0.000	0.180	0.213
1988–1992	0.007	0.392	0.007	0.016	0.206	0.238
EE5						
1988	0.135	0.306	0.055	0.181	0.406	0.381
1989	0.115	0.301	0.049	0.163	0.376	0.361
1990	0.173	0.291	0.043	0.147	0.369	0.369
1991	0.154	0.304	0.074	0.243	0.347	0.334
1992	0.132	0.279	0.021	0.076	0.316	0.286
1988–1992	0.142	0.296	0.048	0.162	0.363	0.346

These results differ from those obtained by Erzan and Goto [*1992*] who generally found higher values. In particular, they obtained much more binding quotas, despite the fact that they defined a binding quota as one with an utilisation rate of 90 per cent or greater. Differences between their results and ours originated exactly from the fact that they had used data in values while we utilised data in quantities.

Our results suggest the following considerations. First, the quota growth from 1991 to 1992 was not totally followed by an alignment in the EE5 exports. The AQUR*, in fact, decreased from 0.347 to 0.316 (and the AQUR fell even more). In contrast with Messerlin's thesis, this seemed to suggest that EE5 exports were not governed by restriction but by production capacity.

Secondly, the fact that in 1992 one-fourth of the EE5 quotas existing in 1991 dropped (from 52 to 38) and the fact that the total exports grew by about

16 per cent, but Q/T fell only by one-twelfth (from 0.304 to 0.279) proved that, above all, superfluous quotas had been liberalised. On the one hand, this meant that EU trade policy was less liberalising than it seemed at first sight. On the other, it also led to the conclusion that the 1991/92 percentage decrease in the EE5 AQUR*, that is, around nine per cent, understated the real average percentage fall in the quota utilisation rates for the 38 remaining restricted categories. Actually, if we had computed the 1991 AQUR* just considering these 38 categories, we would have obtained a value greater than 0.347, since the superfluous categories would not have entered into the average. Consequently, the drop in the quota utilisation rates for the 38 remaining categories was quite relevant, meaning a certain relaxation in the EU trade policy.

Thirdly, further evidence for the un-restrictiveness of the MFA comes from the trend of the binding quotas. On the one hand, in 1992 B/T fell to 0.021, which cannot be taken as proof of a tight restriction in textile and clothing trade, and demonstrates that the Trela and Whalley hypothesis that all quotas are binding could not be applied in this context. On the other hand, from 1990 to 1992 nB/nQ fell from 0.173 to 0.132, and this was not due to a complete liberalisation of some binding quotas, but to a rise in their ceilings, not proportionally followed by an increase in exports. B/Q exhibited the same pattern. Finally, looking at the single countries, Czechoslovakia seems to have been the most restricted one.

VII. THE MFA IMPACT ON OUTWARD PROCESSING TRAFFIC

From 1988 to 1992, OPT trebled and, even if it was still far from the direct trade level, it increased at very higher rates, especially in 1991 and 1992 (see Figures 18 and 24). With the expectation of such an explosion, quotas on many categories were introduced in 1991.

EE5 Q/T showed that in that year half of the total exports was traded within restricted categories (see Table 6 and Figure 18). The percentage lightly decreased in 1992, due to a growth in the unrestricted trade (44.3 per cent), but was not followed by a proportional increase in the restricted one (28.7 per cent). It is difficult to impute this drop to the presence of quotas for at least two reasons. First, the 1991/92 increase in quota levels was around 50 per cent, that is, much greater than the restricted export growth as shown by the decrease in the AQUR and AQUR* (from 0.402 to 0.353 and from 0.438 to 0.391). Secondly, B/Q and nB/nQ were very low in 1991 (0.071 and 0.261) and they did not significantly increase in 1992 (0.138 and 0.294). Therefore, in this case, too, what really matters seems to be not restrictions but export capacity. Again, however, it cannot be discounted that the existence of quotas has led productive resources towards unrestricted categories.

As a matter of fact, the values of Q/T, AQUR and AQUR* over the period

remained substantially higher than those for direct trade. This may be interpreted as proof of the major EU worries towards future trade within OPT. As
far as single countries are concerned, for Bulgaria, Czechoslovakia, and also
Romania, Q/T is greater than 50 per cent in both years. Bulgaria and, above
all, Romania also experienced an increase in B/Q, while Poland never showed
OPT binding quotas (see Table 6).

TABLE 6
INDICATORS OF RESTRICTIVENESS ON OUTWARD PROCESSING TRAFFIC

	nB/nQ	Q/T	B/T	B/Q	AQUR*	AQUR
Bulgaria						
1991	0.000	0.574	0.000	0.000	0.199	0.257
1992	0.250	0.576	0.073	0.126	0.481	0.640
1991–1992	0.125	0.575	0.037	0.063	0.340	0.449
Czechoslovakia						
1991	0.210	0.670	0.095	0.142	0.468	0.505
1992	0.083	0.601	0.039	0.066	0.358	0.373
1991–1992	0.147	0.636	0.067	0.104	0.413	0.439
Hungary						
1991	0.200	0.519	0.097	0.186	0.376	0.468
1992	0.182	0.437	0.088	0.201	0.323	0.404
1991–1992	0.191	0.478	0.093	0.194	0.350	0.436
Poland						
1991	0.000	0.439	0.000	0.000	0.550	0.436
1992	0.000	0.408	0.000	0.000	0.383	0.286
1991–1992	0.000	0.424	0.000	0.000	0.467	0.361
Romania						
1991	0.000	0.526	0.000	0.000	0.434	0.288
1992	0.176	0.519	0.215	0.415	0.560	0.434
1991–1992	0.088	0.523	0.108	0.208	0.497	0.361
EE5						
1991	0.261	0.505	0.036	0.071	0.438	0.402
1992	0.294	0.468	0.065	0.138	0.391	0.353
1991–1992	0.278	0.487	0.051	0.105	0.415	0.378

VIII. FINAL REMARKS

The main conclusion of this chapter is that there is an evident discrepancy
between the formal construction of the arrangement and its real impact on
trade flows. The analysis of the pattern of quotas demonstrates that, up to now,
complete liberalisation has concerned only superfluous restraints. On the other
hand, from the examination of our indicators a general relaxation seems to be

FIGURES 13–15
TRENDS ON OPT IN TEXTILES AND CLOTHING
(categories from 50 to 63 – unit: tonnes)

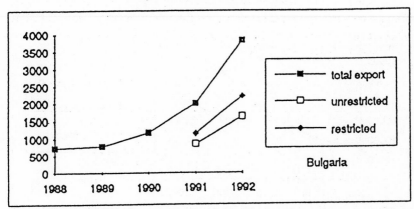

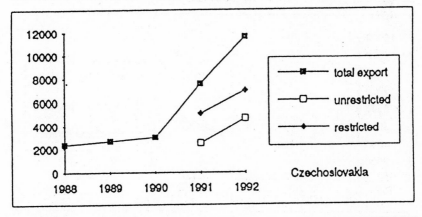

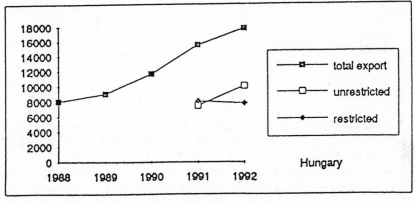

FIGURES 16–18
TRENDS ON OPT IN TEXTILES AND CLOTHING
(categories from 50 to 63 – unit: tonnes) (cont.)

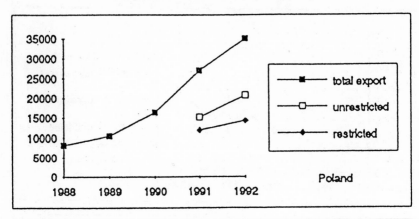

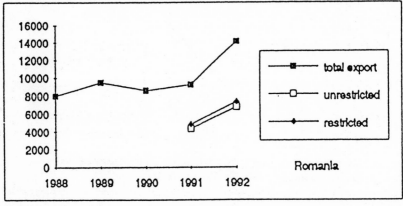

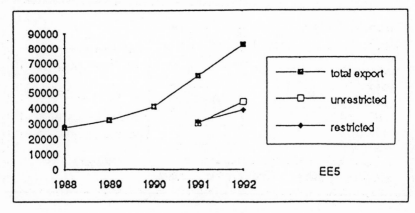

FIGURES 10–21
OPT IN TEXTILES AND CLOTHING: GROWTH RATES
(categories from 50 to 63 – unit: percentages)

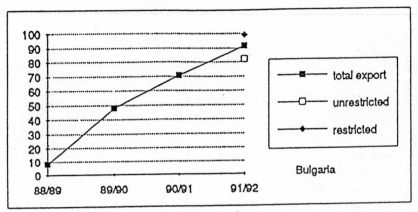

Bulgaria

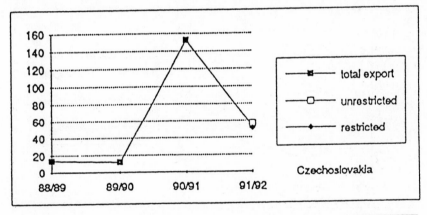

Czechoslovakia

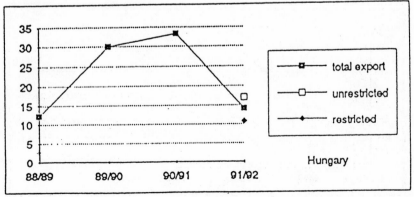

Hungary

199

FIGURES 22–24
OPT IN TEXTILES AND CLOTHING: GROWTH RATES
(categories from 50 to 63 – unit: percentages) (cont.)

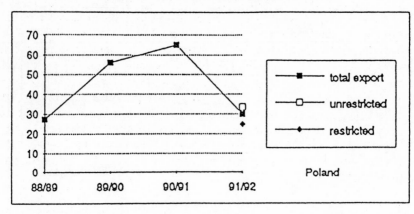

Poland

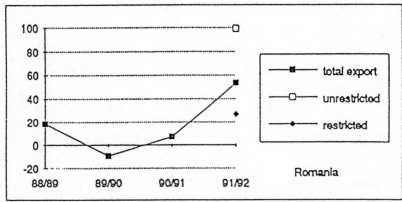

Romania

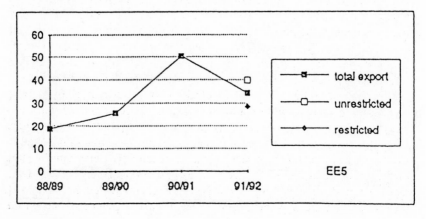

EE5

200

emerging, together with the non-bindingness of present quotas.[28] Therefore, the short-term impact of the MFA on trade flows is marginal. This interpretation is quite different from that proposed in recent literature. It might depend on more than one reason. First, it may be due partly to the existence of differences in the data set (values versus quantities) and in the definition of the relevant variables (that is, un-adjusted versus adjusted quota levels). Secondly, studies are carried out with different methodologies underlying diverse hypotheses, some of which seem unrealistic in some contexts. Thirdly, no one has ever deeply analysed EC-EE5 textile trade in recent years where the pattern of quotas and trade seems to allow conclusions differing to some extent from those derived from a previous period.

The MFA negotiated between the EU and the EE5 in 1986 has been remarkably affected by the transformation process undertaken by these countries since 1989. Quota levels have been substantially increased and several categories subject to restrictions have been progressively liberalised. Although the reduction in the total number of restrictions was due mainly to the liberalisation of regional limits and superfluous quotas, EE5 direct and OPT exports into the EU have increased substantially. Moreover, our indicators show that most of quotas are underutilised (AQUR and AQUR* are generally low) in both trade regimes. It follows that the MFA impact on trade flows has not been particularly restrictive, and that there is still room for further increases of textiles and clothing exports from the EE5.

This conclusion is strengthened by the fact that unrestricted trade growth rates have been accelerating substantially since the beginning of the decade. Finally, we should not forget the effects of the dismantling of the MFA that will ensure to the EE5 a considerable temporal advantage with respect to other MFA suppliers.

OPT might cause some worries since the degree of restrictiveness on exports into the EU is greater than that on direct trade. EE5 are the main exporters to the EC, and most of the clothing industry in these countries is highly dependent on production strategies and orders from European firms. However, subcontracting in production has always played an important role in the competitive strategies of the European firms. Therefore, it is likely that OPT will continue to be used in order to benefit from lower labour and production costs.

It is difficult to draw clear-cut conclusions about this constantly evolving issue, with few data available, and the effects of unpredictable events. However, as our analysis demonstrates, the present level of policy restrictions does not seem to represent a serious obstacle to further increases in the level of trade with these countries, at least in the short term. The long term is more difficult to interpret, since it is not easy to evaluate the real comparative advantages and production capacity of the EE5 in textiles and clothing. Much will depend also on the implementation of the Europe Agreements and on the phasing-out process of the MFA scheduled by the EU, that is, which categories should be liberalised in the early phases and which in the final one. If trends remain as outlined in our analysis, worse fears in terms of restrictiveness of EU trade policy and its responsibilities in the slowing down of the restucturing process in the EE5 do not seem to be justified.

NOTES

1. We would like to thank Professors Carlo Secchi and Sandro Sideri. We are also grateful to the EC officers of DG III for providing data on trade flows and to Christopher Morgan and Gaetano D'Itria for assistance in preparing this study. While this chapter is the result of close co-operation and joint research by the authors, sections II, V and VII can be attributed to Laura Resmini, and sections III, IV and VI to Alberto Brugnoli.
2. Czech and Slovak Republics are treated as if they were a single country.
3. Outward Processing Traffic consists of re-imports into the EU of textile products which have been temporarily exported by the Community and subsequently processed in one of the countries under consideration.
4. MFA I came into force in January 1974, MFA II in 1978 and MFA III in 1982. The current MFA IV was negotiated in 1986 and was due to expire on 31 July 1991, six months after the scheduled conclusion of the Uruguay Round. Instead, it has been renewed on a yearly base until 31 December 1994, in order to allow the conclusion of the Uruguay Round.
5. Flexibility provisions, however, may differ from one agreement to another. East European countries, for example, have been enjoying more favourable conditions since 1990.
6. Poland acceded to the General Agreement in 1967. Hungary was an observer to GATT from 1966. In 1973 it acceded to the GATT after four years of negotiations. Romania's accession to the GATT was ratified in 1971. All these countries renegotiated their Protocol accession after the adoption of market-oriented reforms. Czechoslovakia was one of the 23 founding members of the GATT in 1947. In January 1993, the Czech republic and the Slovak Republic acquired full autonomy in the conduct of their external trade policy and other matters covered by GATT. They became formal members on 15 April 1993 on the same conditions as applied to the former Czech and Slovak Federal Republic. Bulgaria has been a GATT observer since 1967 and asked for accession in 1986. Negotiations are sill in progress.
7. GATT document L/6992, 3 April 1992.
8. The model assumes that all the relevant markets are perfectly competitive. Under this hypothesis, quotas can be assimilated to equivalent tariffs, but in order for the procedure to be correct, they must be binding.
9. They considered the Central and East European countries, EU, US, East Asian Four (China, Hong Kong, Taiwan and Republic of Korea) and all MFA exporters.
10. These indicators are: (I) import share; (II) restricted textile imports (i.e. imports subject to bilateral quotas) as a percentage of total imports of textile products from the MFA suppliers (REST/TOT); (III) textile imports from the MFA suppliers subject to 'binding quotas' as a percentage of total textile imports from the MFA suppliers (BIND/TOT); (IV) textile imports from the MFA suppliers subject to binding restrictions as a percentage of restricted textile imports from the MFA

suppliers (BIND/REST); (V) average quota utilisation rates (AQUR).

11. Nevertheless their analysis presents some limits. First, they: '... proxied capital intensity of the EU's MFA product categories using value added per production worker in the US' [*Erzan and Holmes, 1992: 19*]. While relying on the work of Lary [*1968*] in stating that relative factor intensities of products do not change significantly across countries was made 25 years ago, and things could have changed since, it is obvious that such a proxy is far from being reliable. Secondly, they proxy the relative capital abundance of exporters with their per capita GNP. Consequently, the analysis is extremely senstive to the GNP per capita estimates for EE5.

12. The Hungarian supply price was found to be only two-thirds that of Hong Kong and Portugal.

13. The EU is depicted as comprising seven economies (France, Germany, Italy, UK, Greece and Ireland, Spain and Portugal, the rest of EU) with a single further economy representing the rest of the world.

14. As far as textiles, clothing, leather and footwear are concerned, they computed the effects of the fully liberalisation of trade with a modified version of the computable partial equilibrium model of imperfect competition developed by Smith and Venables [*1988*]. Working with such an aggregate category, they probably over-stated the relevance of the sector to the EC economy since not all the products falling under this category are subject to restrictions. Moreover, the authors did not take into account any possible growth of EC exports to EE5 but focused on a 400 per cent growth in Eastern European exports as a fair assumption of how trade might increase if fully liberalised. They estimated an extra-EU imports' percent-age growth of 28.5 for the EC, greater for Germany (36.4), the rest of EC (33,8) and France (30.8); a percentage change in production of –6.4, greater for Germany (–17.6) and the rest of EC (–6.4); a welfare change of 94.0 million ECU, positive for Germany (101.3), the Rest of EC (27.7) and UK (1.1) and negative for the others, but very small for everyone if related to the base consumption (no more than + or –0.2 per cent); a profit gain of 365.8 million of ECU for the EE5 producers and a trade rent loss of 334 m ECU with a net welfare change of 31.8 million of ECU. Actually, the authors stress that if the trade barrier decrease which originates the trade growth is a tariff reduction, the cost will fall on the EC governments and not on the foreign producers as in the case of non-tariff barrier reductions. In that eventuality, the gains would be greater for the EE5 countries, while the EU ones would meet losses.

15. This system consists of EU limits, subdivided into 12 country levels until 1992; EU sub-limits and regional limits; designed consultation levels, aggregate limits and specific limits.

16. For the EE5 the main textile and clothing categories facing restraints are: 1, 2, 2A, 3, 3A, 4–8, 9, 12–17, 19–21, 24, 26, 31, 32, 36, 37, 38A, 39, 55, 58, 61, 66–69, 67A, 73, 76, 78, 83, 90, 91, 99, 100, 111, 115, 117, 118 and 121.

17. Most MFA producers, mainly the Asian ones, faced OPT restrictions since 1980.

18. The computation of the quota growth rates has been made by considering only EU limits in place for the whole period.

19. In our analysis we adopted the worse scenario that the EE5 could face, that is, none of the categories now facing restrictions will be liberalised in the first stage of the MFA phasing-out process.

20. For each country, the average quota growth rate has been computed as an arith-metic mean of the average growth rates of each quota in the period under con-

sideration. These last have been computed as geometric means.

21. The PHARE programme was born on 26 September 1989 and stands for 'Poland and Hungary: Assistance for Economic Restructuring'. PHARE programme participation is based on two conditions: the first is democracy; the second is the adoption of macroeconomic stabilisation programmes. Romania, Bulgaria and Czechoslovakia were admitted only in 1990.

22. After 1989 the political motive for discriminating against such countries as opposed to other less developed countries has diminished.

23. Textile and clothing products are defined as the sum of categories from 50 to 63 in the tariff and statistical nomenclature of the Community (Combined Nomenclature).

24. Each restricted trade growth rate was computed as the growth rate in the sum of the trade levels of only those categories restricted in both years considered, that is, if a category was restricted, let us say, both in 1990 and 1991, it was included in both the sums of the total restricted trade levels and it took part in defining the 1990/91 restricted growth rate. However, if it was liberalised in 1992, it was neither included in the sum of the total restricted trade level for 1992 nor for 1991 and it did not take part in defining the 1991/92 restricted growth rate. This means that for some years in some countries, we computed two values of the total restricted trade level for the same year (1991 in the example above), depending on its use. Unrestricted trade growth rates were computed using the complementary values of the total sum of categories from 50 to 63.

25. In order to state the exact degree of distortion within the sector we should look at data on production which are not available at the moment.

26. All the following ratios are calculated without considering categories 67A and 121 for which data on trade were not available.

27. This is a weighted AQUR since it gives more importance to the greatest quotas.

28. We define a binding quota as a quota that is utilised more than 85 per cent. In some other papers, the 90 per cent rate is used [*Erzan and Goto 1992*]. With this last definition, our analysis results would be strengthened.

REFERENCES

Erzan, R., Goto, J. and P. Holmes (1990): 'Effects of the Multi-Fibre Arrangement on Developing Countries' Trade: an Empirical Investigation', in C.B. Hamilton (ed.), *Textiles Trade and the Developing Countries*, Washington, DC: World Bank.

Erzan, R. and P. Holmes (1992): 'The Restrictiveness of the Multi-Fibre Arrangement on Eastern European Trade', WPS 860, International Economic Department, World Bank, Feb.

Erzan, R. and P. Holmes (1990): 'Phasing Out the Multi-Fibre Arrangement', *World Economy*, Vol. 13, No. 2, June.

Faini, R., de Melo, J. and W. Takacs (1992): 'A Primer on the MFA Maze', CEPR Discussion Paper Series No. 716, London.

GATT (1993): *Trade Policy Review, European Communities*, Vol. 1, Geneva.

Goto, J. (1989): 'The Multifibre Arrangement and Its Effects on Developing Countries', *Research Observer* 4, No. 2, July.

Hamilton, C.B. (1990): 'Introduction', in C.B. Hamilton (ed.), *Textiles Trade and the Developing Countries*, Washington, DC: World Bank.

Messerlin, P.A. (1993): 'The EC and Central Europe: The Missed Rendez-vous of

1992?', *The Economics of Transition*, Vol. 1, No. 1.

Lary, H. (1968): 'Imports of Manufactures from Less Developed Countries', NBER Working Paper.

Raffaelli, M. (1990): 'Some Considerations on the Multi-Fibre Arrangement: past, Present and Future', in C.B. Hamilton (ed.), *Textiles Trade and the Developing Countries*, Washington, DC: World Bank.

Rollo, J. and A. Smith (1990): 'The Political Economy of Easter European Trade with the European Community: Why so sensitive?', mimeo.

Smith, A. and A.J. Venables (1988): 'Completing the internal market in the European Community: Some Industry Simulations', *European Economic Review*, No. 32.

Trela, I. and J. Whaley (1990): 'Unraveling the Threads of the MFA', in C.B. Hamilton (ed.), *Textiles Trade and the Developing Countries*, Washington, DC: World Bank.

11

Trade Policy and Foreign Investment: Redeployment Illustrated by the Textiles and Clothing Industry

GIORGIO BARBA NAVARETTI

I. INTRODUCTION[1]

Much of the literature on foreign investments examines firms facing the alternative between producing in or exporting to a third country.[2] If trade barriers are raised in the host country, the incentive to set up production facilities there increases. This chapter focuses on foreign investments aimed at reducing costs of production. In this case, trade barriers are expected to slow down the incentive to restructure in the protected areas and, hence, reduce the incentive to redeploy to cheap labour countries. However, this assumption is based on a simplified world where all similar firms based in protected advanced countries compete against all similar firms based in cheap labour countries. If we introduce elements of differentiation between firms in both areas, our initial expectations no longer hold. Redeployment could be an optimal strategy for advanced countries' firms, independent of the competitive threat from developing countries. In this case, trade policy has an asymmetric impact on protected firms. By increasing the cost of redeployment, it is biased against those firms which choose redeployment as their optimal strategy.

The textile and clothing industry provides an ideal ground to examine this issue. The Multi-Fibre Arrangement (MFA) has been protecting advanced countries producers for the last two decades. The industry is relatively labour-intensive (particularly clothing) and the North is facing ever increasing competition from Southern producers. Many firms have redeployed production to developing countries. The phasing out of the MFA agreed during the Uruguay Round is taking place in a context very different from the one prevailing when the agreement was introduced. Today, the industry is characterised by a network of integrated operations spread across every part of the globe.

The understanding of the impact of trade policy on the cost of redeployment is essential to evaluate costs and benefits of the phasing out of the MFA. This

206

chapter examines the major relevant issues and gives some initial evidence. Section II provides the background information on the issue and examines the competitve context of the industry. Section III looks at the role of trade policy and section IV concludes.

II. THE COMPETITIVE CONTEXT

Although the textile and clothing sector in the industrialised countries has been heavily protected against competition from developing countries by the MFA, the industry has undergone dramatic restructuring throughout the 1980s. Restructuring was (and still is) caused by two sets of reasons. The first is that trade barriers have not always been effective in keeping the rising tide of developing countries imports at bay. Quotas have gradually increased throughout the 1980s, barriers are often bypassed, and preferential agreements with neighbouring developing countries exporters have reduced or eliminated import duties (for example, between the Mediterranean countries and the EC). The second is that competition between firms in industrialised countries has been extremely fierce throughout the 1980s. Structural changes have often been caused by the need to confront the competitive threat of producers from other advanced countries.

Changes were not always successful and effective, however. The export shares of Japan and the US in world trade in textiles shrank considerably, whereas the EU managed to keep its competitive edge. (In 1989 the US share of world exports in clothing was roughly two per cent as against 30 per cent for the EC).[3] As we shall see, the nature of the restructuring process was very different according to the segment of the industry (textiles or clothing) and the country that undertook it. In this chapter we focus on Italy and Germany as examples.

Although integrated, textiles and clothing are two different industries, with very different production processes and technologies. The textile industry (both weaving and spinning) is very capital-intensive. In contrast, clothing (particularly sewing) is still a very labour-intensive industry.[4] In this respect, clothing producers have been more exposed to competition from developing countries. Between the early 1960s and the late 1980s, developing countries' share in world exports increased from 16 per cent to 23 per cent in textiles and from 15 per cent to 45 per cent in clothing.[5]

Whereas increased automation has been a key strategy for textiles, clothing producers could not follow the same pattern. They were forced either to decrease their labour costs in some other way, or to increase their value added via product differentiation, increased product quality and so on. Although there is a large variance across individual EU countries, turnover per employee in clothing nearly doubled on average between 1980 and 1989.[6]

In this respect, foreign investments, both direct (FDI) or international contractual agreements, played a very different role in the two segments of the industry.[7] Textiles has seen relatively few foreign investments, mainly concentrated in advanced countries. Foreign production units mostly have been set up (or taken over) to strengthen the competitive position in the export market, that is, to produce goods geared to the needs of the local market, to shorten times of delivery, to bypass trade barriers (for example, European producers in the US), or to implement economies of scale with local producers. Automation did not make it worthwhile to redeploy production to developing countries.[8]

The picture is very different in the case of clothing. FDI and international contractual agreements were key elements of the strategy of garment producers throughout the 1970s and 1980s. On the one hand, like their textile counterparts, many firms started producing in their major export markets or developed commercial agreements with companies there. On the other hand, a large share of production in advanced countries was redeployed to developing countries to reduce the cost of labour.

Consequently, the textile and clothing industry is today composed of a network of different integrated operations, with different degrees of capital intensity: developing countries hold a comparative advantage in only a few of the operations. The increase in imports from developing countries is not always the result of the development of autonomous export capabilities in these countries. Rather, it is often a process of gradual integration between producers in both areas, whereby capital-intensive production phases, design, and distribution are controlled by companies in advanced countries, and labour-intensive production phases are carried out in developing countries. In this respect, redeployment is a key aspect of the process of economic integration between advanced countries and developing countries.

The scattered evidence available shows that redeployment of production to developing countries has not been implemented at the same pace by producers in different countries. The two extremes are embodied by Italy and Germany, the two largest European clothing producers and the two industrialised countries which have been most successful in preserving their competitive advantage in the industry.[9]

Until the last couple of years, investment abroad, and particularly in developing countries, has not been a key element of the strategy of Italian producers. Rather, they have focused mainly on market- (or demand-) oriented strategies. Market-oriented strategies include a mix of sub-strategies (which obviously varies for each individual firm), such as increasing product quality, advertising, differentiating products, developing brand names, and strengthening the distributive network. The final objective of the Italian option is to increase value-added by entering market segments with price-inelastic consumer demand (or by making demand more inelastic by inducing new patterns of consumption).

Market-oriented strategies often need to be backed by highly skilled and flexible production structures. This is sometimes incompatible with redeployment to LDCs: high quality and fast delivery standards are more difficult to match in LDCs. Instead, Italian firms have been able to reduce their labour costs and, at the same time, improve their quality standards by using networks of small domestic subcontractors.[10]

In contrast, German producers have put less emphasis on market-oriented strategies. Neither have they achieved the quality levels of the Italians. Instead, the reduction of labour costs through redeployment in LDCs appears to have been the key strategy of German producers. Table 1 shows the share of 'Outward Processing Trade' (OPT) imports in total imports from LDCs to Germany, Italy, and the rest of the EU for a selection of clothing products. For Italy the shares were all 0 in 1986, increasing in 1991 to values ranging between one per cent and two per cent.[11] In Germany, the shares ranged between 10 per cent and 20 per cent in 1986 and increased further over the period.

TABLE I
IMPORTS IN OPT ON TOTAL IMPORTS (TOTAL DEVELOPING COUNTRIES)
(PERCENTAGES)

	Germany		Italy		EEC	
	1986	1991	1986	1991	1986	1991
Blouses	11.0	19.0	0.0	2.0	7.0	14.0
Shirts	11.0	13.0	0.0	1.0	10.0	8.0
Trousers	14.0	20.0	0.0	2.0	11.0	14.0
Men's Suits	20.0	13.0	0.0	2.0	17.0	9.0
Women's Suits	10.0	10.0	0.0	0.0	6.0	6.0
Average Product(1)	13.2	15.0	0.0	1.4	10.2	10.2

The average product refers to the items listed in the table.
Source: Own computations based on EU data.

OPT figures provide the only statistical ground to compare the relevance of off-shore processing across EU countries, yet they underestimate the pattern of redeployment which occurred in the last two decades. In fact, they only include imports *officially* declared as outward-processed. Such imports are constrained by quotas negotiated among the EU countries (generally on top of the MFA quotas); they include only outward-processing done by European producers (not buyers);[12] and they are subject to a set of restrictions and benefits. Therefore, part of the off-shore production by European producers and all the outward processing done by European buyers are not captured by these statistics. Spinanger and Piatti [*1994*] estimate that almost 50 per cent of

Germany's clothing imports in 1990 can be attributed to German clothing manufacturers, either through foreign subsidiaries or contractual agreements with foreign producers.

The amount of outward processing created by European buyers is also likely to be extremely large. In fact, although distribution of clothing products in Europe is more or less fragmented (depending on the countries), international buying is extremely concentrated. By making extensive use of sub-contracting agreements, a small number of buyers play a very important role in defining production patterns in the developing countries [*Oman, 1989*].

In this context, it would be simplistic to consider redeployment of production only as the result of direct competition between producers in developing countries and industrialised countries. For many textile and clothing products and market segments, the restructuring process is not only the result of increasing autonomous competitive pressure from developing countries. For these products, redeployment (and consequently developing countries imports) is the outcome of direct competition between European producers and buyers.

Distinctions need to be introduced according to products, market segments, and exporting countries. For more complex products (for example, formal menswear), particularly in the high quality range, European firms producing in-house mainly face increasing competition from other European producers which have redeployed their plants in the developing countries. Direct imports from developing countries are relatively low and are concentrated mostly in the low-quality market segment. In contrast, if we consider 'simpler products' (for example, casual wear or shirts) or products in the lower quality range, producers in advanced countries do face direct competition from developing countries.

It is also important to distinguish between different groups of exporting countries. As shown by Table 2, European OPT imports come mainly from neighbouring areas, that is, Eastern Europe and the Mediterranean countries. Table 3 shows that in fact the majority of textile and clothing imports from Eastern Europe consists of OPT. In contrast, most textile and clothing imports from Asian countries are direct. This pattern of specialisation became even more defined between 1986 and 1991.

This evidence raises some important theoretical issues. First, under what conditions may redeployment in cheap labour countries emerge as an optimal strategy when firms are not competing against producers based in cheap labour countries, that is, when cheap labour does not represent the comparative advantage of one or some of the competitors. Second, home markets are on average the largest markets for both German and Italian firms; however, intra-industry trade across the two countries and exports to third European countries are large and increasing. This pattern will be strengthened further by the

TABLE 2

GEOGRAPHICAL DISTRIBUTION OF EU OPT IMPORTS (PERCENTAGES)

	Average Products		Trousers		Men's Suits		Blouses	
	1986	1991	1986	1991	1986	1991	1986	1991
Asia	5.0	2.0	7.0	1.0	8.0	5.0	0.0	0.0
Mediterranean	14.7	17.7	38.0	41.0	0.0	0.0	6.0	12.0
Est	46.0	46.3	23.0	31.0	56.0	50.0	59.0	58.0
Yugoslavia	32.3	31.7	30.0	25.0	34.0	44.0	33.0	26.0
Others	2.0	2.3	2.0	2.0	2.0	1.0	2.0	4.0

The average product is based on trousers, men's suits and blouses.
Source: Own computations based on EU data.

TABLE 3

IMPORTS IN OPT ON TOTAL IMPORTS IN EU: A COMPARISON BETWEEN
DIFFERENT AREAS (PERCENTAGES)

	Average Products		Trousers		Men's Suits		Blouses	
	1986	1991	1986	1991	1986	1991	1986	1991
Asia	1.1	0.3	1.3	0.5	2.0	0.5	0.0	0.0
Mediterranean	5.5	7.6	15.0	16.0	0.0	0.0	1.6	6.8
Est	67.0	79.7	68.0	79.0	0.0	67.0	83.0	93.0
Yugoslavia	73.7	75.7	82.0	79.0	59.0	72.0	80.0	76.0
Others	4.7	0.0	0.0	0.0	14.0	0.0	0.0	0.0

The average product is based on trousers, men's suits and blouses.
Source: Own computations based on EU data.

Single European Market (SEM). Hence, German and Italian firms can be assumed to operate in a unique non-geographically-segmented market. Therefore, how can firms choosing two completely different strategies successfully compete and survive in a non-segmented market?

Barba Navaretti [*1994*] develops a theoretical model which shows that these results can emerge in a vertically differentiated industry, even under free trade, because firms may enjoy a different comparative advantage in quality. The assumption that the cost of quality is partially firm-specific is well supported by the literature.[13] Firms are likely to learn at different rates, with modes and behavioural rules specific to their history and to the environment where they operate. For example, it can be imagined that quality is more expensive for German firms than for the Italian ones, because Italy is better endowed than Germany with highly skilled manpower, networks of subcontractors, and creative/design capabilities. Also, demand factors may influence the decision to invest in quality and, therefore, the cumulated experience in high quality production. Italian demand in the last 20 years has been more quality oriented than German demand.

These results make also intuitive sense. It is quite obvious that quality is a key competitive variable and that firms will engage in a quality race. On the other hand, if some of the competitors have a comparative advantage in quality, the others are in a weaker competitive position. Their only option is to compensate their poorer quality by reducing their costs of production, hence they will redeploy to cheap labour areas. But why do high quality firms not redeploy too? This is because learning costs in developing countries are higher for complex, high quality products. These additional costs offset the reduction in the cost of labour. How does trade policy affect the cost of alternative strategic choices?

II. THE IMPACT OF TRADE POLICY

At first sight, the impact of trade protection on foreign investment is relatively straightforward. Trade barriers are expected to slow down the pace of restructuring in the protected areas, including redeployment of production to countries with cheap labour. However, as argued in the previous section, redeployment is a strategic option that many European producers choose in order to compete with other European firms rather than with developing countries. What is the impact of trade policy when the decision to redeploy is taken within this competitive framework?

Four different trade policy measures need to be taken into account:

(1) the bilateral quantitative restrictions imposed within the MFA;
(2) import tariffs, like the uniform 14 per cent tariff on imports into the EU;
(3) the OPT regulation, agreed between EU countries in 1982;
(4) the changes introduced with the SEM in 1993.

Bilateral restrictions have been particularly binding in countries where European firms have redeployed production under the OPT regime. Utilisation rates of MFA quotas were nearly 101 per cent in 1986 and 139 per cent in 1991, compared with utilisation rates for all LDCs of 69 per cent in 1986 and 110 per cent in 1991.[14]

Bilateral quantitative restrictions may pose three serious constraints to redeployment. First, they can affect the geographical allocation of the investments. European firms can only redeploy into countries where the quotas are not fully utilised or are not expected to be fully utilised in the short term. firms producing high quality and/or complex products are likely to be worse off in this respect. In fact, production capabilities for such products are generally concentrated in a few countries, therefore creating a first mover advantage.

Second, bilateral quantitative restrictions might increase the geographical dispersion of foreign investments for each individual firm. In fact, firms might be forced to distribute their investments in different countries in order to reduce the risk of quota saturation in the future. Once more, dispersion can be particularly costly for higher quality and more complex products. In this case, it takes quite a long period of learning before local producers manage to reach high productivity and quality levels. Obviously, the cost is higher when the learning effort is dispersed across more than one country.

Third, outward processed products imported within the normal MFA bilateral agreements could not circulate freely (before 1993) within the European Community. The major obstacle in this respect was Article 115 of the Treaty of Rome. Under this article, a country may seek to exclude goods subject to a quota when those goods are being deflected via another member state and when such imports pose a threat of serious market disruption [*EIU, 1991*].

Import tariffs also make redeployment in LDCs more costly. European producers are obliged to pay the 14 per cent import duty on the full value of the product imported, even if the raw materials are European and part of the production process (for example, cutting) is carried out in Europe.

Barba Navaretti [*1994*] shows that trade protection favours high quality firms producing at home and hinders the profitability of low quality firms. At the same time, the quality gap between high and low quality firms increases. This implies that a reduction of protection allows redeploying firms to raise their relative quality and to improve their competitiveness. In other words, trade protection is not neutral, that is, equally beneficial, across protected producers. This last point is very well illustrated if the OPT regulation is taken into account.

The OPT regulation provides a partial correction to the negative impacts on redeployment caused by both the MFA and duty tariffs. The OPT regulation, negotiated between the EU countries, defines bilateral quotas for some products and some exporting countries, and these function in addition to the MFA quotas for direct imports. Imports under the OPT regulation can circulate freely into Europe and are charged import duty only on the value-added created through the off-shore processing. At the same time, these imports are subject to a set of restrictions, partly imposed at EU level and partly at national level. The EU restrictions are: (i) only producers based in Europe may use OPT quotas (buyers, with some historical exceptions, are therefore excluded); (ii) OPT must be used for the same products which are produced at home (that is, textile firms cannot do OPT for clothing products); and (iii) the fabric used must be produced in Europe.

Individual EU member states define the amount of OPT processing that each firm can carry out. National rules differ widely across countries. Italy is extremely restrictive: each firm can only produce 30 per cent of its sales in

OPT (independently of whether OPT is done in one or more LDCs), and the authorisation is granted only if the firm's unions agree to the redeployment.

In contrast, Germany is extremely liberal. Until 1 January 1992 each firm could produce 30 per cent of its sales in OPT in each country in which it had established off-shore production. (Thus each firm could produce 100 per cent of its sales in OPT, as long as production in each country did not exceed 30 per cent of the firm's sales.) Since 1992, OPT is no longer linked to the sales of German firms [*Brovia, 1992*].

The introduction of the SEM will have an impact on redeployment in two respects. First, it will be increasingly difficult to implement Article 115 if internal custom controls are going to be abolished. In this respect, bilateral restrictions are also likely to become less binding for outward processing imports which are not covered by the OPT regulation. Second, if imports from extra-EU countries are restricted, redeploying into cheap labour European countries like Greece, Ireland, or Portugal can be advantageous under the SEM even though wage levels are higher than in developing countries.

The discussion above shows that quantitative trade barriers and tariffs are not necessarily beneficial for protected producers when redeployment is taken into account. The negative impact of bilateral agreements and import duties are partially offset by the OPT regulation. However, the OPT regulation is not uniform across the EC, and it is still very restrictive for many European countries. As for the SEM its impact on foreign investment is likely to be ambiguous.

III. CONCLUSIONS: BEYOND TRADE BARRIERS

This chapter has focused mainly on foreign investments aimed at redeploying production to developing countries. Redeployment of production is generally seen as a defensive move of advanced country firms that are defending themselves against growing flows of imports from cheap labour developing countries. Under this assumption, European producers are expected to benefit from trade barriers. Protection provides them with some breathing space, slowing down the pace of restructuring (including redeployment). Yet this is a simplistic view of the restructuring process taking place in the textile and clothing industry. In many segments of the industry, and particularly for high quality products, European firms redeploy due to competition from producers in other advanced countries rather than from developing countries.

This evidence has two very important implications. First, increasing competition from developing countries should be seen partially as a process of gradual economic integration between producers in both areas, whereby capital-intensive production phases, design, and distribution are controlled by advanced country firms and labour-intensive production phases are carried out in developing countries.

Second, trade protection is not necessarily beneficial for European producers. Protection increases the cost of redeployment and introduces a bias in favour of high quality firms. If trade barriers are lifted, redeployment would be less costly and more firms would choose it as their optimal strategy. Thus, trade barriers slow down a process which is beneficial to European producers.

The bias introduced by the MFA bilateral quantitative restrictions is partially offset by the OPT regulation. OPT quotas have been constantly increased in the second half of the 1980s and national regulations (limiting the amount of off-shore processing that each individual firm can carry out) have been loosened in some European countries like Germany. Therefore redeployment has gradually become less expensive, and redeploying firms have been able to improve their quality and their competitive position. OPT imports into Europe have increased dramatically. In this respect, countries like Italy, where national OPT regulations are still very restrictive, are losing competitive ground compared to more liberal countries like Germany.

Under bilateral quantitative restrictions European firms are likely to redeploy in more than one cheap labour country in order to avoid the risk of quota saturation. This is one of the reasons why trade barriers increase the cost of redeployment. One of the expected effects of the increase in OPT quotas is a geographical concentration of off-shore processing. This trend is shown in Table 4: the number of countries in which European firms carry out off-shore processing declines for four out of six categories of products between 1986 and 1991. This result is consistent with the concentration of OPT in eastern European and Mediterranean countries shown in Table 2.

TABLE 4
NUMBER OF COUNTRIES EXPORTING IN OPT IN 1986 AND 1991

	EU	
	1986	1991
Blouses	9	11
Shirts	11	8
Trousers	18	10
Men's Suits	10	6
Women's Suits	7	9
Average Product	11	9

In this Table OPT countries include developing countries exporting in OPT either in 1986 or in 1991.
Source: Own computations based on EU data.

OPT regulation in the EU creates a strong incentive to concentrate production in neighbouring countries because European firms can use OPT quota only if they use European fabric. Transport costs are much lower if production is carried out in neighbouring countries.

The evidence of the increase in geographical concentration of off-shore processing raises two extremely important issues. First, integration between developing countries and European producers is only taking place with a group of developing countries, that is, Eastern European and Mediterranean countries. Asian imports to Europe are mainly direct imports, although in large part channelled through European buyers.

Second, a key competitive factor for the redeploying firm is the learning process which takes place in the developing country. Particularly for more complex products, like formal menswear, production skills are concentrated in only a few developing countries. If European firms can gradually improve local skills through off-shore processing, the cost of producing high quality in developing countries declines. In this way they can improve their competitive position by gradually producing higher quality products. At the same time, if learning is not diffused in the productive system of the host country but is localised in the production units doing off-shore processing, there is a very relevant first mover advantage. In other words, the smaller the skill diffusion externality, the less new investors are able to benefit from the learning process created by previous investors.

The role of OPT regulation provides a good illustration of the impact of a gradual dismantling of quantitative trade restrictions in the industry. In this perspective, the end of the MFA takes place in a world already far in its process of geographic integration, and therefore beyond the constraints lifted by trade barriers.

NOTES

1. This work summarises some of the findings of a paper published in Barba Navaretti *et al.* (eds.) [*1994*]. It is the result of a research project coordinated by the OECD Development Centre and the Centro Studi Luca d'Agliano. Sergio Currarini provided helpful research assistance. Comments by Rodolfo Helg and Ashoka Mody are acknowledged.
2. Coase [*1937*], Hymer [*1976*], Buckley and Casson [*1976*], Rugman [*1981*], Dunning [*1981*], Kindleberger [*1969*], Caves [*1982*], Smith [*1987*], Horstman and Markusen [*1987*] and Motta [*1991*].
3. Economist Intelligence Unit, [*1991*]. The EC share is much larger than the US one even if intra-EC trade is not taken into account.
4. Labour costs are roughly 15–20 per cent of total production costs for textiles against 35–45 per cent for clothing, if production is carried out in industrialized countries.
5. Oman [*1989*], Economist Intelligence Unit, [*1991*].
6. Economist Intelligence Unit [*1991*]. It must be noted, however, that the index is reported in nominal values, thereby overestimating the increase in labour productivity.
7. International contractual agreements differ from foreign investments in that

foreign investors do not hold a major equity share in the local venture (for example, licensing, subcontracting, minority joint ventures, and so on.) Following Oman [*1984*], we consider all forms of international contractual agreements as foreign investments.

8. Oman [*1989*]. Japan has been the only noticeable exception. With the help of Japanese trading companies, small textile producers have been very active in redeploying their obsolete plants to LDCs, via net foreign investment.

9. Oman [*1989*] and EIU [*1991*].

10. Labour costs were lower in Italy than in Germany in the mid-1980s. Today they are more or less equal, as the rate of increase has been much higher in Italy. See EIU [*1991*].

11. OPT are imports of products partially processed in developing countries by subsidiaries or licensees or subcontractors of advanced countries firms.

12. Buyers do not have their own production units. They buy the goods they market from third producers, usually under subcontracting agreements.

13. For a very comprehensive survey of the determinants and effects of innovation (including quality improvement) at firm and sector level, see Dosi [*1988*].

14. Our computation of EU data. Utilisation rates refer to trousers, blouses, shirts, men's and women's suits.

REFERENCES

Barba Navaretti, G. (1994): 'Trade Policy and Foreign Investment: an Analytical Framework', in G. Barba Navaretti, R. Faini, and A. Silberston (eds.), *'Trade Policy, Productivity and Foreign Investment: The Textile and Clothing Industry in Europe'*, Paris: OECD Development Centre.

Barba Navaretti, G., R. Faini, and A. Silberston (eds.), (1994): *'Trade Policy, Productivity and Foreign Investment: The Textile and Clothing Industry in Europe'*, Paris: OECD Development Centre.

Brovia, G. (1992): 'Il T.P.P nell'Industria dell'Abbiglaiamento', Milan: Associazione Italiana Industriali Abbigliamento.

Brovia, G. (1992): 'Traffico di Perfezionamento Passivo', Milan: Associazione Italiana Industriali Abbigliamento.

Buckley, P. and M. Casson (1976): *The Future of the Multinational Enterprise*, London: Macmillan.

Caves, R. (1982): *Multinational Enterprises and Economic Analysis*, Cambridge: Cambridge University Press.

Coase, R.H. (1937): 'The Nature of the Firm', *Economica,* Nov.

Dosi, G. (1988): 'Sources Procedures and Microeconomic Effects of Innovation', *Journal of Economic Literature,* Vol. XXVI, Sept.

Dunning, J.H. (1981): *International Production and the Multinational Enterprise*, London: Allen & Unwin.

Economist Intelligence Unit (1991): 'The Clothing Industry and the Single European Market', Special Report No. 2081, London.

Faini, R. and A. Heimler (1991): 'The Quality and Production of Textiles and Clothing and the Completion of the Internal Market', Discussion Paper No. 508, Centre for Economic Policy Research, London.

Horstman, I. and J. Markusen (1987): 'Strategic Investments and the Development of Multinationals', *International Economic Review,* No. 28.

Hymer, S.H. (1976): *The International Operations of a National Firm: A Study of Direct Foreign Investment*, Cambridge, MA: MIT Press.

Kindleberger, C. P. (1972): 'Direct Foreign Investment and Economic Development', in P. Drysdale (ed.), *Direct Foreign Investment in Asia and Pacific*.

Levin, R. *et al.* (1984): *'Survey Research on R&D Appropriability and Technological Opportunity. Part 1: Appropriability'*, New Haven, CT: Yale University Press.

Motta, M. (1991): 'Strategic Investment, R&D and International Economics', Université Catholique de Louvain, Faculté des Sciences Economiques, Sociales et Politiques, Nouvelle Série, No. 209.

Oman, C. (1984): 'New Forms of International Investment in Developing Countries', Paris: OECD Development Centre.

Oman, C. (1989): 'Les Nouvelles Formes d'Investissement dans les Industries des Pays en Développement: Industrie Extractive, Pétrochimie, Automobile, Textile, Agroalimentaire', Paris: OECD.

Rodrik, D. (1988): 'Industrial Organization and Product Quality: Evidence from South Korean and Taiwanese Exports', National Bureau for Economic Research Working Paper Series, No. 2722, Cambridge, MA.

Rugman, A. (1981): *Inside the Multinationals*, London: Croom Helm.

Shaked, A. and J. Sutton (1983): 'Natural Oligopolies', *Econometrica,* No. 51.

Shaked, A. and J. Sutton (1984): 'Natural Oligopolies and International Trade', in H. Kierzkowski (ed.), *Monopolistic Competition and International Trade,* Oxford: Clarendon Press.

Smith, A. (1987): 'Strategic Investments, Multinational Corporation and Trade Policy', *European Economic Review*, No. 31.

Sutton, J. (1991): *Sunk Costs and Market Structure*, Cambridge, MA: MIT Press.

UNCTC (1986): 'Transnational Corporations in the Man-made fibre, Textile and Clothing Industries', United Nations, New York.

12

The Impact of the Uruguay Round on International Commodity Agreements: The Case of Coffee

ANTONELLA MORI

I. INTRODUCTION

In recent years two issues related to primary commodities have come to the fore of the international political agenda. On the one hand, there have been disputes on agricultural income policies, subsidies, protection, and market access in many OECD. On the other hand, almost all International Commodity Agreements (ICAs) have undergone a period of crisis, facing difficulties in the renegotiation process. As far as the first issue, the Uruguay Round of the General Agreement on Tariffs and Trade (GATT) represented the main international forum of discussion. ICAs have been negotiated among governments of producer and consumer nations to reduce volatility in the prices of primary commodities, to sustain long-term producer income, and to provide an adequate (and at reasonable prices), supply to consumers. However, recently existing agreements have faced severe difficulties. In 1993, talks on a new International Coffee Agreement (ICoA) collapsed in March; the International Natural Rubber Organisation (INRO) failed in June to reach an agreement on the renegotiation of the pact. Finally, after having abandoned their attempts to negotiate a pact based on a stock withholding scheme in March 1993, delegates to the International Cocoa Organisation (ICO) planned a purely administrative agreement.

This chapter tries to show that there was a link between the GATT negotiation on agricultural trade liberalisation and the process for the renegotiation of the primary commodity agreements. It will be argued that the uncertainty surrounding the future of the Uruguay Round represented an external source of difficulties in the renegotiation process of ICAs. Given the liberalisation of agricultural trade within the GATT, it can be expected that ICAs will be renegotiated or extended without economic clauses. On the one hand, consumer countries, that is, developed countries, will more decisively oppose any market support pacts for commodities; on the other hand, primary commodity producers should be more inclined to accept this solution. On the contrary, if the liberalisation of agricultural trade had failed, a revival of ICAs with economic provisions could have been expected.

The chapter is organised as follows: section II reviews recent developments in agricultural trade policies and negotiations. After a presentation of the issue of commodity price volatility and a description of ICAs' experience, section III explores the relationship between the Uruguay Round of the GATT and the renegotiation of the International Coffee Agreement. Given uncertainty about ICAs and unavoidable commodity price volatility, section IV presents different alternatives of domestic schemes for price stabilisation in developing countries. A section with concluding observations ends the chapter.

II. AGRICULTURAL TRADE AND THE URUGUAY ROUND OF THE GATT

Tables 1 to 3 show that primary commodity trade, and especially agricultural trade, is very important not only to developing countries but also to developed countries. In multilateral negotiations both parties have thus strong interests in defending their own agriculture. The case is different for some products which are mainly produced by developing countries, the so-called core IPC (Integrated Programme for Commodities) commodities, which are the following: cocoa, coffee, cotton and cotton yarn, hard fibres and products, jute and jute manufactures, rubber, sugar, tea, copper and tin. In 1990 nearly two-thirds of world exports of the ten core commodities were exported by developed countries (Table 2), whereas developing countries' share of total primary exports (excluding fuels) was about 25 per cent (Table 1).

TABLE I
SHARE OF REGIONS IN WORLD TOTAL EXPORT (IN PERCENTAGES)

	Agriculture		Total primary (excl. fuels)	
	1970	1990	1970	1990
World	100.0	100.0	100.0	100.0
Developed market economy countries	57.1	68.5	57.6	68.1
Developing countries	33.5	25.3	33.1	25.3
Countries of Eastern Europe	7.7	3.5	7.9	4.2
Socialist countries of Asia	1.6	2.7	1.4	2.4

Source: UNCTAD [*1992*].

TABLE 2
SHARE OF REGIONS IN WORLD TOTAL EXPORT (IN PERCENTAGES)

	Total 10 core		Total 18 IPC	
	1970	1990	1970	1990
World	100.0	100.0	100.0	100.0
Developed market economy countries	20.1	29.4	30.6	41.0
Developing countries	75.2	63.8	63.3	53.0
Countries of Eastern Europe	4.1	4.0	5.5	3.7
Socialist countries of Asia	0.5	2.8	0.6	2.3

Source: UNCTAD [*1992*].
The ten 'core' commodities covered by the Integrated Programme for Commodities (IPC), which are mainly exported by developing countries, are: cocoa, coffee, cotton and cotton yarn, hard fibers and products, jute and jute manufactures, rubber, sugar, tea, copper and tin.
The 18 IPC commodities are the ten core plus: bananas, bovine meat, tropical timber, vegetables oils and oilseeds, bauxite, iron ore, manganese and phosphates.

TABLE 3
SHARE OF COMMODITIES IN TOTAL EXPORT BY REGION (IN PERCENTAGES)

	World market economy countries		Developed countries		Developing	
	1970	1990	1970	1990	1970	1990
All merchandise	100.0	100.0	100.0	100.0	100.0	100.0
Primary commodities (excl. fuels)	27.2	15.4	22.1	14.7	49.0	18.1
All food items	14.7	9.4	12.0	9.0	26.8	11.3
Total 18 IPC commodities[a]	9.6	3.6	4.1	2.1	33.1	8.9

Source: UNCTAD [*1992*].
Notes: See Table 2 for the list of IPC commodities.

None the less, trade of primary commodities is relatively more important to developing countries than to industrialised countries. Table 3 shows that the share of primary commodities in total exports is higher for developing countries. Moreover, the share of primary commodity exports in GDP is also higher for developing countries than for developed countries (excluding fuels, in 1989 it was respectively 4.1 per cent and 2.3 per cent [*UNCTAD, 1992*]). Finally, exports of developing countries tend to be less diversified, that is, total exports depends on few commodities. In many developing countries the degree of concentration is very high: the three leading commodities account for more than two-thirds of total exports.

After preliminaries lasting several years, the Uruguay Round was launched

221

in September 1986. It has been the eighth round in a series of multilateral trade talks in the framework of the GATT. The subjects discussed relate to 15 topics, two of which deal with agriculture and tropical products. The round was completed by mid-December 1993, and not by the end of 1991 as expected. A major obstacle to an overall agreement in the negotiations was trade liberalisation in agriculture. After more than six years of negotiations, the US and the European Community (EC) reached agreement on measures to bring agriculture more under the rules and disciplines of the GATT, approving two agreements on trade in oilseeds and on internal farm support and agricultural export subsidies (November 1992). This US–EC agreement came after the EC Common Agricultural Policy reform agreed in May 1992. The reform binds the EC to lower its fixed internal prices and to limit the growth of production by extending the system of quotas. The plan envisages compensatory measures for farmers, who will receive direct payments for lost income [*Commissione delle Comunità Europee, 1993*].

As far as agricultural trade is concerned, the main commitments of the Uruguay GATT deal are: cut of trade distorting subsidies and import barriers over six years; reduction by 20 per cent of domestic farm supports; a reduction of subsidised exports by 36 per cent in value and 21 per cent in volume. Moreover, all import barriers have to be converted in tariffs and cut by 36 per cent. Tariffs on tropical products have been cut by over 40 per cent. Finally, Japan and South Korea will gradually open their closed rice markets.

Tropical products include agricultural commodities produced solely or mainly by developing countries. They are grouped into seven separate categories: tropical beverages (for example, coffee); spices and flowers; certain oilseeds and vegetables oils; tobacco/rice/manioc; tropical fruits; wood/rubber; and jute/hard-fibres (sugar and cotton are excluded). A variety of trade barriers make access to the market of the industrialised countries difficult for tropical products. The main barriers are tariffs, variable levies, quotas, phytosanitary requirements and excise duties. Some unprocessed products are totally exempt from import duties, but always tariffs tend to be higher for products which have been processed (tariff escalation). After the conclusion of the Uruguay Round, products made out from natural resources have a tariff of two per cent for the raw materials but 5.9 per cent for the finished products. In the sector of industrial products, raw materials have a tariff of 0.8 per cent, semi-processed goods a tariff of 2.8 per cent and finished products have a tariff of 6.2 per cent.

The increase in nominal duties from earlier to later stages of processing points to a discrimination against exports of processed goods from developing countries. By limiting developing countries' exports of processed goods, past protectionism has had the negative dynamic effect of impeding the learning process linked to the manufacturing and marketing activities. Hence, even if tariff escalation were completely eliminated, developing countries' producers could experience difficulties in competing with high quality products and strict technical standards of industrialized countries [*Mori, 1992a*].

By eliminating protectionist practices of industrialised countries, international prices for most of the agricultural products are expected to increase [*Goldin and Knudsen, 1990*]. This price increase and enlarged market access are going to be beneficial to developing countries' agricultural exporters, at least in the short term. However, better possibilities for agricultural exports could jeopardise export diversification efforts away from unprocessed primary commodities, and in the longer term could have a negative impact on growth prospects of developing countries.

III. PRICE VOLATILITY AND INTERNATIONAL STABILISATION SCHEMES

Despite efforts towards industrialisation and export diversification, many developing countries are still very dependent on export of few primary commodities. Primary commodities generally experience higher price volatility than manufactured goods. Such variability tends to create macro and micro-economic disruptions to countries with exports concentrated in few commodities. Short-term price fluctuations arise from changes either in supply or in demand. For agricultural commodities price variability is caused mainly by harvest variations, particularly in the case of products with low income and price demand elasticity. Another source of variability derives from protectionist practices of industrialised countries. In the case of minerals, while supply can be affected by political disturbances and strikes, price fluctuations are principally explained by international business cycles. Commodity prices show a high volatility, not only changing frequently but also experiencing exceptionally high peaks.

Considering the annual prices of 13 primary commodities[1] over the period 1900–87, Deaton and Laroque [*1990*] found that (a) prices have high auto-correlation coefficients in the first and second year; (b) shocks do not persist into the near future (except in the case of bananas); (c) year-to-year price volatility is high; (d) positive shocks are more frequent than negative ones. Prices are highly unstable, but their changes are not permanent, that is, after a shock, prices tend to move back towards a given trend. Table 4 reports the Deaton and Laroque descriptive statistics for coffee and the average of the remaining 12 commodities.

Whether commodity price stabilisation is welfare improving is still a discussed issue in the economic literature. At macro level, even if the relationship between price volatility and long-run growth is not clear [*Behrman, 1987*], there is sufficient evidence that sharp increases in prices do have macro-

223

TABLE 4
COMMODITIES' PRICE DESCRIPTIVE STATISTICS, 1900–87

	one year a-c	two year a-c	persistence	C.V.	skewness	kurtosis
Coffee	0.80	0.62	0.11	0.45	1.66	3.82
Other commodities	0.80	0.61	0.17	0.39	1.01	2.27

Source: Deaton and Laroque [*1990*].
One year and two year a-c are first and second order autocorrelation coefficients. Persistence is the normalised spectral density at zero using Bartlett's estimator with 40-year window. Skewness coefficient is $(m_3/m_2)^{1.5}$, where m_j is the j-th central moment. Excess kurtosis measure is $(m_4/m_2^2) - 3$.

economic negative effects. In the literature the term 'Dutch Disease' has been used to describe the macroeconomic costs, mainly through the process of de-industrialisation, that tend to afflict countries experiencing a windfall gain (a bonanza) in trade.[2]

Two categories of approaches towards variability exist: first, initiatives which deal with the causes of variability, such as price stabilisation schemes and quantity stabilisation measures (for example, export diversification, agronomic research). Secondly, initiatives that deal with the effects of variability, by aiming at offsetting its negative impact, such as financial measures to smooth the changes in revenue, futures and options markets. These two approaches can be adopted at international level or at domestic level by individuals and governments. At the international level, ICAs, discussed in the next section, and compensatory finance schemes, are the two basic approaches to commodity market volatility. There are two major varieties of compensation financing arrangements: schemes which provide financial support to country covering their shortfalls in total export revenue (the IMF Compensatory Financing Scheme) and schemes under which a country receives compensation for shortfalls in revenue from export of single commodities (the EC STABEX scheme).

IV. INTERNATIONAL COMMODITY AGREEMENTS

Since primary commodity markets are persistently affected by problems of production uncertainty and price volatility, GATT Article XX allows for the conclusion of ICAs involving both exporting and importing countries, with the aim of regulating trade in specific primary products. In 1964 as a result of increasing pressure from the developing countries, the responsibility for major commodity initiatives was taken over by UNCTAD. The main and direct objective of ICAs is to decrease the volatility of prices. The major instruments are buffer stocks and exports quotas. The major ICAs have been the International Cocoa Agreement, the International Rubber Agreement (two pure buffer stock agreements), the International Coffee Agreement (with economic clauses active until 1989), the International Sugar Agreement (until 1984) (two pure export control agreements) and the International Tin Agreement (a hybrid agreement).[3]

A major problem in the implementation of a buffer stock scheme is the estimation of the long-run equilibrium price. It is difficult to take into account government policy, changes in taste, technology, new suppliers, disease, climatic change, and new substitutes. All these factors affect the long-run supply and demand schedules. Another problem is the cost of maintaining buffer stock – financing and capital immobilisation – since the size of the required stock is generally considerable. Apart from the practical problems, the sustainability of a price fixing buffer stock is controversial. Townsend [*1977*] showed that a buffer stock programme, which attempts to fix a relative price over time, eventually fails.[4]

Export control agreements attempt to balance supply and demand through supply control. Supply reduction may be carried out by storing, by disposing of excess production or by cutting production. The advantage of export control agreements is that they do not require foreign currencies expenditure. The introduction and the removal of controls and the revision of overall quota size are typically triggered by an indicator price. The major difficulties are the allocation of the total quota among the exporting member countries, the determination of the indicator price, the control of trade between member and non-member countries, the control of smuggling, and the forecasting of consumption and imports.

Another major problem of all ICAs is that they are not robust with regard to exchange rate changes, if target price ranges are not specified in terms of a basket of currencies. For example, the fluctuations of the dollar in the 1980s indirectly introduced variability into the price range fixed in dollar terms such as in the Coffee Agreement. Precisely to limit this problem, in the last Cocoa Agreement the price range was denominated in SDRs.

The International Coffee Agreement

First established in 1962 for a period of six years, the International Coffee Agreement (ICoA) was renewed in 1968, 1976 end 1983. Since July 1989, when negotiations to renew the 1983 Agreement were suspended and economic provisions lifted, ICoA continues on purely administrative terms. Member exporting and importing countries accounted respectively 99 per cent of world production and 90 per cent of world import. The four ICoA's had all incorporated similar rules. The ICoA operated entirely through export controls: the price in the quota market was kept within a target range through a global quota, which was allocated among exporting countries. According to a World Bank study over the period 1981–86 [*Akiyama and Varangis, 1989*] the ICoA' export quota system had a stabilising effect on world coffee price.

In 1989 renegotiations foundered on three major issues: quota allocation among exporters, as well as the related issue of quota selectivity between different groups of coffee, and the existence of a two-tier market with lower prices to non-quota countries. After the suspension of the organisation's export quota system, prices collapsed, reaching the lowest levels for more than 20 years.

Since the ICoA collapsed, there have been continuos negotiations among producers and consumers. At the beginning of 1993, both sides agreed that any new agreement should be based on a universal quota system. This would cover all coffee exports, regardless of destination, thus avoiding the development of a second cheaper market with consumer countries not participating to the agreement. However, parties did not agree on quota for different kind of coffee (selectivity) and on rules for changing individual's country quotas (automaticity). At the end of 1993, Latin American coffee producers (more than half of world production) agreed to retain 20 per cent of their exports in order to lift prices. On 30 March 1994 the International Coffee Council unanimously adopted the text of a new five-year International Coffee Agreement to begin in October 1994. It does not have the power to intervene in the market to control prices (that is, no economic clauses). The new Agreement provides a forum for discussion between coffee producers and consumers, and provides for the continued collection and distribution of trade statistics. The Council may decide by a two-thirds majority to negotiate a new Agreement with economic measures

For more than five years of negotiations, producer and consumer countries were not able to agree on the features of a new agreement. Consumer countries in particular did not show a clear position in favour or against a new coffee pact. It appears that some parties continued to bargain on provisions, and contemporaneously to remind others that they were against a new agreement. This contradictory behaviour could have been motivated by uncertainty about external factors that influenced the coffee market. In particular, the overall trade regime for agricultural products, which was going to emerge from the GATT negotiations, was indeed important for the coffee market. Developed countries were unwilling to accept an increase in coffee price brought about by a new ICoA in the case of an overall reduction of agricultural protectionism, which would have implied a loss of part of domestic and international markets. On the contrary, in the event of a failure of GATT negotiations on agricultural trade liberalisation, developed countries would have probably accepted renewing an ICoA with economic provisions, as part of an international system of economic co-operation with developing countries. In

March 1994, that is, only after the conclusion of the Uruguay Round, the International Coffee Council adopted the new text of the agreement.[5]

V. POLICY IMPLICATION: THE DOMESTIC RESPONSE
TO MARKET UNCERTAINTY

International commodity prices are volatile and their volatility may have serious consequences for individuals and countries which are not able to diversify risks. Since the future of ICAs is uncertain and their experience has been rather disappointing, policies and instruments that can be adopted at national level have a crucial role to play. Uncertainty can be reduced through crop diversification. By changing the mix of crops they grow, farmers can reduce the total risk which they face if the return to different crops is imperfectly correlated (see, for example, Newbery and Stiglitz [*1981*]).

At individual level, agents have four alternatives: storing, saving/borrowing, selling forward, or hedging with futures and options. Storing and saving/borrowing require an efficient credit market, a condition that is not always met in developing countries. Forward contracts face the problem of commitment and international enforceability. In developing countries, lack of knowledge, lack of adequate access to credit, controls on foreign exchange transactions and the almost total absence of domestic futures[6] markets are all impediments to the diffusion of market instruments, such as futures and options.[7] Moreover, local price does not always vary consistently with prices in major commodity markets because of exchange rate fluctuations, government policies and freight changes.

Since individuals in developing countries still face severe limitations to the use of market instruments for hedging against risk, the issue of domestic price stabilisation schemes has recently acquired importance on the agenda of both economists and policy-makers. At the national level, the authority has different alternative policies. The most common schemes are: price bands, buffer fund, export marketing boards and progressive export taxes. Governments may also aim at reducing production uncertainty by improving extension services, by investing more resources in developing new and more resistant varieties, or by implementing an accurate weather forecasting system.

Price band schemes are used mainly in the case of importables, competing with domestic production. The authority establishes the floor and the ceiling of the band generally on the basis of past prices and the system to keep prices within the band. The system may consist of government intervening in the market by buying at the floor price and selling when the price reaches the band ceiling. In this case the government must have both financial resources and stocks of the stabilised commodity. Alternatively, the government may establish a flexible tax, which increases when the price reaches the ceiling, while decreasing when the market price is at the floor price.

Price band schemes with public buffer stock have been criticised because they tend to discourage private storing and because they are not robust to speculative attacks at the ceilings. When market price is near the ceiling, speculators have an incentive to purchase huge quantities of the commodity because they know that eventually this will exhaust the stock and the price will increase ('speculative raid') [*Salant, 1983*].

A buffer fund is established usually for pure stabilisation aim, that is, it is a zero expected profit scheme. The government fixes a formula for a reference price (for example, a moving average of past prices) and then collects levies when the price is higher than the reference price, and pays bounties when the price is below the reference price. In buffer fund schemes as well as in price band schemes, the estimation of reference prices is probably the major problem. Bad estimates may cause the early collapse of schemes and may give wrong signals to producers, leading to inefficiencies.

Export marketing boards are generally state organisations with monopsony power in the marketing of specific commodities. Marketing boards usually fix prices for an agricultural season, announcing them to the farmers before the planting time. Hence, they have a stabilisation function by eliminating price uncertainty within a season. However, marketing boards may also be the instruments for taxing producers and collecting fiscal revenue. Some time ago, it was recognised that it was very dangerous to plan fiscal policy on the revenue from export taxes of commodities which have high price volatility [*Helleiner, 1964*], since international price volatility would automatically carry across to fiscal revenue variability. Marketing boards require the control of smuggling in order to be effective, otherwise when they offer a price lower than the border price an outflow of commodities would occur; however, with a support price higher than the international one there would be an inflow. The existence of marketing boards tends to discourage intra-seasonal stockholding [*Knudsen and Nash, 1990*]. Many developing countries, especially in Africa, use marketing boards to control prices. However, removing price uncertainty in this way can be costly and inefficient. It can be achieved only through 'heavy taxation' of the producers, that is, by constraining the price always below the international level, or by transferring uncertainty to the authority/ marketing board and eventually to taxpayers.

Most developing countries tax their primary commodity exports but generally with the aim of collecting fiscal revenue. If taxation is progressive, it has a stabilisation effect: by varying the marginal rate of the tax with the world export price, the impact of international price volatility on domestic producers is reduced. Gilbert [*1991*] argued that a country should tax its exports in order to increase fiscal revenues, only if it is difficult to tax incomes and expenditures. The reason is that trade taxes distort production and consumption decisions, while income and expenditure taxes, by affecting allocation between goods and leisure, cause typically small distortions.

A study of the Colombian stabilisation policy in the coffee sector [*Mori, 1992b*] showed that, on the one hand, domestic stabilisation schemes can be very helpful and effective and, on the other hand, in order to be effective a scheme should be flexible and discretionary and not based on simple and given rules, as some international organisations are suggesting (for example, the World Bank). The coffee price stabilisation scheme in Colombia can be seen as a mixture of a price support scheme and variable export taxes.[8] The policy was effective in stabilising domestic price to growers over the period 1960–90. The coffee authority was also able to limit macroeconomic negative impacts of coffee booms, especially during the 1986 boom.

Figure 1 shows the movements in the real Other Mild Arabicas price (a proxy for the international price) and the domestic support price between 1960 and 1990.[9] The international price was very unstable and the variability was characterised more by sharp peaks than by falls, as the theory suggests [*Deaton and Laroque, 1990*]. The domestic price was much more stable than the one for Other Mild Arabica, showing that coffee policy in Colombia played a clear stabilising role of the average price that coffee growers receive. Various measures of price variability show that coffee policy shifted the risk from domestic coffee growers to private exporters primarily, and to the Federación Nacional de Cafeteros (it appears reasonable to protect thousands of farmers instead of few exporters). Colombia is certainly a special case among developing countries. It is a rather stable country, with high social and political cohesion. The effectiveness of a 'discretionary' scheme depends on many idiosyncratic characteristics of the country and the ruling authority.

VI. CONCLUSIONS

For more than five years there were parallel international negotiations, on the one hand, for agricultural trade liberalisation within the Uruguay Round of the GATT and, on the other hand, for the renewal of the ICoA. In the Uruguay Round the position of the contracting parties was fairly clear: almost everyone supported a less protectionist environment, and the bargaining concerned the extent of this liberalisation. On the contrary, the negotiations at the International Coffee Organisation meetings appeared characterised not only by different position on technical aspects but also by unclear willingness of renewing the ICoA. This chapter has argued that the ambiguous position of industrialised countries (the consumers of coffee) derived from the uncertainty about the process of liberalisation of agricultural trade within the Uruguay Round.

FIGURE I
OTHER MILD ARABICA PRICE

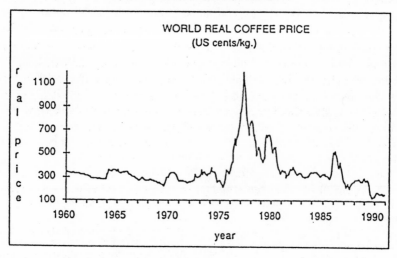

FIGURE 2
REAL OTHER MILD ARABICA PRICE AND REAL DOMESTIC PRICE

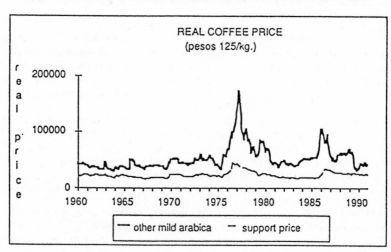

It is worthwhile to note that in a longer-term perspective the renegotiation of economic clauses within the ICoA can be more convenient to developed countries. In fact, with higher international agricultural (but tropical) prices

230

and low coffee prices (without an ICoA), LDCs will diversify their primary production by decreasing tropical production and increasing other agricultural products. Over time, coffee prices as well as prices of other tropical products could increase.

As a consequence of the uncertain future of ICAs, national schemes for commodity price stabilisation become very important. After having briefly reviewed various alternatives that can be used either by individuals or a central authority, the author argues that in developing countries the latter is more feasible. The Colombian coffee policy shows that a domestic scheme can be effective in decreasing price volatility for growers, and that a flexible and discretionary scheme is probably more effective than a simple rule.

NOTES

1. The 13 commodities are: bananas, cocoa, coffee, copper, cotton, jute, maize, palm oil, rice, sugar, tea, tin and wheat. Their nominal US dollar price has been deflated by the US CPI.
2. The bonanza can be due either to an extraordinary increase in the production – the case of a permanent boom as a consequence of a natural discovery or a technological innovation [*Corden, 1985*] – or to an extraordinary increase of the international price of an export good, the case of a temporary boom. For a discussion of experiences of Dutch disease see Edwards [*1984*] and Bevan *et al.* [*1993*] and Cuddington [*1989*].
3. See Gilbert [*1987*] for a discussion of the functioning of ICAs.
4. Townsend modelled a pure exchange economy with two goods. The supply of the goods is stochastic and the series are i.i.d. over time. If a policy fixes their relative price, consumers will demand the two goods in constant shares. Since availability of the goods is random, a succession of realisations with the supply of the first good low relative to the availability of the second good must be expected. Hence, the stock of the first good would be depleted with probability one.
5. The same happened to other ICAs: negotiations for a new International Tropical Timber Agreement ended on 21 February 1994; the UN Conference on Natural Rubber in April 1994 agreed on about 80 per cent of a new text, and will meet again from October 1994 onwards.
6. Futures trading allows agents to hedge their revenues and to reduce their exposure to the spot price at the delivery date. While price stabilisation attempts to mitigate price volatility, futures markets mitigate the negative effects of this volatility.
7. Options are in principle more flexible than futures and allows agents the possibility of insuring themselves only against extremely low or high prices.
8. The actual institutional framework is very complicated (see Correa Ordoñez [*1989*] and Mori [*1992b*].
9. The price for 'Other Mild Arabicas' has been used as the international reference price for Colombian coffee, even if Colombian coffee generally obtains a premium on the 'Other Mild Arabicas' quotation for its higher quality. US dollar prices have been deflated by the US CPI to obtain real values, while prices in pesos are deflated by the Colombian CPI. The international price has been converted in pesos using the monthly average market exchange rate (IMF), although until Law 444 of

1967 there was a coffee exchange rate different from the official one and during 1977–80 a different exchange rate was also adopted.

REFERENCES

Akiyama, T. and R. Duncan (1982): *Analysis of the World Coffee Market*, World Bank Staff Commodity WP No.7.

Akiyama, T and P. Varangis (1989): *Impact of the ICA Export Quota System on the World's Coffee Market*, World Bank, International Commodity Markets Division, Feb.

Behrman, J.R. (1987): 'Commodity Price Instability and Economic Goal Attainment in Developing Countries', *World Development*, May.

Bevan, D.L. *et al.* (1987): 'Consequences of a Commodity Boom in a Controlled Economy: Accumulation and Redistribution in Kenya 1975–83', *The World Bank Economic Review*, Vol.1, No.3.

Commissione delle Comunité Europee (1993): *La situazione dell'agricoltura nella Comunité. Relazione 1992*, Brussels.

Corden, W.M. (1985): *Protection, Growth and Trade Essays in International Economics*, Oxford: Basil Blackwell.

Correa Ordoñez, M.C. (1989): 'Politica de Estabilizacion Cafetera en Colombia', *Ensayos sobre Economia Cafetera*, Bogota, No. 3.

Cuddington, J. T. (1989): 'Commodity Exports Boom in Developing Countries', *Research Observer*, Vol.4, No.2, July, Washington, DC: World Bank.

Davis, J.M. (1983): 'The Economic Effects of Windfall Gains in Export Earnings, 1975–1978', *World Development*, Vol.11, No.2.

Deaton, A.S. and G. Laroque (1990): *On The Behaviour of Commodity Prices*, NBER.

Edwards, S. (1984): 'Coffee, Money and Inflation in Colombia', *World Development*, Vol.12, Nos.11/12.

Gilbert, C.L. (1987): 'International Commodity Agreements: Design and Performance', *World Development*, Vol.15, No.5.

Gilbert, C.L. (1991): 'Domestic Price Stabilization Schemes for Developing Countries', Queen Mary and Westfield College, London, April, processed.

Goldin I. and O. Knudsen (eds.) (1990): *Agriculture Trade Liberalization. Implications for Developing Countries*, Paris: OECD; Washington, DC: The World Bank

Helleiner, G.K. (1964): 'The Fiscal Role of the Marketing Boards in Nigerian Economic Development, 1947–61', *Economic Journal*, 64, Sept.

Hertel, T.W. (1990): 'Agricultural Trade Liberalization and Developing Countries: a Survey of Model', in Goldin and Knudsen (eds.) [*1990*].

Knudsen, O. and J. Nash (1990): 'Domestic Price Stabilization Schemes in Developing Countries', *Economic Development and Cultural Change*, Vol.38, No.3, April, pp. 539–58.

Massell, B.F. (1969): 'Price Stabilization and Welfare', *Quarterly Journal of Economics*, May.

Mori, A. (1992a): 'The Prospects for EC-LDC Trade Relations in Traditional Consumer Goods: The Case of the Agro-industry', in S. Sideri and J. Sengupta (eds.), *The 1992 Single European Market and the Third World*, London: Frank Cass.

Mori, A. (1992b): 'Domestic Policies for Commodity Price Stabilization: The Case of Coffee in Colombia', Ph.D. Dissertation, Dottorato di Milano, July.

Newbery, D.M.G. and J.E. Stiglitz (1981): *The Theory of Commodity Price Stabiliza-*

tion, Oxford: Clarendon Press.

Oi, W.Y. (1961): 'The Desirability of Price Instability under Perfect Competition', *Econometrica*, Vol.29, No.1, Jan.

Salant, S.W. (1983): 'The Vulnerability of Price Stabilization Schemes to Speculative Attack', *Journal of Political Economy*, Vol.91, No.1.

Townsend, R.M. (1977): 'The Eventual Failure of Price Fixing Schemes', *Journal of Economic Theory*, 14.

UNCTAD (1989): *Protectionism and Structural Adjustment*, TD/B/1240/Add.1, 14 Dec. 1989.

UNCTAD (1992): *UNCTAD Commodity Yearbook 1992*, New York: United Nations.

Waugh, F.V. (1944): 'Does the Consumer Benefit from Price Instability?', *Quarterly Journal of Economics*, Aug.

13

The External Impact of the New Common Agricultural Policy: An Assessment in Terms of Strategic Trade Policy

FRANCESCO PASSARELLI

I. INTRODUCTION

The recent reform of the Common Agricultural Policy (CAP) will exert a direct and an indirect influence on the agricultural policies and on competitive strategies of third countries. By converting direct support for producers (guaranteed prices) into an indirect one in the form of deficiency compensations, the reform aims at reducing excess production, decreasing subsidy levels and making the CAP compatible with international trade policy agreements.

The complexity of the liberalising negotiations is also reflected by the difficulties in understanding the impact of each domestic agricultural policy on prices, trade flows and welfare. This chapter tries to show that governmental policies, by affecting the oligopolistic competition among big agricultural producers and traders, can be used strategically for improving welfare. Positive levels of protection are compatible with a non-co-operative game among governments. Co-operation is not a stable equilibrium in non-repeated or finitely repeated games. In case the game is infinitely repeated, a sort of co-operative outcome will imply a lower, but still positive, amount of protection.

II. THE MODEL

A three-countries world has been considered: the domestic country, the foreign one and the rest of the world. Attention has been focused on the interactions between the two national countries' actors; the rest of the world's market is perfectly competitive and it is also the most efficient one. Consumers can buy two kinds of good, the agricultural good and another numeraire good; the demand functions are obtained from the solution of the usual maximisation problem. Agricultural producers decide how much to produce for the domestic market and how much to export to the foreign country, in order to maximise profit; symmetrically, foreign producers decide how to partition their production between the foreign and the domestic markets. National governments implement policy strategies aimed at maximising welfare. Domestic governments can either fix the guaranteed price and eventually sell the domestic excess production on the rest of the world's competitive market, or set the amount of the deficiency compensations. A foreign government chooses the tariff on imports from a domestic country.

Following Brander and Spencer's analysis of the tariff protectionism under imperfect competition [*Brander and Spencer, 1984*], a two-stage game can be depicted. Governments play their policy strategies first; second, producers play a Cournot game by price discriminating between the two national segmented markets.

Guaranteed Prices, Domestic Monopoly and Duopoly on the Foreign Market

A simplified domestic demand for the agricultural good arises from the following utility function:

$$U = u(X) + N \tag{1}$$

where X is the domestically consumed quantity of the agricultural good and N is the expenditure on the other numeraire good. X can be partitioned into domestic production, y, and imports, x; then $X = x+y$.

Maximising (1) gets the inverse demand:

$$p = u'(X) \tag{2}$$

Let us denote with '*' the variables referred to the foreign country; then $Y = y+y^*$ is the total domestic production. A production function for the agricultural good can be specified:

$$Y = f(h) \tag{3}$$

where h is the cultivated land. By assumption, h is the only factor; its marginal productivity is decreasing, $f_{hh}<0$. Let us assume that f is invertible too; then,

$$h = h(Y) \tag{4}$$

with $h(Y) = f^{-1}(Y)$; $h_Y>0$ and $h_{YY}>0$.

One possible cost function could be:

$$C = F + c(Y) \tag{5}$$

where F measures the fixed costs. This function presents economies of scale. It is convenient to assume growing marginal costs, $C_{YY}>0$.

Domestic government fixes a guaranteed price p_g and a prohibitive import tariff. The domestic monopolist will produce for the internal market probably more than the demand. The entire excess of production is bought by the government and sold to the rest of the world for the fixed price p_w. The net domestic welfare is then:

$$G = u(X_g) - p_g \cdot X_g + \pi - (p_g - p_w) \cdot (X - X_g) \tag{6}$$

where X_g is the quantity purchased by the private domestic consumers; denotes the domestic producer's profit.

The foreign government sets the tariff t^*; then its welfare function is:

$$G^* = u^*(X^*) - p^* \cdot X^* + \pi^* + t^* \cdot y^* \tag{7}$$

At the first stage, the domestic and the foreign governments choose p_g and t^* in order to maximise (6) and (7) respectively. This will influence the equilibria in the domestic market and in the foreign one. These equilibria represents the solutions of the second stage, when private producers play. The domestic firm maximises its own profit function:

$$\pi = p_g \cdot y + p^* \cdot y^* - c(y + y^*) - F - t^* \cdot y^* \tag{8}$$

The foreign producer maximises:

$$\pi^* = p^* \cdot x^* - c(x^*) - F^* \tag{9}$$

In order to get the sub-game perfect equilibrium, let us solve the Cournot-Nash equilibrium of the second stage:

$$
\begin{aligned}
\pi'_y &= p_g - c'(y + y^*) = 0 \\
\pi'_{y}{}^* &= p^{*\prime} \cdot y^* + p^* - c'(y + y^*) - t^* = 0 \\
\pi^{*\prime}x^* &= p^{*\prime} \cdot x^* + p^* - c^{*\prime}(x^*) = 0
\end{aligned} \tag{10}
$$

The solutions of the system will depend on the values of p_g and t^* set at the first stage; then the two oligopolists' reaction functions will be determined by the policy variables.

A Special Formulation

In order to solve the game and make some comparative static analysis, (1), (3) and (5) can be specified conveniently:

$$U = a \cdot X - \frac{b}{2} \cdot X^2 + N \tag{11}$$

$$Y = \frac{1}{d} \cdot \sqrt{h} \tag{12}$$

$$C = F + \frac{c}{2} \cdot Y^2 \tag{13}$$

where a, b, c and d are positive parameters. Let us also assume that $U = U^*$ and $C = C^*$.

Second Stage

Using (11) and (13) in the First Order Conditions (FOC) system, the domestic and foreign firms' explicit reaction functions on the foreign market are respectively:

$$x^* = \frac{a - p_g - t^*}{b} - 2 \cdot y^* \tag{14}$$

and

$$x^* = \frac{a}{2b - c} - \frac{b}{2b - c} \cdot y^* \tag{15}$$

Graphically,

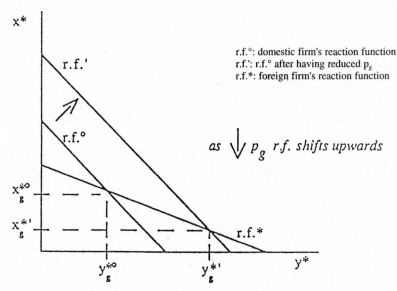

Proposition 1: If the domestic government raises the value of p_g, then on the foreign market the domestic firm's quota decreases and the foreign firm's increases; X_g^* decreases.

Proof: the solutions of the second stage are:

$$y_g = \frac{3b^2 p_g + 4bp_g c - cba + 2cbt^* + c^2 p_g - c^2 a + c^2 t^*}{cb \cdot (3b + 2c)} \tag{16}$$

$$y_g^* = -\frac{2bp_g - ba + 2bt^* - cp_g - ca + ct^*}{b \cdot (3b + 2c)} \tag{17}$$

$$x_g^* = \frac{pg + a + t^*}{3b + 2c} \tag{18}$$

Then, $\qquad \dfrac{\partial y_g}{\partial p_g} > 0; \qquad \dfrac{\partial y_g^*}{\partial p_g} < 0; \quad \text{and} \; \dfrac{\partial x_g^*}{\partial p_g} > 0.$

The equilibrium price is:

$$p_g^* = \frac{ba + ca + bp_g + bt^* + cp_g + ct^*}{3b + 2c} \tag{19}$$

Then, $\dfrac{\partial p_g^*}{\partial p_g} > 0.$ Q.E.D.

First Stage

The governments' best-reply functions are defined by the $\dfrac{\partial G}{\partial p_g} = 0$ and $\dfrac{\partial G^*}{\partial t^*} = 0$ equations, after having substituted the solutions of the second stage into (6) and (7). The functional forms of these policy functions are quite complex; however, their slopes depend on specific characteristics of some parameters. If the foreign government raises t^*, then the domestic firm's export net marginal revenue decreases; since this firm behaves as a price discriminating oligopolist, it will try to equate the marginal revenues on both markets, since the domestic marginal revenue is constant, then y_g increases and decreases. Moreover, domestic excess production will increase and will cause G to decrease. Then the best response to higher t^* is to lower p_g in order both to increase the consumer surplus and to decrease excess production. However, this policy decreases also the domestic firm's profit. The net effect on G is an ambiguous one; it will be positive if the domestic demand elasticity is high and the foreign residual demand is rigid. This means that p_g is sufficiently higher than p_g^*. In this case the domestic government's best-reply curve has a downward slope.

Following the same argument, it is possible to assert that the foreign government's best-reply function is upward sloped under similar conditions.

Proposition 2: perfect sub-game equilibrium exists and can imply positive values for p_g and t^*, for appropriate values of the parameters.

Proposition 2 can be proved by solving the model.

Proposition 3: the equilibrium is not Pareto-optimal and any co-operative agreement is not a stable solution of the game.

A graphic demonstration of proposition 3 can be obtained by looking at the form of the iso-welfare curves:

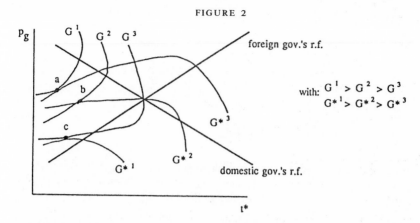

FIGURE 2

The Pareto-optimal points *a*, *b*, and *c*, are not optimal responses.

Deficiency Compensations and Symmetric Duopolies

In trying to introduce the deficiency compensations as a trade policy, one possibility is to make it fit with non-cultivated fertile lands. One could imagine a linear relationship:

$$S(h) = \begin{cases} \bar{S} - r \cdot h & 0 \le h \le h_g \\ 0 & h \ge h_g \end{cases} \tag{20}$$

with $r>0$ and h_g denoting the amount of land cultivated under the p_g regime:

$$h_g = h(y_g + y_g^*).$$

Using (4) and (12), (20) becomes:

$$S(Y) = \begin{cases} \bar{S} - \frac{s}{2} \cdot Y^2 & 0 \le Y \le Y_g \\ 0 & Y \ge Y_g \end{cases} \tag{21}$$

where $s = 2 \cdot r \cdot d^2$ and $Y_g = y_g + y_g^*$.

By using the same simplified specifications, namely (11) and (13), and the symmetry hypothesis, the domestic firm's objective function is:

$$\pi = [a - b(y + x)]y + [a - b(x^* + y^*)]y^* - F - \frac{c}{2}(y + y^*)^2 - t^*y^* + \bar{S} - \frac{s}{2}(y + y^*)^2 \tag{22}$$

The foreign firm maximises, with respect to x and x^*, the following profit function:

$$\pi^* = [a - b(y + x)]x + [a - b(x^* + y^*)]x^* - F - \frac{c}{2}(x + x^*)^2 \tag{23}$$

239

Second Stage

From the maximisation conditions,

$$\frac{\partial \pi}{\partial y} = -2by + a - bx - c(y + y^*) - s(y + y^*) = 0$$

$$\frac{\partial \pi}{\partial y^*} = -2by^* + a - bx^* - c(y + y^*) - s(y + y^*) - t^* = 0 \qquad (24)$$

$$\frac{\partial \pi^*}{\partial x^*} = -2bx^* + a - by^* - c(x + x^*) = 0$$

$$\frac{\partial \pi^*}{\partial x} = -2bx^* + a - by - c(x + x^*) = 0$$

The system (22) defines the four implicit reaction functions of the two firms for the domestic market and the foreign one. Since the marginal cost and the deficiency compensations depend on both the domestic production and the production sold abroad, the system is not partitionable and each firm's behaviour in one market is strictly interrelated with what happens in the other one; the quantities are strategic substitutes.

Let us consider the solutions of (22):

$$y_g = \frac{4c^2t^* + 6cba + 5cbt^* + 3b^2a + 4cst^* + 4sbt^*}{3b \cdot A} \qquad (25)$$

$$x_g = \frac{2c^2t^* - 4cbt + 6cba + 3b^2a + 2sbt^* + 6sab - 2cst^*}{3b \cdot A} \qquad (26)$$

$$y_g^* = \frac{-4c^2t^* + 6cba - 11cbt^* + 3b^2a - 6b^2t^* - 4cst^* - 4sbt^*}{3b \cdot A} \qquad (27)$$

$$x_g^* = \frac{2c^2t^* + 3b^2t^* + 2sbt^* + 4cbt^* + 6cba + 6sab + 3b^2a + 2cst^*}{3b \cdot A} \qquad (28)$$

where $A = 8cb + 4c^2 + 3b^2 + 4sc + 4sb$.

The equilibrium prices are the following:

$$p_g = \frac{12cba + 12ac^2 + 3b^2a + 12asc + 6sab - 6c^2t^* - cbt^* - 2cst^* - 6sbt^*}{3 \cdot A} \qquad (29)$$

and

$$p_g^* = \frac{12cba + 12ac^2 + 3b^2a + 12asc + 6sab + 3b^2t^* + 7cbt^* + 2cst^* + 2sbt^* + 2c^2t^*}{3 \cdot A} \qquad (30)$$

From comparative static analysis it is possible to assert what follows:

Proposition 4: if the government raises the per-unit deficiency compensation payment, *r*, the domestic firm's reaction functions shift downwards.

The External Impact of the New Common Agricultural Policy

Proof: the domestic firm produces until the difference between total marginal revenue and marginal cost is greater than the marginal subsidy, $s \cdot Y$. When r raises, the firm reduces total production up to the point where total marginal profit equates the opportunity cost $s \cdot Y$. Q.E.D.

Proposition 5: if the foreign government raises t^*, *then* y_s increases, y_s^* decreases and x_s^* increases; X_s^* decreases and X_s increases.
   Proof: from (25) – (30) one gets:

$$\frac{\partial y_s}{\partial t^*} > 0; \quad \frac{\partial y_s^*}{\partial t^*} < 0; \quad \frac{\partial x_s^*}{\partial t^*} > 0; \quad \frac{\partial p_s}{\partial t^*} < 0; \quad \frac{\partial p_{s^*}}{\partial t^*} > 0. \quad \text{Q.E.D.}$$

Proposition 6: if the domestic government raises r, then x_s increases and, if t^* is sufficiently low, y_s^* and y_s decrease (by the same amount), and x_s^* increases.
   Proof: from (25) – (28) one gets:

$$\frac{\partial x_s}{\partial_s} > 0 \text{ and, if } t^* < \frac{2ca + ba}{c + b}, \quad \frac{\partial y_s}{\partial s} = \frac{\partial y_s^*}{\partial s} < 0 \text{ and } \frac{\partial x_s^*}{\partial s} > 0 \text{ Q.E.D.}$$

First Stage

The domestic and the foreign governments play a non-co-operative game aimed at maximising the welfare functions:

$$G = u(X) - p \cdot X + \pi - s \tag{31}$$

and

$$G^* = u^*(X^*) - p^* \cdot X^* + \pi^* + t^* \cdot y^* \tag{32}$$

where the strategic variables are r and t^*, respectively. Once the second stage behaviours have been depicted, G and G^* depend only on s and t^*.
   The FOC's of the simultaneous maximisation define the best-reply schedules. In the first stage of the game, build using equations (11) – (13) and $u(X)=u^*(X^*)$, s and t^* can be alternatively strategic substitutes or complements, depending on the starting values. However, one important conclusion is the following proposition.
   Proposition 7: for appropriate values of the parameters, a sub-game perfect equilibrium exists and implies positive values for s and t^*.
   This proposition can proved by solving the FOC's system of the first stage.

III. CONCLUSIONS

The hypothesis of growing marginal costs causes the domestic and the foreign market to interact. If the equilibria depend on the trade policy variables, then the governments can influence the competition of the firms in the two markets.

Actually the non-co-operative trade policy equilibria have been determined and they involve positive levels of protection.

This chapter presents two games which can be adapted to the international negotiations for the liberalisation of the agricultural trade flows. Counter intuitively the first game (with guaranteed prices) predicts the improvement of the foreign welfare as the guaranteed price rises. In fact, the model does not take into account the negative impact of selling domestic excess production in the market of the rest of the world. Moreover, the model does not consider the foreign share of the domestic market which should fall as the guaranteed price increases.

The second game (with deficiency compensations) predicts a positive impact of increasing compensations on the foreign country's welfare. In this case, the absence of excess of supply makes improvement even more credible.

The new CAP, more largely based on deficiency compensations, has played a positive role in reaching an agreement in the Uruguay Round of the GATT.

REFERENCES

Brander, J.A. and B.J. Spencer (1984): 'Tariff Protection and Imperfect Competition', in H. Kierzkowski (ed.), *Monopolistic Competition and International Trade*, Oxford: Oxford University Press.

Brander, J.A. and B.J. Spencer (1985): 'Export Subsidies and Market Share Rivarly', *Journal of International Economics*, 18.

Dixit, A.K. and G.M. Grossman (1986): 'Optimal Trade and Industrial Policy Under Oligopoly', *Quarterly Journal of Economics*, 101.

Helpman, E. and P.R. Krugman (1989): *Trade Policy and Market Structure*, Cambridge, MA: MIT Press.

EADI is 20 years old

The European Association of Development Research and Training Institutes (EADI) started its activities in 1975.

In fact, the decision to create the Association was taken in Ghent, and a founding conference took place in 1974 for this purpose; but the constitution was adopted only a year later, in Linz. The theme of the first general conference was *A New International Order: Economic, Social and Political Implications*. From then on, conferences were held every three years, in Milan, Budapest, Madrid, Amsterdam, Oslo and Berlin.

Quite a number of these venues, as well as the years the meetings took place and the themes chosen, symbolically characterise the vicissitudes of very recent European history and the changing orientations of development co-operation. As early as 1981 in Budapest, reflection was made on the nascent opening of Eastern Europe. Later, in 1987 in Amsterdam, participants dealt with the initial evolution towards globalisation and the problems that it created for the welfare of people: the theme was *Managing the World Economy or Reshaping World Society?*

In those years, much attention was dedicated to the theme of environmental degradation, and because of this the relation between development and environment was thoroughly discussed during the Oslo conference in 1990. The theme of the conference also concerned *Changes in Europe* as the Berlin Wall had just come down. But this major event and its consequences were thoroughly examined three years later, in 1993, at the Berlin conference. It was also at that time that Eastern European colleagues substantially increased their participation in EADI and that attention started shifting slightly from the problems of the South to those of the East. In relation to the profound changes taking place the world over, the next conference, which will be held in Vienna in 1996, will focus on *Globalisation, Competitiveness and Human Security*.

Entering its 21st year, EADI has now come of age, and has proved that it was indeed the missing link between development researches, decision-makers, and aid agencies in Europe, as well as international organisations, NGOs and colleagues in the South. With 220 institutional members and more than 150 individual members, EADI's prestige and reputation is increasing every year. EADI was the missing link 20 years ago; it is now an essential link in development studies and training.

EADI BOOK SERIES